MOMENTS IN PI

Dedicated to the late Brian Williams and Mark Harris
whose separate and untimely deaths during 2007
meant we lost two more extraordinary contributors
to the rich life story which is probation.

Moments in Probation

Compiled by Paul Senior

Shaw & Sons

Shaw's
Since 1750

Also published by
Shaw & Sons Limited

The Probation Directory incorporating Offender Management and Interventions – Formerly *The NAPO Probation Directory*, this is now supported by the National Probation Service as well as Napo and is considered to be the "bible" of the Probation Service.

History of Probation: Politics, Power & Cultural Change 1876–2005 by Philip Whitehead and Roger Statham – Tells the story of probation from 1876 through to the present day, exploring probation by alluding to crime; imprisonment; politics and power; increasing central control and bureaucracy; criminology; and penal and social policy.

Modernising Probation & Criminal Justice: Getting the Measure of Cultural Change by Philip Whitehead – Explores modernisation and cultural change in the Probation Service, particularly with reference to the significant developments of the last decade. It takes a philosophical journey, investigating bureaucratic developments and implications for practitioners.

The Companion Guides Series – The outstanding series on law and practice for probation officers, social workers, lawyers and other practitioners in the criminal justice system. Simple, clear, authoritative, user-friendly guides to the most troublesome areas of practice.

For full details of the above and Shaw's other products and services, visit
www.shaws.co.uk

Shaw & Sons Limited, Shaway House, 21 Bourne Park, Bourne Road, Crayford, Kent DA1 4BZ. Tel: 01322 621100; Fax: 01322 550553; E-mail: sales@shaws.co.uk

Published by
Shaw & Sons Limited
Shaway House
21 Bourne Park
Bourne Road
Crayford
Kent DA1 4BZ

www.shaws.co.uk

© Shaw & Sons Limited 2008

Published October 2008

ISBN 978 0 7219 1780 1

A CIP catalogue record for this book is available from the British Library

Printed in Great Britain by
Athanæum Press Limited, Gateshead

Table of Contents

TABLE OF CONTENTS

Table of Contents by Category

TABLE OF CONTENTS BY CATEGORY

RESEARCH & THEORY

TRAINING & STAFF DEVELOPMENT

AFTERWORD

Alphabetical Table of Contents

ALPHABETICAL TABLE OF CONTENTS

Acknowledgements

This volume first appeared as individual papers on the Community Justice Portal (www.cjp.org.uk) during the year of the century of probation, 2007. Each day a new Moment would appear and I thank the industry and commitment of all those writers who submitted their Moment for editorial comment and publication. The one person who made this all possible, after the editing was complete, was Ian Buczynski. He worked tirelessly to convert each Moment into the agreed style, to squash the wordage onto the single page format we had agreed, to make the snapshots look as good as possible and to do this in time for people to wake up to their next Moment there on the Portal. This work was only possible because of the energy and enthusiasm of Ian to complete those last vital pre-publication tasks. Thanks, Ian: a sterling effort.

We were contemplating how to turn such a wonderful series into reality when a chance conversation with one of our collaborators, Owen Wells, suggested Shaw and Sons Ltd to us. Conversations with Crispin Williams led quickly to the hard work of putting this volume together. Thanks must go to all the staff at Shaw and Sons for making such a timely intervention and for producing such an attractive and quality product in such haste.

At the end of the day, the words in these Moments belong to the authors. They are expressions of the mysteries of what 'probation' really is and I hope you will find something in there which strikes a note of accord and agreement. I also hope that you will take up the challenge of the book's final Moment!

Thank you to all the contributors.

Paul Senior
September 2008

Author Index

Introducing the Moments Series

Professor Paul Senior, Director of Hallam Centre for Community Justice, Sheffield Hallam University, Sheffield, UK

It was 1974. In the basement of Minshull Street Probation Office, Manchester, a bolshy left-wing student (see picture) – theoretically compromised as a potential teacher by the musings of Illich, A.S. Neill, Montessori and the de-schooling movement – was seeking to discover a challenge where theory and practice might interact more helpfully. I was shown around the 'day centre in the dungeon' by a committed Christian who lived in a catholic commune, an ex-police officer and a politics graduate. I had found a home. The intellectual curiosity that probation training encouraged, via a youthful diet of Keith Bottomley and Adrian James (admittedly as a counterpoint to what the Napo newsletter had announced as the 'death of rehabilitation') was exciting and affirming. The Action Group offered a ferment of socialist reflection and a bolthole from my first job where the prefix 'red under the bed' followed me around.

Seventeen years in the Service plus a further 15 years working in and around the Service has failed to dim that sense of purpose, innovation and challenge which my first encounter with probation clients (sorry ... service users? offenders? hoodies? performance targets?) engendered that day in Manchester. Keeping an empathy with people who could provoke many different and not always productive emotions whilst seeking to humanise their experience of the criminal justice system and, when necessary, protecting others, has remained a meaningful goal. Today we may challenge, confront and enforce but we should always do this, even a century on, in the spirit of 'advise, assist and befriend'.

Work with probation clients throws up exceptional and extraordinary challenges. This year-long '*Moments in Probation*' series seeks to capture such endeavours. Whilst the nascent service of the police court missionaries of 1907 may not recognise the probation officer of today (and I won't tempt fate by saying 'and tomorrow') the process of engagement with probation show many continuities. We want to capture those personal reflections in this series. There are five interlocking themes. First, accommodating policy and legislative change is a seemingly daily occurrence today, but no less important be it the 1907 Act itself (see tomorrow's Moment), the 1991 Act, the Morison or Streatfeild Committee to name a few. The second theme is developing positive practices, be it psycho-dynamic or task-centred casework, Heimler social functioning, cognitive-behavioural work, the Milan school of family therapy, or a myriad of other attempts to construct positive solutions. Research and theory forms our third theme, drawing on insights that have informed our perspectives. What books have influenced you the most? For me it was Bruce Hugman's *Act Natural*, Walker and Beaumont's *Radical Socialist Practice* and, from a personal vantage point, the writing of the fifth edition of *Jarvis* (rather like painting the Forth Bridge, but giving you an intimate knowledge of the supervisory requirements of offenders on the British Army on the Rhine, a fascinating office-party debate). Fourthly, a theme dear to my heart is training and staff development. What might distinguish those who were direct entrants, from Rainer house products to those from CQSW, CSS, DipSW and DipPS? What will be the training of tomorrow? Does in-house training shape the culture and attitudes of workers? To pursue these aims, an International Conference was held in September 2007.

We wanted this to be an inclusive project. We invited those who were involved in an innovative project in the past. We asked the following questions:

- What figure or book influenced you?
- What was it like to work in a rural setting?
- How did a particular Act impact on you?

I was delighted to receive offers to write a Moment.

Certainly, it has been a long time since 1974. My enthusiasm remains undimmed about the importance of this work. I guess I am still bolshy and, even if the passage of time dulls the revolutionary zeal, still seeking to be creative and innovative in my approach.

I hope you enjoy these Moments as they appeared each day in 2007. There was a rush of daily contributions until March 17th and then the series was kept alive throughout the year by further contributors.

This Tremendous and Progressive Step: The Probation of Offenders Act 1907

David Phillips, Senior Lecturer in Probation Studies, Hallam Centre for Community Justice, Sheffield, UK

The Probation Service was born in the first decade of the 20th-century, a time of public anxiety and rapid political and social change. In 1906, the Liberal Party (with its 'new liberalism') was elected by a landslide vote, largely on the issue of free trade. However, it soon found itself responding to a number of challenges that it had perhaps not anticipated. Public confidence had been shaken by the recent Boer War when badly armed farmers, fighting a guerrilla war, had held the British army at bay and challenged imperialism. The Rowntree and Booth reports had highlighted the extent of poverty and deprivation that underpinned growing industrial unrest. The Victorian prisons were full.

The response to these challenges was a series of social reforms, up to the outbreak of war in 1914, that included provision for the first old-age pensions, unemployment insurance, labour exchanges and free school meals. The state acknowledged that it had a responsibility to remove the shackles of poverty, unemployment and ill-health to allow people to be free to exercise choice and realise opportunity.

In addition to the welfare measures, a number of new penal measures were introduced, including probation, borstal training, preventive detention and licensed supervision. These were designed to remove some offenders from prison. The Probation of Offenders Act 1907 enabled, but didn't compel, courts to appoint paid probation officers for the first time and to impose probation orders on offenders. Royal assent was granted on 21st August 1907 and the Act came into effect on 1st January 1908, marking the birth of the Probation Service that is only now (2007) being dramatically transformed.

Probation officers, of either sex, could now be appointed by courts and paid a salary and expenses, often from fine receipts. They supervised youthful offenders, first offenders and, in some areas, the old and habitual offenders. Work also extended to prison aftercare and intervention in domestic disputes. No training or support was provided but some probation officers also worked for voluntary organisations, such as the

Police Court Mission or the Church of England Temperance Society, in addition to the court.

Published memoirs of these early days describe a new way of dealing with offenders through this "tremendous and progressive step" (Harris (1937): p.20). Jo Harris, an early probation officer working in Lowestoft, describes how he would initially interview probationers at home in his study for a "solemn half hour" in this initial "surgical" part of the order. Through this discussion he familiarised himself with the world of the offender and then followed these inquiries with the "advisory talk". If he thought it appropriate, Jo Harris could request the court to impose conditions in the order. In Lowestoft, this would most likely be an order to keep away from the fish dock, where all manner of temptations arose.

During the course of the order, the offender might attend a club that Jo ran from his own home or be referred to other agencies. Jo recommended that records should be kept but not be "verbose or exaggerated" (p.31). The offender, if he had kept out of trouble, would hand back the probation document to Jo on the expiry date, and both would ceremoniously watch it burn to ashes.

As the 'Century of Probation' arrived, the Service was undergoing a transition to the National Offender Management Service (NOMS). It was hoped that we would not 'ceremoniously watch it burn to ashes'. The last words should go to Jo Harris: "Keep officialism in its right place, it is only the under servant of the great movement, but unless this is closely watched it could become a dictator" (p.32).

End Note

Our thanks are due to the Nottingham Galleries of Justice who made records available and to Jo Harris for his book: *Probation*, published 1937 by Robinson and Co. in Lowestoft.

Report of the Advisory Council on the Treatment of Offenders, 1963

Professor Anthony Goodman,
Principal Lecturer in Criminology,
Middlesex University, Enfield, UK

In April 1961, the Advisory Council on the Treatment of Offenders was asked to review the arrangements for statutory and voluntary after-care for both adults and juveniles. Chaired by The Hon Mr Justice Barry, they subsequently produced their report in October 1963, the year after the Morison Report had already highlighted the need for the Probation Service to take on after-care.

Barry consulted widely and Part One of the report includes a fascinating history of the growth of the Discharged Prisoners' Aid Societies (DPAS). The National Association (NADPAS) had recently 'been charged with the important function of recruiting social workers for employment in prisons' (p.1). The exchequer paid for the running costs of NADPAS.

Back in 1953, the Maxwell Committee had produced a report on the needs of discharged prisoners (the Maxwell Committee), though this had only been concerned with voluntary after-care. Barry agreed with its conclusions that "the central object of after-care is to provide such guidance and moral support as will help the ex-prisoner to cope with his personal and peculiar difficulties" (p.4). There were a number of different DPAS groups at the time of the report and Barry did not want there to be differences between them regarding services offered to ex-prisoners.

Barry recognised that ex-prisoners needed much support: "A job, a home and a friend may still be the essential needs, but the task of helping each individual to find them in the form which best meets his personal needs requires patience, skill and imagination of a high order" (p.4). These skills were seen as a form of social work, requiring special qualities, training and experience. Sadly, the report made the following comment:

> "Many of the local aid societies, for reasons of financial stringency, have of necessity had to employ as after-care officers persons with other sources of income who may not be adequately equipped for the work."

This was a delicate way of saying that after-care should not be left to the rich to indulge in a bit of philanthropic do-goodery!

NADPAS felt that the solution to this 'flagging voluntary movement' was for them to become the central point for after-care, but Barry saw that this would result in two, wholly Exchequer-financed, parallel systems: one for compulsory after-care using probation officers as its field agents; one for voluntary after-care and employing social workers in prisons and in the community. The report could see no logic for two separate systems of after-care, especially as offenders could oscillate between compulsory and voluntary after-care. In Part Two, the report then considered how this could be brought about.

The report considered whether the Probation Service would be linked too strongly with the prison system if it took over the social work role within the prison. It concluded that this was the case, with the possible exception of detention centres (for short-sentenced young offenders) as their (locally-based) probation officers were likely to be able to visit them. At the time of writing the report, following the earlier Maxwell report, there was a social worker appointed to every local prison in England and Wales, with more than one in the bigger institutions. Barry recommended that all prisons should have social work support as long-sentenced prisoners were in as much need for this as short-sentenced ones.

Finally, the report concluded that there was a strong case for concentrating on a single service in the community and opted that this should be undertaken by an expanded Probation Service. As the Morison report had commented, after-care could be the 'Cinderella' of the Probation Service and probation officers could regard after-care as secondary to their 'normal functions'. Barry felt that this could be overcome and that the new title should be 'The Probation and After-Care Service'. Professor Leon Radzinowicz and two others disagreed in this amalgamation. By 1966, probation had taken over all through- and after-care functions and NADPAS became the National Association for the Care and Resettlement of Offenders (NACRO).

The Victim's Charter

† *Brian Williams, Professor of Community Justice and Victimology, De Montfort University, Leicester, UK*

The Victim's Charter was welcomed by Victim Support but criticised by shadow home secretary Roy Hattersley as a 'cynical gesture' when it was introduced in 1990. It came as something of a shock to the Probation Service, which was given new responsibilities without any new resources. Consultation had been minimal.

The only big idea Major's Government had in relation to victims of crime was that victims should be provided with more information about the offender, at least in the most serious cases. Unlike some of the other charters' provisions (and much other policy-making in relation to victims of crime), this was based upon sound evidence about what victims wanted. The Victim's Charter suggested (in a very tentative way) that it might be a good idea for the Probation Service to offer victims and survivors regular information

in cases where the offender received a life sentence; for example, explaining what the sentence meant at the outset, offering information as the sentence progressed, and consulting the victim at key points in the sentence. This was not true consultation, because victims' views did not count for much (particularly in the early days), but it was to prove an historic step, introducing the principle of such consultation for the first time. Towards the end of lifers' sentences, victims/survivors would be informed in general terms of the release plans. This had radical implications for probation officers working with the offender: release plans could not be vetoed by victims' survivors, but they often provided information which threw the intended plans into doubt. Not surprisingly, this was unpopular with some through-care specialists.

By the mid-90s, it was apparent that the Victim's Charter was not being consistently implemented around England and Wales. Generally speaking, big metropolitan probation areas had invested resources in establishing a service for the victims and survivors of offenders sentenced to life imprisonment (although some had not) and most rural probation areas had done nothing. There was controversy about the merits of setting up a specialist service as opposed to adding Charter duties to those of supervising probation officers – and in most areas, specialist provision won the day. As offenders and victims moved around the country and probation staff tried to transfer cases, the disparities between different levels and models of provision became very obvious. Probation staff and managers were well aware of the iniquities of 'justice by geography' and there was growing disquiet about these variations.

The problems were brought to the attention of members of parliament in a number of cases, and the government acted (perhaps to avoid political embarrassment, or perhaps from nobler motives), first by issuing circulars requiring the implementation of the provisions concerning victim contact in lifer cases, and later by re-issuing the Victim's Charter and widening the requirements it made of probation.

It was in 1994 that I, with a group of colleagues, first became involved in evaluating the impact of the Victim's Charter. We found considerable resistance to involvement with victims, and our work confirmed that the Charter's provisions were being implemented very patchily. Soon afterwards, the government issued a new version of the Charter widening the information service to victims to include all cases where the offender received four years or more in prison (later further extended to one year). What had begun as a small, bespoke service to a few hundred offenders rapidly became a major component of the work of the Probation Service and a huge cultural shift was under way: probation became a service working with offenders, communities and victims.

End Note

Brian sadly died during 2007, leaving a wife and young family, and will be sorely missed by colleagues inside and outside probation. He was co-editor of the *British Journal of Community Justice* with Paul Senior and the three issues of Volume 5 of 2008 have been dedicated to his memory (www.cjp.org.uk). We thank his wife for permission to publish this Moment.

Intermediate Treatment:
Treats or Therapy?

*Charlotte Knight, Principal Lecturer in Community
and Criminal Justice, De Montfort University,
Leicester, UK*

The concept of 'intermediate treatment' was introduced by the 1969 Children and Young Persons Act at a time when 'therapeutic' work with young offenders was probably at its peak. Legislation enabled local authorities to provide resources for young people at risk of, or involved in, offending to participate in group, residential and community projects, as an 'intermediate' option between 'normal' supervision and custody.

As a student on the probation pathway of the CQSW programme at Leicester University in 1972/73, I undertook my fieldwork placement with Leicester City Probation Service. Fired with the 'rehabilitative ideal', and keen to make an early contribution to such work with young offenders, myself and a fellow student presented a case to the Chief Probation Officer, with regard to running a camp for young offenders. With the support of newly qualified officer, Mike Othen,[1] we were successful in gaining a small sum of money, plus permission that enabled us to take a group of ten young male offenders to camp in Derbyshire for a long weekend. The following year, encouraged by our 'success', I became involved with another probation officer in running a more comprehensive IT project involving three residential trips, with intervening weekly evening programmes of activity for a mixed group of male and female young offenders aged 14 to 16.

The underlying philosophy of IT schemes was to promote positive alternatives to an offending lifestyle that introduced young people to outdoor and group activities beyond their current experiences, alongside opportunities to promote a sense of personal and collective responsibility for behaviour. I guess we could have called much of this 'pro-social modelling'. It was very challenging work being in such close and regular proximity with some quite disturbed young people. We had some success in instilling a sense of group responsibility in undertaking tasks and determining rules of behaviour, with sanctions for 'breach', collectively agreed.

The concept of intermediate treatment was subsequently challenged on two rather different fronts. The right-wing press had something of a field day in highlighting examples of young offenders being taken on 'holiday' and seemingly being rewarded for bad behaviour. Left-wing commentators, supported by some research, were able to argue that intermediate treatment was 'net-widening' and, although well-intentioned, was bringing increasing numbers of non-convicted, 'at risk' young people into the system too early and thus pushing them up the sentencing tariff when they were subsequently convicted, on the grounds that 'treatment' had been tried and failed. The concept of 'non-intervention' for significant numbers of young people who had committed minor acts of delinquency but subsequently 'grew out of' crime, gained sway along with the temporary rise of the 'Nothing Works' era, and intermediate treatment was relegated to the history books.

It is quite salutary to recall the level of creativity and autonomy that was permissible in the early 70s for 'young', 'inexperienced' and pretty 'naïve' probation staff to work with young offenders. I learnt a great deal more about the young people on these schemes than I ever did from office interviews and I like to believe that the strong relationships I built with quite a few of them did have a positive impact on their lives. Sadly, I have no proof of this. We were required to write an evaluative report of both schemes at the end of the respective projects but I recall no link to re-offending being expected. What I do recall is the strong sense of personal accountability I felt for the work and the confidence invested in me by the chief officer (which now no doubt would be seen as misguided), that gave me a strong platform for developing my professional practice over the years.

End Note

[1]   Mike Othen tragically died from cancer six months after his partner was killed in a car crash in 1983, leaving three young sons to be brought up by their grandparents.

Flagging Standards

*Professor Rob Canton, School of Applied Social
Sciences, De Montfort University, Leicester, UK*

In the autumn of 1992, at the time of the implementation of the Criminal
Justice Act, I was working as the senior probation officer of a busy city
team. The Act was to be supported by National Standards. We had come
across this idea a few years earlier when Standards on Community Service
had been issued. The new edition covered all the Service's core tasks.

Our team was particularly exercised by the sections prescribing levels of
contact. It is widely believed that, until that time, contact depended on
the idiosyncrasies of supervisors, but in some Services, including ours,
there were already attempts to make sure that the level of contact would
be determined by assessment of risk and need. Standards cut across all of
this.

Whether intentionally or not, the Standards also effectively brought an
end to voluntary after-care. Once, a serious sex offender came into our
office, released after a long sentence. Having always been considered too
risky to release on parole, he was therefore subject to no form of statutory
supervision. He told us that through-care work had convinced him that
he posed a continuing danger to children and asked for our help in
avoiding re-offending. I experienced considerable difficulty in persuading
my manager that we should respond to this request at all: such work was
not covered by National Standards and might therefore be abandoned.
Meanwhile, irrespective of risk, need or the amount of work to be done,
probationers convicted of minor offences had to be seen every week.

It is instructive to compare the Standards with the Code of Practice
promulgated by the Crown Prosecution Service, an organisation that was
the same age then as the National Probation Service is now. The Code
required staff to make judgments within a framework of stated principles
and objectives: it was a document written by lawyers, for lawyers. The
Standards were written for practitioners by civil servants. In answering
questions that are often complex, the Code invoked principles of fairness
and public interest; Standards, with a complacent disregard of the challenges
of securing compliance, answered questions of no less complexity with

'four times a month – and no slacking'. They confused consistency with sameness, often losing sight of purpose in their preoccupation with detail. They also wrongly assumed that accountability and good practice meant that discretion, increasingly circumscribed in successive editions, should be ever more constrained.

Teams were already busy and years later, in the opinion of the Carter Report and Her Majesty's Chief Inspector, the Service became swamped. Standards effectively prevented the Service from responding to this by intelligent prioritisation according to risk and need. While the core principles of effective practice – risk, responsivity and criminogenic need – call for differentiation and judgment, the Standards indiscriminately prescribed the same for everyone. Their neglect of diversity is a particular shortcoming. As Barbara Hudson puts it, "Once the subject of justice is given back his/her social context and flesh and blood reality, it is clear that difference is the standard case, and that differences are routinely irreducible" (Hudson 2001, p.166). This entails discretion and indeed calls into question the whole idea of National Standards as they are now prescribed.

Conformity with the Standards was increasingly mistaken for quality. More plausibly, such conformity is a sign of efficiency and this is, to be sure, a virtue of organisations. However, Standards have never been evidence-led (they are really Rules rather than Standards), and indeed have been defiantly indifferent to findings of research (for instance on the matter of enforcement and programme completion). Drafted and implemented differently, it could all have been otherwise. What we needed and did not get was professional guidance to support the core tasks of a Service dedicated to bringing out the best in people. It's what we are; it's what we do.

Reference

Hudson, B. (2001). 'Punishment, Rights and Difference: Defending Justice in the Risk Society' in *Crime, Risk and Justice: The Politics of Crime Control in Liberal Democracies* by Kevin Stenson and Robert Sullivan (eds.) (Cullompton: Willan).

Report on the Departmental Committee on the Probation Service, 1962

Professor Anthony Goodman, Principal Lecturer in Criminology, Middlesex University, Enfield, UK

The report on the Departmental Committee on the Probation Service, published in 1962, should be compulsory reading for our policy makers as a study on why it is important to retain a Probation Service that is capable of listening to, and working with, offenders. It is steeped in the language of casework and the recognition by the courts that work with offenders is a skilled and challenging activity.

It begins with a definition of probation from the United Nations, Department of Social Affairs, from 1951: "probation is a method of dealing with specially selected offenders consisting of the conditional suspension of punishment while the offender is placed under personal supervision and is given individual guidance or treatment". The Criminal Justice Act 1991 made probation a sentence in its own right, but the notion of 'personal supervision', forgotten in more recent attempts to deconstruct the offender into constituent parts that could be worked on separately, ignored the essence of probation, namely that the offender needs a focal point of contact that they can relate to.

The report is not by any means a sentimental attempt to portray the offender as a victim. The Departmental Committee did not like the word 'client'. The caseworker "needs the fullest possible insight into the individual's personality, capacities, attitudes and feelings and he must also understand the influences in the individual's history, relationships and present environment which have helped to form them" (p.24). It commented that the general view of those that gave evidence to it was that it was valuable for the probationer to accept being placed on probation, however grudgingly, and that this was valuable for the future conduct of the offender. "Probation extracts from the offender a contribution, within the limits of his capacity, to the well-being of others, whether it be through his useful employment in the community or through his participation in the life of the family or other social group" (p.4). In this succinct sentence, the report pre-dates the work of writers like Stephen Farrall and Shad Maruna by highlighting the importance of what is now called 'social capital' and the need to get offenders into employment as well as keeping them linked into family support.

The object of the probation order is the "ultimate re-establishment of the probationer in the community" (this is actually a quotation in the 1962 report from a 1936 report). It continues: "[W]e should deprecate any tendency to regard such purpose as other than therapeutic even although its fulfilment requires guidance and control of the probationer" (p.5). The report was not afraid to use words that one could not imagine emanating from contemporary politicians that seek to punish, control and monitor.

The report describes the research of the 1958 survey, conducted by the Cambridge Department of Criminal Science, that examined the records of over 9,000 offenders placed on probation. It reported a success rate of 73.8% for adults and 62.4% for juveniles. It acknowledged the lack of matched control groups. It summarised the value of probation as follows: "There is a moral case, in a society founded upon respect for human rights, for a system which allows an offender to continue to live and work in the community" (p.9).

The report commented that the demands on the Service should increase, referring to prison after-care, which had been the remit of the Discharged Prisoners' Aid Societies. At the time of writing, this was under review by ACTO, which is the subject of a different entry in this series (see p.5). It saw after-care work as not being "extraneous to the normal functions of the Service" (p.151), thus it paved the way for its inclusion into the professional task of probation. Morison's report was far-sighted and, sadly, many of its messages have been forgotten.

Alternatives to Custody Rarely Means Substitution for Custody – A Tale of Net-Widening and Sentence Confusion from 1975

Professor Ken Pease, Visiting Professor, Loughborough University and University College London, UK

I think it was on April Fools Day 1975 when our first report on community service orders, as they were then, was published by HMSO. If it wasn't, it should have been. It had been a long time in the editing, or should I say 'emasculation', by the civil servants in the Probation and After-Care Department of the Home Office. Bill McWilliams and I later (in 1980) edited a book in which we said some of what needed to be said. The message which needed to be screamed loud and clear was that if a sanction is marketed as an alternative to another, confusion and injustice will result.

Dick Sparks had already shown that suspended sentences of imprisonment were only imposed in place of unsuspended sentences in around 50% of cases, the problem being compounded by making the suspension of imprisonment mandatory in some circumstances. The confusion permeated the introduction of community service orders both here and overseas.

Charlie Rook in Tasmania did a particularly elegant piece of research making the point for that antipodean former penal colony. The confusion matters less if in any particular case everyone knows the score, but research by Tony Vass and others showed that this was not the case, so that people who were not at risk of custody could be imprisoned on revocation of an order, and those who really did get a community penalty instead of custody could again avoid imprisonment on revocation because the revoking could readily mistake the intention of the sentencing court. The confusion also made a nonsense of consent to a community sentence. This lesson has not yet been learned.

Alternatives to custody remains a topic on the Youth Justice Board website and that of Women in Prison, and is the title of a recent report from the Scottish Parliament Information Centre. It is the topic of a recent independent report for the Esmee Fairbairn Foundation, a 2006 Oxford conference, and so on – organisations like SmartJustice campaign under the banner. Apart from the confusion and injustice, using custody as the benchmark in sentencing obscures what you really want to achieve. Google 'alternatives to custody' and see what I mean. The canny Baroness, Barbara Wootton, had avoided the phrase in her 1970 ACPS sub-committee report with the words 'Non-Custodial and Semi-Custodial Penalties' which begat community service orders in the first place.

How would you answer a right-wing cynic who sees 'alternatives to custody' as politicians' moral pressure on kindly people who would prefer not to lock other folk up? How would you respond to her perception that prison overcrowding through tardy prison building is a device to make community penalties more palatable, and who recognises Home Office research on confidence in community penalties as missing the point of why one should have such confidence? How the cynic would smile at the most misleading of comparisons, the routine Home Office way of calculating reconviction rates by starting the risk period for those given custodial sentences upon their release from sentence, and from the date of imposition of the sentence for those given community sentences. Only by leaving incapacitation out of the equation can community penalties look as good as custody in terms of public protection.

Thus, two insights dawned with April Fools Day in 1975 – that labelling some rungs on the penal ladder as alternatives to custody invited confusion and that many subtle pressures precluded a clear-eyed official look at the benefits of such sanctions. Bill McWilliams was a liberal cynic. When a nurse in a mental hospital before becoming a probation officer, he was once cornered by a violent patient who addressed him thus "W**ker's doom, you b***ard Bailey, I'll get you for this you f***ing swine". Bill thereafter used this as a surreal comment when things became incomprehensible to him. I find myself saying it ever more often.

References

Pease, K., Durkin, P., Earnshaw, I., Payne, D. and Thorpe, J. *Community Service Orders. Home Office Research Study 29.* (1975: London: HMSO (p80).)

Pease, K. and McWilliams, W. (1980) *Community Service by Order.* (1980: Edinburgh: Scottish Academic Press: p149.)

Creating the Diploma in Probation Studies 1997

Professor Paul Senior, Director of Hallam Centre for Community Justice, Sheffield Hallam University, Sheffield, UK

There was a collective sigh of relief when Michael Howard's draconian plans for probation training were shelved in the light of the election defeat of 1997. The worst excesses of a competence-based approach without any higher education involvement were removed, and early statements by Jack Straw confirmed that the aspiration for probation to be a graduate profession would in the short term be preserved. Sadly, the anathema, which had become social work methodology as the core underpinning for probation officer's practice, was still firmly out in the cold. As the mist settled, the new terrain for training probation officers resembled a rather different set of policy imperatives: changing higher education frameworks and incorporating National Vocational Qualifications. Whether the loss of social work as an explicit theory system was crucial, only history will judge.

In the later years of DipSW provision, curricula for probation had already begun to take on a distinctive feel reflecting the greater attention paid to risk assessment and management, public protection and, as yet just a nascent, 'What Works' agenda. It was questionable whether social work, as a philosophy and as a set of theories, represented a sufficient enough basis for the shaping of this new award. Institutionally, this decision was taken out of university hands. For some institutions it contributed to a feeling that now was the time to exit from this training and this, for some, was reinforced by the new arrangements as they began to emerge. For others, the chance to update the form and content of such training, and to make it more employer-focused, was a difficult but necessary condition of the changes and, utilising emerging credit framework structures from the new universities, a very differently sculpted award began to grow.

The key elements were: employer-led structures and curricula; achievement of an NVQ integrated academically into the degree award; a single level of performance assessed at degree level; a tight, some would say impossible, timetable of 24 months to achieve it all; and the requirement that at any one-time trainees were a mixture of students, NVQ trainees and employees. The elements are represented diagrammatically. As someone who helped shaped this structure, I can reflect that it was mistrusted by almost all recipients. The loss of an illogical but strongly held mixed economy of awards at non-graduate, graduate and post-graduate levels was deeply resented by higher education; the permissive approach to the curricula driven too by the demands of an NVQ was mistrusted; the attempt to academically accredit an NVQ powerfully resisted as somehow anathema to liberal education; the 24-month timescale

Developing the Professional

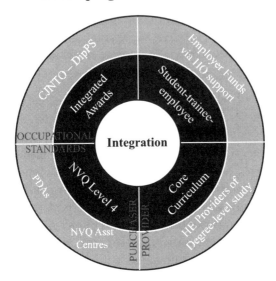

allegedly dumbing down education; the ability of services to organise and deliver the sort of learning environment this question demanded; the regional approach to delivery lambasted; and the precise role of the (Practice Development Assessor) PDA, coined as a term to meet various needs in one role, distrusted. These and many other innovations conspired to breed debates, arguments and resentments in equal measures.

Change the world of training professional workers in probation it certainly did. Producing competent, fit for purpose, probation officers it certainly did. Finding ways to integrate academic and practice learning, history will judge, but I would say it has been a hugely innovative and ultimately successful structure. The one potential downfall is that, although built on a model of partnership, one element has had control and this has increased. This, more than any other element, can undermine a shared framework for future developments in such as offender management. I hope everyone involved can be kept on board and help shape the next generation of professional awards if we are not to lose the many exciting elements the DipPS helped create.

Turnips and Life Graphs

Kit Barton, Assistant Chief Officer, North Wales Probation Area, UK

I never knew you could live off turnips, but apparently you can.

I first met Alistair, (not his real name), when I was a newly qualified probation officer working in Westminster in 1976. Initially, he was just like the majority of my clients (yes, that was what we called them then), in that he was in his late 20s, homeless, living in a cardboard box, and up in court for a minor offence of theft. What steered him in my direction was partly the reference to homicide in his very short list of previous convictions and something about his lost and vacant manner in court. Both the Stipendary Magistrate and I felt that he needed some 'advice, assistance and befriending'.

With some difficulty I managed to find him a bed in one of the local hostels, as well as arranging access to money, first from the court 'poor box' and then, on a more regular basis, from the DHSS. I wondered whether he would turn up for his first appointment but he did. At that stage I started to wonder what I could usefully do with him. Perhaps it was my youthful ignorance or perhaps it was intuition, but something told me he wanted to talk about what had happened to him – so that's what we agreed to do. We would spend the next few weeks (in the end it was nearly 12 months) going over his background and life history in whatever detail he felt was necessary. I would listen and ask questions and he would talk. We would write down what was necessary.

Over the next weeks and months the story came out, with some questioning, particularly when we got to very painful memories, but mainly I just seemed to provide the space and the ear. His story was one of loneliness and childhood abuse on a sparsely populated Scottish island, culminating in him shooting up at the ceiling with his father's gun, whilst his father was raging at him from upstairs. Unfortunately, the shot went through the ceiling and killed his father. He was arrested and sent to an approved school for some years before being released to his Aunt. One day on his way to work, and for no apparent reason, he left the town, his job and his Aunt, and went on the road.

For the next few years he lived the life of a vagrant, mainly living off vegetables (primarily turnips) stolen from the fields around. He had drifted into London and the hostel bed I had found for him was the first time he had slept under a roof for many years. At one point, he asked me to contact the local Island council for some information about his past. At the first mention of his name the person I spoke to said, "Not the person who killed his father?". This was many years after the event. He might have been nobody in London but clearly he was a celebrity at home.

Alistair never missed an appointment and he was always on time. He remained at the hostel and got a job. He didn't offend and it was clear that he hugely valued our work together. He became much less vacant and seemed to be developing a sense of the future. However, one day towards the end of his order, and very much at the conclusion of our work together, he disappeared again. I will never really know what good the whole thing did or whether what I did with him was the right thing. However, I don't think I've ever felt such a strong need in anyone to talk about their life history and it was clear that he was getting some dreadful life experiences into some kind of perspective. Perhaps he went back to a life on the road, perhaps even back to a diet of turnips, but I like to think that, if he did, it was more as a matter of choice than it was before, and that he was at least a little happier and less confused. As far as I am aware, he never offended again but, unlike today where reduction in offending is the primary goal, that would have been as a by-product of the work we did, not as its main purpose. The real focus was on him and on his own, very real needs.

So what has all this to do with today's modern world of probation? In part, it shows up the differences in approach and philosophy between now and then. Equally it shows up that some of the fundamentals remain. Life graphs are now a frequent feature of modern probation practice and their usefulness is well-understood. Similarly, much group work activity is based around getting offenders to review and take stock of their behaviour and attitudes, and to discover how some of their thinking distortions might have arisen. The research base is now much more solid and there is perhaps less reliance on intuition.

For me, Alistair is a client I will never forget. He helped me to understand, and feel, a harsh and lonely world I had never known. I probably learnt more from him than he learnt from me and for that I will always be grateful.

The Birth of Community Service by Offenders in England & Wales, 1973–1975

John Harding, former Senior Probation Officer,
Nottinghamshire Probation Service/
Community Service 1972/1974,[1] UK

Community service was the brainchild of a criminal justice think tank, the Advisory Council on the Penal System. In 1966, Roy Jenkins, the then Home Secretary, appointed a criminologist, Barbara Wootton, to lead a committee on non-custodial and semi-custodial penalties. Following governmental acceptance of the premise that it provided "an opportunity for offenders to perform constructive activity in the community and the possibility of a changed outlook on the part of the offender", the Home Office set up a working party of probation chiefs. The pilot areas included, Nottinghamshire, Inner London, Kent, Durham, SW Lancashire, and Shropshire. The use of a small number of pilot areas had much to commend it; the worst mistakes could be avoided, and the possibility of failure is acknowledged. The pilots were evaluated by Ken Pease (see the Moment dated January 8th, p.15). The empowering legislation appeared in the 1972 Criminal Justice Act.

I was appointed as the senior probation officer for the Nottingham pilot, but was given little guidance from the Home Office about whether community service was an alternative to imprisonment or a sentence in its own right. We were asked to have suitable tasks in place within four months. Each area was shaped by the views of the local chief, the courts, and indeed, the persuasion of the pilot SPOs and their staff. There were three major components to be accomplished before the launch: the identification of tasks for offenders; awareness setting and training of court staff; and referrals through social inquiry reports written by probation staff.

In Nottinghamshire, we had a particularly strong association with the Councils of Social Service and thus links to voluntary and neighbourhood groups. Extensive meetings took place with education services; community centres and youth clubs; Social Services, in particular, old peoples homes, disability and day centres; housing associations, parks, canal sites, etc. Following my own training in community development, I was interested in locating neighbourhood tasks that were relevant and appropriate to offenders' lives. The New Careers catchphrase of the 70s, borrowed from the USA, whereby offenders could be legitimately empowered from being recipients of aid to dispensers of service, had a certain compelling resonance. In fact, a significant minority of those early community service graduates went on to take up para-professional roles in public services. Tasks were located either in a group setting with a paid supervisor or in individuals being placed with voluntary organisations in ones and twos. We were careful to avoid conflicts with paid work situations, though later on, this became blurred.

Sentencers were supportive; a few diehards wanted it to be unpleasant, even degrading, but the majority quickly silenced the critics, regarding community service as a positive penalty, 'a fine on an offender's time' that made imaginative sense. Probation officers were sometimes less than wholehearted; some doctrinaire colleagues considered that staff would become 'screws on wheels' in a punishment mode, failing to see that community service represented an indirect form of reparation. Overall though, colleagues were supportive and enabling.

The first community service order in the world was made in Nottingham Crown Court on 2nd January 1970. The order was for 120 hours and was given to Peter Giles, a cannabis supplier, by Mr Justice James, the Presiding Judge in the Great Train Robbery. On the day of the sentence, the steps leading to the court were littered with TV cameras from the Western World. Peter Giles, with shoulder-length hair and a suede caftan, became a minor celebrity before he proceeded to work in an old people's home.

Community service orders then flourished in the six areas. The scheme was viable; orders were made and completed. Even though the research left many unanswered questions, the government had sufficient confidence to sanction a national roll-out after 1975. Replication of community service spread across Europe, North America and Australasia, within ten years. It is estimated that a quarter of £1billion worth of unpaid work has enhanced the social capital of numerous towns and cities in the past 30 years.

Those of us who were fortunate enough to have been involved in the pilots were part of a belief system that probation can make a difference to changing offenders' lives, provided that hard-work, clarity of purpose and vision underpinned all our efforts.

End Note

[1]   Currently Visiting Professor of Criminal Justice at Hertfordshire University.

Probation Joins the Criminal Justice System – Reflections on the Probation Service in the 1980s

David Faulkner, Senior Research Associate Centre for Criminology, University of Oxford, UK

When I first encountered the Probation Service in 1962, it functioned essentially as a group of independent practitioners, loosely co-ordinated by principal probation officers who were not so much managers as first among equals.

In that respect, not much had changed when I became the Deputy Secretary for Probation in 1982. The service was now involved in prison after-care, parole supervision and community service, but most probation officers still saw their main responsibility as being to their clients, or sometimes to the courts, certainly not to the public or the government. Many were motivated by a sense of justice for their clients, whom they often saw not so much as offenders but as victims of an unfair social system. All were jealous of their professional and operational independence. Their political sympathies were usually with the left, but their – quite numerous – political friends were more often in the House of Lords and among 'traditional' Conservatives than in the Labour Party or in Margaret Thatcher's Government.

Like all public servants, probation officers felt the effects of the Thatcher Government's impatience with professional service-providers. They had to face the decline of 'liberalism' and the emergence of new public and political values. Despite their still potentially influential friends, the future in 1982 was beginning to look quite precarious.

In the event, the Government needed the Service to provide convincing 'punishment in the community' and so help limit prison overcrowding. Few probation officers could quarrel with that, although there were misgivings about probation having a role in punishment. Most came to accept that the FMI and its standards and indicators were necessary if the Service was to survive. Some saw them more positively (as I did) as the means by which the Service could be more effective.

The service also needed a stronger sense of direction and leadership. ACOP, NAPO and the Inspectorate had their own functions and agendas, but none of them were able to provide it. Probation officers more or less accepted the Home Office 'Statement of National Objectives and Priorities', drafted by my colleague Bill Bohan, but it was not a professional vision owned by the Service. Even so, we were still a long way from a situation in which the Home Office thought it could, or wanted to, give orders.

It was also my job to 'join up' the criminal justice system. That brought probation into closer contact with the police, the Prison Service, and with the Home Office. Early suspicions and sometimes outright hostility (police and probation officers had often thought of themselves almost as natural enemies) gave way to an increasing sense of mutual respect. Officers of ACOP had more contact with Ministers and a stronger influence on the formation of national policy, such as in framing the Criminal Justice Act 1991. Through the courts' increasing confidence in community sentences, and with political support from government, we were able to bring the prison population down from 50,000 to about 42,000. Graham Smith, then Chief Probation Officer for Inner London, emerged as the professional leader of the Service and later, as HM Chief Inspector. He was able to secure the Service's survival when its existence came under more serious threat.

At the same time, individual casework began to give way to less personal case management, and the probation officer's relationship with the offender (no longer to be called the client) came to rest more on compulsion and less on consent. More emphasis was placed on enforcement, and support for victims became increasingly significant. The service was expected to work more closely with voluntary organisations, for which some probation officers still saw no place. Probation officers had been among the first to recognise what came to be called 'institutional racism', but it was harder to work out the implications for their own professional practice.

None of that was easy or straight forward, and some of it was quite painful. However, I believe the Service and the Home Office, with Philippa Drew as Head of the Probation Service division, were able to work constructively together, and that the 80s were, for most probation staff, a period of relative optimism and professionally rewarding progress.

End Notes

[1]   The developments described here took place 'on his watch' as the responsible deputy secretary in the Home Office from 1982 to 1990.

[2]   The story is told in Chapter 7 of *Crime, State and Citizen: A Field Full of Folk*, Second Edition (2006: Winchester: Waterside Press).

Taking Anti-Racism Forward in the 1980s

Steve Collett, Chief Officer, Cheshire Probation Area and Honorary Fellow of the Department of Sociology & Social Policy, Liverpool University, UK

During the 1980s, race relations and problems of inequality began to challenge probation to respond constructively in a way that seemed to bypass some of our criminal justice partners. This was a period in which economic de-industrialisation led to unprecedented levels of unemployment and economic disadvantage. In the conurbations, racial tension expressed itself in what was ubiquitously and simplistically reported as race riots. As with Brixton and the disturbances of April 1981 (which prompted the setting up of the Scarman Inquiry), Merseyside experienced significant disturbances in both 1981 and 1985. However, unlike today's debate about cultural differences, immigration and terrorism, we were faced with the unpalatable truth that integration and assimilation of one of Britain's oldest black communities did not protect individuals from discrimination and racism in housing, employment, social services and criminal justice.

Evidence was emerging that, whilst there was little variation in the level of crime generated by black and white communities, black men and women appeared to be caught up in a system where decision-making from the street to the court ultimately propelled them disproportionately into our prisons. On 30th June 1989, our prisons held some 48,532 individuals. Both black men and women were significantly over-represented compared to their proportion within the general population (by a factor of 3 and 5 respectively). The explanations were complex, and a broad range of research was beginning to show the relevance of differences between Black and Asian communities, the impact of age and the double discrimination experienced by black women. Practitioners and managers within probation were trying to make sense of the research to better understand the processes (indirect and institutional) that were resulting in over-representation within custodial institutions and under-representation on community alternatives.

Like other Probation Services, Merseyside committed itself to a comprehensive anti-racism training strategy as one mechanism for tackling these complex organisational problems. It is fascinating to look back to what we would now see as the duty to promote racial equality under the

Race Relations (Amendment) Act, 2000. A backward glance also provides a timely reminder of the expectations that were being placed on the Service in advance of the implementation of the 1991 Act. David Mathieson, Merseyside's then Chief Probation Officer, summed it up in the foreword to *Managing and Developing Anti-Racist Practice within Probation* (1992: Merseyside Probation Service: Liverpool) which myself and others wrote:

> "This is a time when the Probation Service is being urged to move centre-stage in the criminal and civil justice systems. Of all the agencies involved, the Probation Service ought to be able to give a clear lead in respect of anti-racist practice in view of our traditional social work values which emphasise respect for people without discrimination."

I believe that the Merseyside strategy represented a key strand in developing anti-racist practice. The argument that racism could only be understood in terms of its institutional nature is striking. It took the murder of Steven Lawrence and, in 1999, the MacPherson Inquiry to get full ownership of this view across all the agencies. MacPherson defined institutional racism in terms of unwitting behaviours. In our strategy, we stressed the impact of our behaviours rather than the intentions as the key. We also eschewed the saris and samosas approach, which emphasised better understanding of cultural diversity. Within our strategy, the political use of the term 'Black' was to denote the fact that skin colour rather than cultural differences was the important factor in understanding discrimination.

The training strategy included every member of staff and took two years to complete. In retrospect, some of our approaches were mechanistic. Promoting an understanding of racism in the context of skin colour to the exclusion of cultural differences may have been short-sighted. However, it was just months after the main training for staff was completed that Steven Lawrence was murdered (22nd April 1993), and why? Essentially, because he was a black youngster.

The criminal justice system continues to be littered with serious racist incidents as well as the everyday mundane actions, by ignorance or intent, that impact upon black and minority ethnic offenders, victims and colleagues. We have learnt that humanitarian values alone are insufficient to tackle discrimination but, as a Service, we should be proud of our long-standing commitment to act in ways that promote anti-racist practice. These early attempts to tackle racism were ultimately about the aspiration of delivering justice to all offenders and all victims. As Blairite modernity seems to be pushing us beyond, or perhaps even off centre-stage, commitment to criminal justice will be more important than ever.

Social Work with Offenders: 1990 – The Beginning of the End

Professor Adrian James, Professor of Applied Social Sciences, University of Sheffield, UK

There have been many important moments in the history of the Probation Service: moments relating to its organisation and training, its relationship with other criminal justice agencies, and to its operations. Few have been more important, however, than the publication of the Green Paper *Punishment, Custody and the Community* (1988: Home Office: Cm 424). Why? Because it marked the end of the ethos on which the Probation Service was founded and built.

This ethos was embodied in its social work with offenders. Based on its founding mission, which was to reclaim the souls of drunken offenders, the Service was rooted in an understanding of offending behaviour that rightly recognised the importance of a range of variables – alcohol, poverty, unemployment, low educational achievement, heredity, peer-group pressure and psychopathology – that historically were varyingly seen as contributory factors.

Punishment, Custody and the Community, and the subsequent White Paper *Crime, Justice and Protecting the Public* (1990: Home Office: Cm 965), finally dismissed this ethos. They drew to a close 15 years of debate about the effectiveness of a probation practice based on such understandings. It was a debate triggered by the widely quoted, widely misunderstood, but probably not widely read study published by Martinson in 1974, which lent itself to the erroneous but devastating claim in relation to such interventions that 'nothing works'.

As the titles of these policy documents so clearly signalled, they embodied a sea-change in the philosophy underpinning work with offenders, promulgating an approach based on a profoundly different understanding of the causation of offending behaviour, and thus of the role not only of the Probation Service, but of the criminal justice system as a whole. Rather than focusing on the treatment and rehabilitation of offenders through the social work intervention traditionally offered by the Probation Service, the new approach saw a radical shift of emphasis towards their punishment in the community, crime reduction and the protection of the public, and where necessary, through the use of custody.

This reflected a fundamental shift in the way the government sought to present and explain the causes of offending behaviour. As John Patten, the Home Office Minister responsible for taking this policy initiative forward, made unequivocally clear in an interview in the New Society (Jenkins, 25.11.88), this shift, and thus the re-orientation of the Probation Service, was based on the view that 'people commit crime because they are bad', therefore, attempts to explain crime by sociological phenomena like unemployment or affluence are 'cop outs". In these few words, decades of work based on an understanding of the relationship between structural constraints and other factors beyond the immediate control of the individual and their offending behaviour, were swept aside and with them the entire ethos of the Probation Service.

It also marked the emergence of the disingenuous desire of government to distance itself from any responsibility for crime that might be laid at its door through accusations of failure and to address the wide range of social inequalities that the welfare state had been intending to address in post-war Britain (a political motivation subsequently shared by both Conservative and Labour Governments). In spite of the current mantra of evidence-based policy and practice, the criminal justice system continues to fill our prisons with increasing numbers of people whose biographies are a telling condemnation of the failure of government to address such structural factors but whose crimes, we are led to believe, are committed because 'they are bad' and therefore deserve to be punished.

How It Was

*Owen Wells, Retired Probation Officer (Retired
2006) and Editor of The Probation Directory
incorporating Offender Management & Interventions
(Formerly Napo Probation Directory) since 1974*

It is now difficult for anyone to remember the huge respect enjoyed by the
Probation Service in the early 70s. When I gave up working in publishing I
knew I was losing out in salary terms (I think my salary declined by about
one third) but I was gaining more than that in public reputation. We
were almost universally respected for doing a poorly paid but eminently
worthwhile job. When we stood up in court, we were listened to with respect
(I keep coming back to that word, but it is the only appropriate one).

We were nearly all second-careerists. On my training course at Cromwell
Road there was a former TV set-designer, an engineer, a drug company
rep, a soldier, a miner, a policeman, and two Methodist Ministers; a fairly
eclectic mixture. Since all had decided to become probation officers late
in life it gave a tremendous stability and breadth of experience to the
Service.

Our caseload was about 40; less than 35 cases and one would twiddle
one's thumbs and complain about not having enough to do; over 45 cases
was regarded as fairly intolerable. Most of those 40 would be seen weekly,
some fortnightly, very seldom more infrequently. An interview would
usually last half an hour or more. Since we each had a half share of a
clerical officer, we were not expected to write up case notes. Good practice
was to dictate them to the clerical officer, who would then type them up.
Sharing an office was regarded as something distinctly unusual, so it was
normal to have our own office, in which we could conduct our interviews.
This meant that we could make it into our own workspace, with our own
pictures on the walls and our reference books close to hand. A proposal
for an open-plan office and impersonal interview rooms would have
been laughed into oblivion. Interview rooms came into existence on the
supposition that they were safer. However, I do not know of any research
that has shown that assaults are any more or less frequent as a result.

An SPO would have half the usual caseload. ACPOs might have the odd
case or two, and I remember one CPO who still had one or two clients
as he did not want to become too divorced from the reality of front-line

work. I would never have respected a senior who did not have a caseload; after all what would he or she know about the real dilemmas of the job or the pressures encountered in face-to-face work?

Home visiting was expected, and there was an expectation that you would know your patch. Going for a stroll to see who was hanging around, or which factory was advertising vacancies, was accepted as quite normal. It was later that, following riots in the North East, a committee of enquiry observed that the Probation Service had largely withdrawn into its offices and had little contact with the communities it served.

An advantage of home visiting was that one then knew the families of clients. It was quite commonplace to sit down in a kitchen and, over a cup of tea, talk to a mother about her delinquent son, or to a wife about the problems of having a husband in prison. Because people tended to work in the same office for very many years, one might well have supervised more than one generation of the same family.

As a high proportion of clients were employed, evening reporting was the norm. My chosen pattern (as a single parent) was to work very late one evening a week up until 9.00 or 10.00pm, instead of working until 7.00pm two or three times a week. On a late reporting night, it was considered acceptable not to come into the office until lunchtime, or to go home for a couple of hours in the afternoon. Given that we also worked about every third Saturday morning (covering the Saturday court) our hours were considerable. It was only when the Home Office (believing that we were not putting in the hours) introduced time sheets for a while that we all realised just how long we were working, and started claiming time off in lieu.

The CPO, Mr McGillivray, would regularly visit field offices, putting on an old mackintosh before going into the reception area and asking to see a probation officer. He did this to discover what sort of reception was given; as in those days, casual callers, asking for a handout or advice on almost anything, were a regular and accepted feature. I always thought that if the time came that the general public no longer believed they would get a civil welcome when calling at a probation office we would cease to deserve respect; it would mean that we were no longer interested in the great mass of humanity, which was often poor and in desperate need, because we had decided that it was someone else's job to deal with them, even if there was no 'someone else' to whom they could turn.

Street Prostitution – A Reflection

Anne Robinson, Senior Lecturer,
Hallam Centre for Community Justice,
Sheffield Hallam University, Sheffield, UK

Before the 1980s, many women charged with prostitution-related offences (soliciting, loitering) were made subject to probation orders. This was in addition to other women who had more diverse patterns of offending but who were also involved in prostitution activity. Sentencers tended to see these women as in need of welfare intervention and support, rather than punishment, and so were increasingly reluctant to impose fines. They felt that fines provided a perverse incentive for women to go back out onto the streets.

Two major developments created a heated debate about whether probation supervision was appropriate for prostitution offences and how probation officers could be more pro-active: the feminist movement and the Criminal Justice Act 1982. The feminist movement and its influences:

(a)   highlighted social inequalities and restricted life opportunities for women;

(b)   campaigned on rape, domestic violence and the sex industry within an analysis of patriarchal power relations;

(c)   ensured that the voices of women involved in prostitution were heard, and supported women prostitutes in organising (although this caused much dissent with the movement); and

(d)   informed the work of academic writers and researchers, creating a huge expansion in knowledge about women in the Criminal Justice System and those involved in prostitution.

These influences were picked up by interested probation officers concerned about the implications of 'being sentenced to social work', the tariff escalation effect of non-compliance and, more generally, about promoting anti-oppressive practice with these highly-stigmatised women.

The Criminal Justice Act 1982 made soliciting and loitering non-imprisonable offences, although women could still be imprisoned for non-payment of fines imposed for soliciting. Indeed, NAPO identified an increase in women imprisoned by the latter route which was brought to the attention of the 1986 NAPO conference by Mary Davies and Gillian Stewart, both practitioners from the North West. Their motion called for a NAPO policy of recommending Absolute Discharges in Social Enquiry Reports on prostitution offences (this was in the days when we made recommendations!) Although the conference eventually accepted an amended motion, the two proposers subsequently wrote a passionately argued article in the *Probation Journal*[1] in June 1987, entitled *Probation and the Absolute Discharge Strategy*, explaining the reasons for their original unequivocal stance.[2]

Both this and the resulting NAPO guidance clearly impacted on probation policy, but was later eclipsed by the CJA 1991 and its notions of offence seriousness and proportionality in sentencing. In the then social climate, soliciting and loitering were classed as minor offences and there was, in addition, a huge overall reduction in women receiving probation orders on welfare grounds. This was beneficial in terms of reducing the number of ineffective and unnecessarily intrusive orders made but, as a consequence, the Probation Service has been largely absent from subsequent debates around prostitution and, with the exception of a small number of initiatives in courts and day centres, developments in services.

The question of prostitution and legal and policy remedies has again been raised in the public consciousness by the tragic deaths of five women street sex workers in Ipswich during November and December 2006. This occurred within a relatively short space of time after the major Home Office consultation in 2004, *Paying The Price*, followed by the publication of *A Co-ordinated Prostitution Strategy* in January 2006. Sadly, although the consultation seemed to offer the best opportunity to re-examine law and policy in this area since the Wolfenden Committee and the Street Offences Act 1959, the opportunity for bold and informed change was not taken. Within an abolitionist framework, the Home Office has stated that it is not in favour of toleration zones and will continue promoting the use of ASBOs for street prostitutes, whilst increasing routes for exiting prostitution, backed by court orders if women do not access those services voluntarily.

Yet, as I write, no policy changes have been implemented and the potential for influencing change in prostitution policy still remains.[2] Two questions to leave you with: will probation officers make their voices heard this time around? And what is our role two decades on?

End Note

[1]   *Probation Journal* (1987) 34: pp51–53.

[2]   July 2007 saw the launch of a major report of the results of a Symposium, '*Women, Human Rights and Prostitution*', which looked at these issues in the UK and across Europe and sought to ensure that women have a voice on future measures in this area.

Groupwork with Male Sex Offenders in the 1980s

Malcolm Cowburn, Principal Lecturer in
Criminology, Sheffield Hallam University,
Sheffield, UK

In the 1980s, groupwork with male sex offenders in the UK was shaped by two non-mainstream sources: social skills training and cognitive-behavioural psychology (CBT). The main aim of 'social skills training' courses was to help people convicted of offences to rehearse and develop their ability to interact socially in an effective and positive manner.

Social skills training did not directly address offending behaviour; CBT provided this focus. However, sex offender groupwork in the 80s was different to current probation practice in many ways. Professional training encouraged probation officers to understand the origins of crime. Psycho-dynamic understandings of human behaviour sought explanation in the individual psyche, whilst sociological understandings of crime offered explanations rooted in a structuralist analysis of society.

Probation officers were trained as social workers, subscribing to psycho-dynamic values of approaching 'clients' with 'non-judgemental positive regard'. However, as most sex offenders invariably minimised responsibility and denied harm to their victim(s), working from this standpoint could lead to collusion with an offender's version of his offending behaviour. Moreover, at this time, probation work eschewed involvement with victim-related issues; the focus was on people who had committed offences. They were viewed as victims, either of their own history or of the social structure.

Some early groupwork programmes were influenced by feminism. Feminist-structuralist understandings of male sex crime provided a counterbalance to 'non-judgmental positive regard' by locating male sexual offending within a social analysis of gendered power. This drew attention to the gendered nature of sex crime, in particular male responsibility for offending and the harm caused to victims (most of whom were female). Whilst the male sex offender may be a victim of individual and social criminogenic forces, he was also responsible for his offending behaviour (as a man) and for the harm that he caused his victim(s).

However, a feminist perspective on male sex crime did not, by itself, provide a clear means of working with sex offenders: CBT provided this.

All groupwork programmes featured a detailed deconstruction of an offender's account of one of his offences and then, in turn, concentrated on issues such as responsibility for starting and sustaining offending behaviour and on harm to victims. Additionally, following the analysis of offending behaviour, programmes helped offenders to consider ways of avoiding future offending (Relapse Prevention (RP)). It was at this point that social skills training was used.

Most programmes were initiated and sustained by the insight and energy of key groups of probation officers in different parts of the country. Programmes were run in both the community and in prisons. They ran either on a weekly basis over many months, or more intensively for two, five-day blocks. The continuance of these programmes was often dependant on particular staff remaining in post. Although the programmes had similar components and methods of delivery, they were not standardised.

In 1991, the Prison Service introduced its first version of the Sex Offender Treatment Programme (SOTP). The programme was very similar to many of the established groupwork programmes and used their exercises. Psychologists became responsible for developing this initiative, and there are now nationally accredited programmes in the community as well as in prisons. Whilst the increased standardisation of groupwork programmes is an aspect of the greater involvement of psychology in programme management and delivery, it has also led to a narrowing of the vision in relation to understanding male sexual coercion. Programmes no longer have an explicit value-base that locates sexual coercion not merely as an individual 'dysfunction' but as a social problem. With the loss of a feminist perspective on sex offender groupwork programmes, male sexual coercion can (falsely) be viewed merely as an individual problem that only requires a psychological response.

Targets for Probation Boards:
Partnership Expenditure

Peter Johnston, Business Development Manager,
Yorkshire and Humberside Probation Region, UK

The Home Office Probation Unit's Circular (PC 77/2000) notified probation Areas of the withdrawal, from 1st April 2001, of the requirements for each Area to spend at least 7% of its revenue budget on partnership activity (via sub-contracts and grants) and to report on their actual expenditure at least twice a year.

The Circular justified the removal of this target on the grounds that retaining the target was "inconsistent with business effectiveness models, principally the Better Quality Services (BQS) framework and European Excellence Model". The Circular did, however, go on to suggest that areas needed to ensure that partners "continue to play a significant part in the delivery of services to offenders".

Prior to 1st April 2001, most Areas had made steady progress in meeting or exceeding the 7% target.

The removal of the 7% target coincided with the Home Office's development of Joint Commissioning approaches to the delivery of offender services. Substantial funds have been re-directed to bodies such as Drug Action Teams, Supporting People Joint Commissioning Arrangements (Housing), and Learning and Skills Councils, who now lead in contracting directly with voluntary and private sector providers of offender services.

In addition, from 2001 the National Probation Directorate's sharper focus on Probation Board performance (with financial penalties for failure), the introduction of accredited programmes and the experiment with enhanced community punishment for offenders subject to community service (unpaid work) combined together to force many long-established partners out of the offender services market. The 'quality standards', set by the Home Office for the delivery of such services by partners, were simply too onerous and costly for many medium and small providers to justify continued partnership arrangements to their management committees.

At the time of writing this Moment, the average Area spend was only 3.6%.

In 2006, the Home Office's paper, *Improving Prison and Probation Services: Public Value Partnerships*, had concluded that private and voluntary sector providers were generally only being offered opportunities by Boards to get involved in working with offenders on a 'peripheral' basis. Probation Circular 33/2006 thus re-imposed targets for partnership expenditure – Probation Boards are now required to spend at least 5% of their revenue budgets in 2006/07 on such partnership work, with at least 10% in 2007/08. Moreover, boards now have to seek approval for their sub-contracting plans from their regional offender manager and demonstrate that such arrangements will also deliver value for money. It is not yet clear what sanctions will be imposed on Boards which do not meet the requirements.

Home Office Ministers have recently been unrelenting in their criticism of Probation Boards' current level of partnership spending. Most NOMS officials involved in work relating to the current probation partnership targets express genuine surprise that targets were once set, reported on by Boards and then removed by the Home Office.

There is only a very recent understanding within NOMS of the long-term impact of the removal of the 7% target in 2001 and the potential de-stabilising impact of such an immediate re-imposition of the new and challenging partnership targets. It will take time for Boards to re-build their partnership arrangements to a level where they can achieve the new targets set and deliver value for money.

Will the Home Office accept that policy decisions drove many voluntary and private sector organisations out of the offender services market at a time when the level of actual spend by Probation Boards on sub contracting arrangements was at its highest? Probably not, but it is important that the recent history of probation partnership activity is accurately recorded and fairly presented.

Convoy 2000 – Romania

John Harding, Visiting Professor of Criminal Justice,
Hertfordshire University, UK

On 1st January 2007, Romania joined the European Union. As part of the assimilation process of entry into Europe, the Romanian Ministry of Justice was required to undertake crucial reforms in the administration of justice, particularly in the modernisation of the prison estate, the training of prison staff, and the development of a Probation Service. The modernisation initiative was spearheaded by the Inner London Probation Service in 2001 when, together with the Spanish Prison Service, they were given a three-year contract by the European Union to reform the penitentiaries and enhance the probation system. Over the three-year term, the commissioned agencies set up training centres for prison and probation staff, linking prisons and Probation Services to a computerised communication network, providing information about prisoners on remand. Seconded staff from London trained local Romanian probation officers in delivering information on offenders appearing before courts. They also prepared Romanian criminologists in the vital role of training future local probation staff in Romania.

The Probation Service's interest in Romania was inspired by an earlier joint initiative between the Metropolitan Police Service and the Inner London Probation Service, with further assistance from Rotary International and the Essex Police Service, to bring aid and relief to Romanian orphanages. Part of the tragic legacy of the Ceausescu dictatorship, which dominated Romania from 1965 to 1989, was the abandonment of children to state orphanages. Women under the age of 45 were expected to have five children or more. With rising levels of poverty and insufficient food to feed families, parents placed children in orphanages, often ill-equipped and starved of resources. By 1999, some 40,000 Romanian children were in orphanages.

In that year, the new Metropolitan Commissioner, Sir John Stevens, the Inner London Chief Probation Officer, John Harding and other senior representatives, met to agree a three-year mission of goods, services and volunteer staff to orphanages in Romania, at first in Constanza and Bucharest and later in remote towns in the countryside, where orphanages were located.

The first convoy in May 2000 consisted of 15 fully-loaded articulated lorries, driven by Metropolitan Police Officers, who journeyed from London to Bucharest and beyond. The Probation Service's contribution to the first convoy involved a large-scale logistical exercise. The project notched up several notable firsts. It was the first time community service offenders had been involved in a project of this type, the first major co-operative venture between the four organisations, and the first time most of the group had visited Romania.

To a degree it was also a leap into the unknown. Some group members made an advanced visit to Romania, including the Hackney workshop manager, Don Gibbs, who visited orphanages in Bucharest and made a careful assessment of what was needed to be done. Gibbs, with the help of a second community service workshop in Greenwich, commissioned an ambitious work schedule of goods and materials to be installed in Bucharest orphanages. Over a period of nine months before the convoy set off in 2000, the workshop-based community service offenders, under supervision, built 75 bunk beds and made adventure playground equipment, including swings, climbing frames and wooden toys. Police and probation staff also persuaded London-based wholesale outlets to donate duvets, pillows, soft furnishings and building supplies such as paving slabs, wood, paint, etc., for the construction of play areas in the orphanages.

A few weeks before the official launch, the Romanian Ambassador to the UK, Radu Onofrei, hosted a reception for 110 volunteers from the four agencies at the Romanian Embassy. The convoy's work in the first week was covered by the Sun newspaper and Sky television who also donated £25,000 towards the cost of the mission in exchange for the publicity. The Inner London Probation Service sent ten volunteers for the two-week assignment including the Chief Officer, the senior probation officer for community services, the workshop manager and three community service offenders, whose presence had been sanctioned by the Home Office with the full support of the Metropolitan Commissioner.

Looking back, the value of the mission was shown in the expression of children clambering over bunk beds and testing playground equipment with delight and pleasure. There were several lessons for us too. The police volunteers were stunned by the quality of the goods. They, like the public, did not sufficiently understand the demands of the community penalty and the discipline of the workshop setting, whereby offenders, often with little practical skills, can be taught how to use equipment safely and to a high standard of quality and finish. In addition, offenders not only gained the satisfaction of producing equipment for a social purpose, but acquired foundation skills in the world of work.

End Notes

John Harding is the former Chief Officer of Inner London Probation Service, and worked there from 1993 to 2001.

Romanian orphanage convoys took place over three years from 2000–2002.

A Lesson in Styal

Mike Denton, National Probation Service
(HMYOI Thorn Cross),
Cheshire Probation Area, UK

The staff mobility policy of the Probation Service has generally dealt me a good hand over the years, and in 1989 it provided me with an ace in the form of a six-year secondment as Senior Probation Officer at HMP Styal Women's Prison.

Up to that point I had had no special interest in, and little experience of, working with women offenders. Anyway, there were debates about whether, as a male, I was capable of understanding the issues. Never mind that though, I saw my job primarily as managing a well-established probation team, and only secondarily as an opportunity to learn about, and act on, some of the factors affecting women in prison. However, of the variety of experiences I have had throughout my time in the Probation Service, this was the best.

What leads me to say this? Some people, often never having seen or experienced a women's prison, described Styal to me as sad and sombre. They stressed the pain and the privations, the injustices and inequalities. They overlooked, maybe through ignorance, maybe through an unwillingness to admit, the counter to this (I am reluctant to use the word 'positives', when there can be few positives to being locked up when it is not necessary). However, it continues, now as it did then, to pose uncomfortable dilemmas; how was it that numerous women chose prison as the place to disclose that they had been the victims of abuse? Why did some of them not want to leave? What point were those campaigning for reform of the Criminal Justice System as it related to women trying to make?

Although tempting at the time, it would have been wrong to think of myself merely as an observer in a six-year experiment. I sometimes needed reminders that I was not there just to watch what was going on, but to do a job. It was not the job I thought I had gone there for (i.e. to manage a functioning team, and occasionally tinker around the edges). Instead I discovered that there was an industry built around reform of the women's prison system, and secondly, my biggest lesson, I realised that it was not only well-motivated, but it was right. All the assertions about women in prison were exactly as the campaigners were saying. Huge numbers of them did not need to be there; imprisonment severely affected their families and relationships, caused them to lose their children, their homes and their jobs, and stigmatised them deeply. The system itself penalised them in comparison with their male counterparts: they were treated more harshly by the prison disciplinary processes, over-medicalised, and more often diagnosed as mentally ill. They also got longer sentences, earlier in their criminal careers, than comparable males.

My own research showed me that the prison disciplinary system did bear more heavily on them than on males. It provided some of the many funny moments amidst the more serious business, though plainly not amusing for the women involved; the 'nicking' of a woman for being in possession of a marmalade sandwich, for instance, and another for 'allowing herself to be sat on' during a mock fight.

This was the time when Styal emulated the Holloway practice, and established a day-visits scheme for mothers and their children. Brilliant! It reflected a growing awareness of the importance of the bond, and the need to preserve it. You get an impression of how this was seen by looking at the impressive range of people and organisations that played a part in setting up the scheme.

I want to finish on a sad note, sad in the sense that the wrongs of those six years still in large part need to be righted. The undeniably good work that now goes on at Styal and other women's prisons speaks for itself, but the underlying injustices still live. I want the campaigning to continue until it does itself out of a job.

Styal Prison

The main prison buildings were built as an orphanage in the 1890s which closed in 1956. The site opened as a women's prison in 1962 when female prisoners from Strangeways were transferred in.

From 1983 Young Offenders were admitted and in 1999 a wing was added to accommodate unsentenced female prisoners following the closure of Risley's remand centre, increasing the prison size by 60%.

The prison was featured in the BBC2 documentary 'Women on the Edge – the Truth about Styal Prison' on February 27th 2006.

(Taken from official website.)

Therapeutic Authority

Roy Bailey, Senior Research Fellow, De Montfort University (UK), Formerly Principal Probation Officer, Devon, Exeter and Torbay; and Secretary to the (then) Central Council of Probation Committees, UK (retired)

In the mid-20th century, after the turmoil of the Second World War, the Probation Service was a small but enviable service in which to work.

The Home Office Training Course at Rainer House was, for its time, thorough and well-grounded, and graduating entrants to the Probation Service found themselves, after their practice placements, in an environment in which they could exercise a great deal of personal discretion and professional initiative.

At about the same time, the Home Office had discovered the merits of psycho-therapeutic casework (the 'medical model' being explored in some detail) and had begun to disseminate its principles as something of a panacea for all offenders.

This had led to a wholly explicable in-service conflict between the old school of traditional 'commonsense' officers and the new wave of practitioners trained in psycho-therapeutic theory.

Rather less explicable was the hostility from psycho-therapists and some social caseworkers in other agencies, especially Psychiatric Social Workers, to any claim by probation officers to be able to use their (perceived) authority constructively and psycho-therapeutically in their work.

Into this tri-partite conflict of theory and professional interest waded Bob Foren (then a senior lecturer at the University of Bradford after working as a Home Office Inspector), and I (then Principal Probation Officer, Devon) to explore the function of authority in all its forms in social casework processes across a number of agencies. Our book, *Authority in Social Casework* (1968: Eslevier), was virtually the first comprehensive textbook on this topic and remained a useful *vade-mecum* on applied authority for the rest of the century.

The book included much detail about the proper (and improper) use of authority – legal, professional and cultural – in the then-prevailing psycho-therapeutic approach to social casework, although attention was paid also to those agencies in which the more traditional processes of working with clients were practised. It is significant that, at that time, the thrust of the book was towards the effectiveness of processes of individual (and, sometimes, group) intervention which relied substantially on the professional experience, skill and discretion of practitioners.

Over the succeeding half-century the question of authority has been raised in a different and perhaps even more cogent form. Successive governments have gradually assumed control over the criminal justice services, both in policy and in practice, to the detriment and virtual abolition of professional authority and discretion.

It would be interesting today to discover how Bob Foren and I would analyse the ways in which aspects of the authority of, for example, probation staff have been skewed in order to provide much less rehabilitative casework, a great deal more of a sense of punishment, and in many ways a less effective Service.

Probation and Mediation –
Are They Compatible ?

John Walters, Former General Secretary, CEP

In May 2003, I attended a CEP workshop in Prague with the ambitious title 'Justice and Balance: Victim, Offender and Community Perspectives'. When I retired from the Probation Service in 2001, I had taken up the position of Secretary General of the CEP, the *Conférence Permanente Européenne de la Probation*, and I had a wide range of contacts among both well established and newly developing Probation Services. There was a keen interest to develop probation in the so-called new democracies and a corresponding interest in how probation was being done in well established services. Not all the learning was one way, however, and the position in the Czech Republic was especially interesting. I had followed the development of the Czech Probation Service with a great deal of personal interest because it was led by a small group of very well-informed, young professionals who had only recently been social work students together. During their studies they had been motivated by a wish to develop a social work contribution to criminal justice, and they had been hugely influential in gaining government and judicial support for the establishment of a probation and mediation service.

Key among the convictions of this group of workers was the belief that mediation had an important role to play in criminal justice. They were well informed about the principles of restorative justice and were active in European networks to promote restorative practice. The workshop provided an opportunity to look at practice across Europe and what emerged very quickly was that, while the principles of restorative justice were very clear, the evidence of their penetration into probation practice was slight, with a few notable exceptions such as the Czech Republic and Austria. The Czechs were alone in taking the title of a probation and mediation service. Apart from these few exceptions, much of the best victim offender mediation work across Europe appeared to be taking place away from the services concerned with the supervision of offenders.

I was therefore particularly interested in the presentation of Ivo Aertsen of the Catholic University of Louvain and the President of the European Forum for Victim Offender Mediation and Restorative Justice. I subsequently asked him to write a piece for the *CEP Bulletin* focusing on why mediation and the supervision of offenders did not seem to fit well together. Since there is so much evidence of the benefits to both victim and offender of a well-conducted mediation, it must be of interest to look into why this practice has had so little influence on probation work in most countries in Europe.

Aertsen drew attention to a distinction between the social work model of practice and the independent model of mediation. He suggested that mediation based on social work principles tended to focus on the benefits that mediation might have in influencing the future conduct of the offender. True mediation on the other hand, should be seen as a service provided equally to the victim and the offender. The mediator's role was facilitative and not directed to any particular outcome. That was a matter for agreement between the victim and the offender. Can a service with objectives concerned with the rehabilitation of the offender, let alone a correctional service, allow power and decisions about outcomes to pass to the victim and the offender? Aertsen identified many other reasons, some organisational, some cultural, why restorative justice struggled to take hold in probation practice. However, it seemed to me that the key issue concerned the empowerment of the victim and the offender. For all the high levels of expressed concern about victims, empowerment seems a step too far.

It may be that this kind of discourse sounds entirely irrelevant at a time when even the principles of rehabilitation struggle to assert themselves in a firmly correctional climate. There may, however, be more than the usual range of reasons for visiting Prague and it would be interesting to learn how the bold adoption of the principles of restorative justice is faring in the Czech Probation and Mediation Service.

Training and the New CQSW

*Colin McCulloch, former Deputy Chief Probation
Officer, Middlesex Probation Service;
currently Branch Manager, South Buckinghamshire
Alzheimer's Society, UK*

In 1972, whilst employed as an ancillary worker at the newly named Crown Court (previously, Quarter Sessions), I applied for training. I remember a thorough psycho-analytic grilling by a senior probation officer, which was followed by a day with the Home Office. There I joined a group and was interviewed on my own by a panel. I remember their curiosity that a middle class young man should have worked in the building trade. They asked me if this gave me any insight into the mindset of the working class! This was followed by a stopwatch-timed intelligence test set by the British Psychological Society. The final part of the day was participation in a group discussion about the merits, or otherwise, of imprisonment.

It was a long time before I was informed that I had been accepted for the course at the Home Office, Cromwell Road. During the wait I was told about a new qualification that was about to be implemented, the Certificate of Qualification in Social Work (CQSW). It was suggested that my probation and social work career prospects would be better served by the CQSW, which at that time was not offered by Cromwell Road.

Subsequently, I applied to a college of higher education. Having undergone the rigour of Home Office selection, I was taken aback by being interviewed by a gnome-like man in a tiny office, slouched back in his seat, thumbing through my papers and mumbling about something being 'alright'. He didn't ask me any questions and so I asked him how things stood. He replied that I would be accepted.

Probation was rather peripheral to the course and badly taught. Sociology was more stimulating and casework was the core subject. In those days we imbibed Helen Harris Perlman, Florence Hollis, Roberts and Nee, Reid and Shyne and Jehu *et al.* Group work was also important. Social policy was a joke. The gnome-like man who interviewed me delivered these lectures by turning the pages of those small books from the Routledge Library of Social Work to prompt some mumblings about Malthus, the workhouse and the less deserving poor. He later told me that he had been a senior probation officer and that the job had been very easy as he had

had such a massive caseload. He explained that this enabled him to justify doing a large proportion of his supervision by telephone.

The lecturer who covered the sociology of deviance looked as though he had come straight from Woodstock and had scant regard for authority. When we asked him how his teachings squared with our joining the Probation Service, we were told that that was our problem and that it was not a job that he would want! Most of the lecturers on the course were conscientious and constructive but the exceptions left a lasting impression. Their views chimed with the times when all conventions and authority were subject to question, if not ridicule. Intellectually it was all great fun and a doddle, but it bred a lack of realism and not a little arrogance among some of us.

With Harry Potter spectacles above his full-set white beard and moustache, the psychology lecturer looked the part. He warned us to be wary of animal lovers. Our understanding of psychiatry was heavily informed by the works of Satz, Laing, Esterson and Cooper, who blamed so many social ills on the institution of the family. This was, perhaps, not the best way to prepare me for my final year-long placement in a crumbling former mental asylum.

I therefore gained my CQSW with a probation option. I regret that social work has ceased to be the qualification for probation work. Properly taught, it equipped us to engage with offenders. Later, with the help of the Service, I was able to further my training and academic studies and for that I will always be grateful.

Once Upon a Time in a Land Without National Standards

Tina Eadie, Senior Lecturer in Community and Criminal Justice, De Montfort University, Leicester, UK

In the 1980s, I worked in the Leicestershire Probation Service Community Service Unit (now Unpaid Work). Before that, I had worked as a probation officer in a city field team and, along with most of my colleagues at the time, was completely unversed in taking breach action. It came as something of a shock, therefore, to find that this was to be my main role in the unit!

Soon getting the hang of it, I found that I most enjoyed considering each instance of failure to attend on its own merits, and in the light of the offender's particular circumstances at that time. By using my professional judgment, I tried to ensure that whenever I chose to take breach action for failure to attend (whether at the start of an order or later when commitment was flagging) it was the right time for that particular individual. In this way I tried to ensure that the order would be completed, achieving the combination of punishment for the offence and reparation to the community for which community service was designed. In addition, the high costs of imprisonment (both to the offender and to society) were avoided. For some of the offenders in my caseload, this was one of very few achievements in a life full of disappointment and failure.

Addressing a group of probation students at the Leicester School of Social Work in 1987, my approach to breach as a positive tool to encourage the completion of orders was received as heresy – breach action equalled imprisonment in their minds, and was something no right-minded probation officer should contemplate! To illustrate my point I used the example of Joey who, at the age of 20, had appeared in court for the tenth time and received a CSO for the maximum (at the time) 240 hours. His attendance was sporadic from the start; he so wanted to complete his hours but life seemed to conspire against this. His reasons were many and varied:

- Did not hear the supervisor knock on the door.

- Assaulted by brother – taken to hospital to have stitches.

- Returned to hospital to have stitches removed.

- Argument with girlfriend – found himself homeless.

- Involved in another fight, more stitches, unfit for work.

And so on ...

Working just prior to the introduction of National Standards in 1989, I was able to exercise my discretion about how to respond to the absences, and to decide at what point breach action would be most appropriate. In fact, I breached him twice: once when the order had been in force for several months and less than half the hours had been worked, and again when he chose to spend the afternoon in the pub rather than return to the work party. On both occasions he was given another chance and subsequently completed his hours within the one-year timescale.

As I was to later write with Andrew Willis (Eadie and Willis, 1989) this case is not untypical. The Joeys of the world oversleep regularly, fight intermittently and sometimes get thrown out of home. Their lifestyle is characterised by disorder, chaos and ill-discipline. For them, unpredictability becomes routine. Why should it be any different when they are on court orders? What is at issue is not whether breach should be used at all, but when and how to use it. The skill of the probation officer is to assess whether, and at what point, breach action to gain compliance is appropriate. This is one of a myriad of reasons to retain professional training. The conclusion to our article remains, for me, as pertinent today as it was 20 years ago (1989: p.419):

> "If the threat of breach is a genuine aid to finishing community service, then inflexible rules may have to give way to an imaginative interpretation of reasonable excuses by probation officers, combined with the artful manipulation of formal and informal warnings. Rigid criteria and no discretion will not work. For offenders whose social circumstances are often characterised by instability and chaos, a probation officer's discretion may be the only barrier between their fecklessness and imprisonment. Penal rhetoric may trumpet the new vogue of discipline in community service, but good penal practice suggests otherwise."

Probation officers hover uncertainly between unpalatable extremes of immediate breach and infinite excuses; this is the challenge of the role.

Reference

Eadie, T. and Willis, A.. 'National Standards for Discipline and Breach Proceedings in Community Service: An Exercise in Penal Rhetoric'. *The Criminal Law Review.* 1989: June: pp.393–460.

On the Touchline of Probation History, 1968

John Birkbeck, former Probation Officer, South Yorkshire Probation Area (retired)

Remember the 1960s and you weren't really there. However, anyone who was at the 1968 anti-Vietnam War demonstration which ended with violent clashes in Grosvenor Square, always recalls being involved. I was there but had returned to my lodgings for tea by the time the situation turned ugly! Nevertheless, I had at least been on the touchline of national history. Less dramatically, I was on the touchline of probation history a few weeks later.

During my gap year, I was a Community Service Volunteer at the Homeless After-Care Unit of the Inner London Probation Service. Essentially an early 'ancillary', I was mainly engaged in finding bedsits for homeless ex-prisoners. In an age before job descriptions or widespread risk assessment, I worked closely and unsupported with some seriously dangerous and damaged individuals. At the age of 19, I knew all the ruses employed by probation officers to dump inappropriate work on unqualified colleagues!

When the first ever prisoner was released under the new parole provisions, I had a minor role to play. After he reported to our office, I was sent immediately across town to the Home Office with written confirmation of his arrival. In a gloomy cell-like room, I toasted the historic moment with a cup of Home Office tea along with three excited clerical officers who seemed to be the entire Parole Section of the Home Office.

However, it seemed only a matter of days before our celebrated parolee asked to go back to prison and was duly returned to the Isle of Wight! He was unprepared for and unsettled by the media interest which, by today's standards, was quite modest. It was also apparent that he was uneasy about the strict requirements of parole and the ever-present threat of recall if his behaviour did not meet some expectations which to him seemed fairly ill-defined. Lastly, as someone with no family or friends outside prison, life in the relatively bleak Rowton House hostel where, I believe, he was lodged, offered few bright moments or rewards.

With almost 40 years experience, I think we are now better at assessing and preparing prisoners to cope with the pressures of release on licence, particularly where there is strong media interest. I am worried, however, that the trend to increasingly demanding licence requirements may lead an increasing number of people preferring to stay in prison or quickly return there like our first parolee.

One of my great disappointments is that we are no better prepared to resettle homeless ex-prisoners now, than we were in 1968! We don't even have Rowton Houses let alone after-care hostels. There are precious few lodging schemes, and local authorities generally make poor provision for homeless ex-prisoners.

What we do have in profusion, are grumpy old men who will moan about the present and wax nostalgic about the past.

Yes, 1968 was a great year to be on the touchline of probation and national history. My only regret is that in May of that year I couldn't get a ticket to be on the touchline to watch my boyhood hero Jeff Astle win the FA Cup for West Brom. A few years later I became a Probation Officer. Jeff became a window cleaner and on the side of his van it said "Jeff Astle Window Cleaner – Never Misses the Corners".

Priceless!

End Note

The Parole Board is the independent body that protects the public by making risk assessments about prisoners to decide who may safely be released into the community, and who must remain in, or be returned to, custody.

The Parole Board was established under the provisions of the Criminal Justice Act 1967 to advise the Home Secretary on the early release of prisoners. The Criminal Justice and Public Order Act 1994 established the Board as an Executive Non-Departmental Public Body.

How Volunteers Are Coming of Age

Mike Denton, National Probation Service
(HMYOI Thorn Cross), Cheshire Probation Area, UK

I qualified as a probation officer in 1979 via two journeys; the first was a period spent as a volunteer at a local probation and bail hostel, and the second, a two-year course at what is now Manchester Metropolitan University.

My second probation officer post was at Withington Office in Manchester (now, like so many places I have worked, no longer there!). The office had a long tradition of using volunteers to support the work of the paid staff. My colleagues, a committed and very supportive team, had not the time to devote to the 20 or so volunteers, but recognised their value and wanted the group to continue. My proposal to them was that, in return for them relieving me of half my caseload, I would run the volunteer group. They agreed.

Now in today's climate, that in itself would constitute a story. While it illustrates how volunteers were seen at the time as a 'good thing', they also needed considerable investment in terms of recruitment, training and support for a diverse range of tasks, from supporting a women's group, to driving family members to prison visits. It was the sheer diversity of tasks that reflected the nature of volunteering in probation, or at least, in those areas that supported it. It was mainly unco-ordinated, existed on good will, and was, in the best sense, aimless.

Even though the value of involving volunteers from within the community in rehabilitating 'its' offenders was a laudable and generally accepted aim, the reality often differed from the intention. It was hard to articulate a SMART objective to frame the outcomes of volunteer engagement. 'It works in practice, but we don't know if it works in theory' seemed to be the underlying ethos. In fact, the theory was hardly tested, mainly because of a reluctance to become involved in what was seen in probation as a fringe activity. A volunteer co-ordinator, as I was, had not only to take on responsibility for recruiting and training volunteers, but also for deploying them for work with the client group, and for devising a system of recording what they had done and how they had done it. It was hard work, even with colleagues willing to make the ultimate sacrifice.

Not surprisingly therefore, few probation officers stuck their hands in the air when the option of becoming a volunteer co-ordinator was suggested.

Perhaps that is a generalisation, but it serves to highlight the fact that, even then, pockets of excellence, and some real commitments to action, existed among Probation Services of the time. A contemporary survey showed that only a few had a real commitment to encouraging the use of volunteering as part of their business. Nevertheless, the fact that most probation staff would probably have said that volunteering was 'a good thing' in principle, was testament to the belief that for many offenders they worked with, the involvement of someone from outside the structured world of probation would be beneficial. The ideal candidate for volunteer engagement was often an isolated offender, with poor social skills and a need of a higher level of support than the probation officer was able to provide.

The Withington Volunteer Group went from strength to strength. Its staying power was one thing, and so was its expertise, but the count of how many of its members went on to think seriously about careers in the Probation Service (and in some cases to pursue them) was another. To my mind, that is a mark of how volunteers not only viewed the worth of the work they were doing, but also of the respect they were given by the probation staff who worked alongside them. In addition, I detected another measure – the significant number of new volunteers who had been introduced into the group by existing members.

However, times change, probably nowhere more than in probation. In more recent years, volunteering has gradually become transformed into mentoring, and in so doing is able to offer even more. If evidence of this progress were needed, one only has to look at the way that some probation areas, notably Cheshire, have embraced mentoring with offenders. Its mentors are well supported, they work to a specific brief, and they are managed by a dedicated mentor co-ordinator. They carry out difficult and imaginative tasks that fit with sentence planning targets, and they account for what they do. Their value to the organisation and to its offenders is not in question.

The next big thing is how we evaluate the real impact of mentoring, but that's a story for the next 100 years!

Probation Reaching Out:
Working in the Community
During the 70s and 80s

David Pidwell, Senior Probation Officer,
South Yorkshire Probation Area, UK

When he started urinating on the centre's locked front door, I could tell that my efforts to divert Eric from returning to St. Mary's that night and smashing the place up were not making much headway. Averting my gaze, I caught my colleague's eyes looking from the office window, clearly amused at my dismal skills of persuasion. After a while Eric moved off, staggering under the influence towards the park, where he was certain to bump into fellow drinkers who would meet his need for more.

This was a regular occurrence at St Mary's House. Called a 'Probation Support Centre', its main purpose was to provide a day centre and residential accommodation. St Mary's was funded by the Nottinghamshire Service for around 15 years from the early 70s. Community work theory had influenced probation thinking, and St Mary's was one of several projects across the country (all with locally determined aims and practices). Such projects were probation's approach to community outreach, to experiment with client interaction other than in the traditional office environment, and to engage in direct preventative work.

The day centre opened most mornings and every night, including weekends, and provided a range of services including a café, TV lounge, pool table and access to pastimes and sporting activities. In so doing, it offered a cheap, alcohol-free zone, an alternative to the pub. Staff were active in assisting clients with a range of issues around benefits, housing, alcohol use, literacy and budgeting. Initially, the idea was for field teams to refer clients to use it to occupy their time and to structure their leisure time (or, if you prefer, their long-term unemployment). That model never really took off, and day centre visitors came to be drawn heavily from the local area. Many were not on supervision, or not even offenders, but were representative of the area's red-light function and its high number of bedsits and lodging houses.

The residential unit offered an abstinent environment for those seeking to deal with their drink problems. Residence had to be earned, usually by an acceptance interview before other residents and attending the day centre sober for two weeks (including released prisoners). Many became residents on several occasions as they zigzagged their way to sobriety. In later years, we diversified to take long-term prisoners who wanted sanctuary before venturing into the world.

The unit's ethos was located within a self-help philosophy, not too far removed from Alcoholics Anonymous, and St Mary's hosted one AA meeting a week. Residency was voluntary, not a condition of any probation order, and staff worked hard to assess 'motivation' as being intrinsically driven rather than externally imposed. Residents took responsibility for much of the unit's running and there was a weekly resident's meeting. Residents had to account to peers for current attitudes and behaviour, and new ones had to sit in the 'hot-seat' to discuss their past life and future intentions. Residents developed self-responsibility, a strong loyalty to, and respect for, the group and the unit's rules, the most important being 'one drink and you are out'.

This was successful in moving people on. I can't recall if Eric was one that made it but Bill moved into his own council flat and re-established contact with his daughter. Michael and Charlie, after years of street living and niggling public order offences, regained their dignity and sobriety in older age, council accommodation and a niche in their community by becoming volunteers to various community enterprises.

St. Mary's provides an interesting insight into how probation staff contemporaneously approached their work. We relied heavily on volunteers. Residential workers did 24-hour shifts, alone once the day centre closed; the job was viewed almost as a vocation with tremendous staff interest in, and commitment to, client progress. Defusing potentially violent behaviour was commonplace.

Always expensive, St Mary's fell victim to the emerging new 80s philosophies of working with more heavily convicted offenders and in sponsoring activities that provided alternatives to custody. In such an environment, St. Mary's became a costly anachronism to a service repositioning itself less in terms of the community it served and more in relation to its utility to the Criminal Justice System.

Probation Service as Co-ordinator for the Implementation of a Sentence – A Swedish Model of Offender Management

Gunilla Nilsson, Swedish Prison & Probation Service, Sweden

The Swedish Prison and Probation Service (SPPS) is the combined body of three fields of activities: remand prison, prison, and probation. Since the present Penal Code came into force in 1974, SPPS has worked towards a coherent implementation of each sentence for its clients. Each field of activity is guided partly by its own regulations, but also by general SPPS regulations.

From the main objectives of the SPPS, it is evident that the whole organisation needs to co-operate to make sure that clients are rehabilitated in the best way possible during their time in prison.

The internal revision of the SPPS made a report a couple of years ago concerning the Probation Service. There was the suggestion, among other things, that the Probation Service should be responsible for all of the sentencing process. It suggested that the Probation Service should be involved from the very beginning during the pre-sentence investigation and throughout the time in custody until the last day under parole. This would mean an integrated and evidence-based sentence planning, following the client through the different stages of sentence.

In order to try this way of working, the SPPS is now carrying out a countrywide project, which calls for the Probation Service to be responsible for the whole implementation of a sentence. This means that the Probation Service will participate in the sentence planning even when the clients are still serving their sentences in an institution. In this way, the Probation Service will focus on parole and gradual release from the very beginning of their involvement with the clients.

The working method is based on a scheme, following the sentence, that includes compulsory co-operation activities and operations in which prison officers have to consult the Probation Service. The main tool is the sentence plan which should be based on risk and need assessment, including static and dynamic risk factors. A special document that includes the most important areas is filled out. Areas that are most important in reducing relapse must have the highest priority.

The plan must also be carried out in consultation with the client. The motivation to change must be considered. Goals should be realistic, measurable and activity-oriented. It is important to start with small steps instead of aiming too high and there is also a need to define who is responsible for things to be done. Finally, it is important to follow up and revise planning, set new goals according to what has happened, and learn from mistakes.

The information from the sentence plan should be followed up during the client's time at an institution. Therefore, the task of the Probation Service will be to make sure that the sentence plan is followed correctly, to provide support for the client, and to act as a supervisor for the officers working as contact persons at the penal institutions.

A coherent sentence plan for the entire time through custody and parole for each client, is the basis for the SPPS to successfully reduce re-offending. The most important barrier is the inability to co-operate around the client, who loses out in a system that does not work.

The aim of the project will be to identify risks and/or success factors, to spread information about this new method of working, and to facilitate the implementation of a fully deployed activity in 2008.

Punishment, Control and Probation –
A Personal Reminiscence

Cedric Fullwood, Chair, Cheshire Probation Board,
UK

Sitting in the library at the Cambridge Institute of Criminology in the late 80s, I took down the *Justice of the Peace for 1908* – the year in which the Probation of Offenders Act was brought into effect. Within weeks of its enactment, a worried correspondent wrote asking whether it would be possible to combine corporal punishment with the new-fangled order of probation. The reply was that 'the matter is not free from doubt', but, after some tortuous sentences, the opinion was that it would not be in keeping with the spirit of probation. In the 40s, the use of corporal punishment by the juvenile courts increased. Even as 'modern' probation was in its infancy, Home Office Committees reported on whether the diameter of the canes used in Approved Schools should be changed.

In the 60s, as Secretary to the Manchester Criminological Society, I invited the formidable editor of the *International Journal of Offender Therapy* (note – not Offender Management!) to speak to us. Melitta Schmideberg was besotted with the work of probation officers, praising their ability and commitment to bring structure and some sense of order to the troubled and chaotic lives of offenders, and admiring their relaxed ability to show both care and control in their professional supervision. I did not realise that she was the daughter of Melanie Klein – one of the pillars of psycho-analysis whose emphasis was on the childhood experiences of early years. None of that for Melitta; how the present was handled was all important.

In my paper, *Bot, Wite and the Dooms of Alfred* (1983), I urged the engagement of local authorities. It has taken over 20 years for them to begin to accept their responsibilities for their offending citizens. Despite the shock waves from the Prison Disturbances, Lord Justice Woolf's report was enlightening. Having said that, at the same time, Professor Radzinowicz sent me his paper warning of the international hunger for more and more imprisonment round the world.

Despite pioneering work in the Probation Service throughout the 80s, it ended for me at a regular forum on crime (which was organised by a respected senior civil servant, and included four eminent professors of law and criminology), when emerging thoughts on what became known as 'Punishment in the Community', including, to our great dismay, electronic monitoring, were outlined. A year or so later, a group of chief probation officers were entertained in Westminster by the Minister. He was trying to charm us into embracing 'punishment' as a central part of probation. It felt as if every time the Minister made some profound statement about probation needing to embrace punishment, there were gales of laughter from the adjoining room (where Neil Kinnock was celebrating his 10th year as Leader). Voices, even from within probation, were insisting that it be rebranded as punishment and that the term 'client' be banished. Nevertheless, some enlightened elements did appear in the Criminal Justice Act. However, with the seismic ripples from the brutal death of James Bulger, and some chief constables courting tabloids with stories of 'bail bandits' and 'rat boy', the pressure for imprisoning more and more showed no signs of waning.

During the lean years of the 80s with the mantra 'Prison Works' as the dominant political cry, a courageous group of managers, academics and practitioners lit the flame of 'What Works', only to see it almost extinguished at the turn of the century by a bureaucratic implementation and political mismanagement. The pressures on probation, for me, were exemplified when Eric Cantona was made subject to a Community Service Order. The Minister at the time was in my office and said, "I hope you will humiliate this man." The following Monday, the senior civil servant at the Home Office phoned me, "Without putting any pressure on you, Cedric" to encourage me to ensure the Community Service was punitive. I was subsequently publicly criticised for refusing to "obey".

The theme of my reminiscence, from those early days in 1908 – can we whip this probationer? – to the current policy miasma, is that there has always been an uneasy tension between the humane and constructive principles that underpin probation and the pressures to punish, control and, to quote one Minister, to humiliate. There has been excellent progress and creative changes. Its true leaders and committed practitioners must keep up a brave and robust defence of their work with offenders, their families and communities, shore up the positives that demonstrably work, and unashamedly espouse care and rehabilitation.

Drop-in Day Centres:
A Different Challenge?

Sue Raikes, former Chief Executive,
Thames Valley Partnership, UK

For about 20 years from the mid-70s onwards, Oxfordshire Probation Service ran a drop-in day centre in the Centre of Oxford for the homeless, street drinkers and people who were living in hostels, night shelters or on the streets. That client group was seen as meriting a specialist resource and considerable investment, and it was acknowledged that meeting their needs required a different sort of Probation Service from that offered by colleagues in the rest of Oxfordshire.

The Day Centre had showers, a kitchen, a games room and a wet room where people who had been drinking were allowed to hang-out provided they didn't cause any difficulties. The Centre opened at 8.30am as the Oxford Shelter closed. I have since wondered whether the trail of those who simply moved between the two places indicated dependency rather than positive intervention.

There was no doubt that the Oxford Day Centre was meeting a need and that it required not only a different approach from within probation staff, but also different relationships with other organisations such as the 'Oxford Network' (which included hostels, drugs and alcohol agencies, Alcoholics Anonymous and local churches) and our more familiar partners, the courts, the police and the Housing Authority. Networking, or what we would now call 'partnership' work, was the bread and butter activity of the team. The Day Centre's crucial role in supporting and co-ordinating the work of these agencies would now be called 'capacity building'.

There was one particular moment that cast this otherwise understated resource into the local and national spotlight. In September 1982, I was on court duty alongside my colleague from the Day Centre who was on 'cell duty'. This meant going down to the court in the early morning to visit those arrested overnight in order to pass information to court duty officers, to find hostel places, or to provide stand-down reports on people who we knew well. That day, access was denied, not only to us but also to defence lawyers. The previous day, the DHSS and the police had collaborated to set up a trap designed to catch people staying in Oxford's many bed and breakfast establishments. Over one hundred people were allegedly fraudulently claiming bed and breakfast lodgings payments whilst sleeping rough or in the night shelter. DHSS had written to those claimants instructing them to sign on in a different temporary office which turned out to be a 'sting'.

What followed was a national scandal. About 150 claimants were instantly remanded in custody, and miraculously, that same number had been shipped out of Oxford Prison the night before. Access was denied to legal advice and nobody got bail. NAPO secured the attention of local and national press and was supported by CHAR (Campaign for Homeless & Rootless) and the Child Policy Action Group in exposing the breach of human rights and the way in which homeless people had been stitched up in a highly discriminatory process. Most pleaded guilty and got short prison sentences. However, in all cases where not-guilty pleas were entered, the evidence collapsed. The real culprits were the bed and breakfast landlords, one of whom had been encouraging fraudulent applications and taking a large cut from individuals over many months. He was never prosecuted. The story was subsequently published in a book called *Poor Law*. I have lost my copy but I hope there is one on a top shelf in Chivalry Road!

Meanwhile, back in the Day Centre, the daily routine of providing food, shelter, company and access to drugs, alcohol and other treatments continued. This client group would not receive a service from probation these days, let alone command such specialist and committed interventions. Although the Day Centre now no longer exists, the network of agencies working together to respond to this needy and difficult group still thrives – and the legacy of Oxford's Probation Service is still recognised with those with long enough memories.

Operation Major: An Experience of Exclusion

Paul Goodman, Chief Executive, Ley Community; previously Oxfordshire and Berkshire Probation Services 1980–1998, UK

What an opportunity to look back through rose-tinted glasses! There really was a time when probation officers were employed to 'advise, assist and befriend'! In the early 1980s, the Oxford Day Centre (Ebor House) for the homeless and rootless provided the small team of probation officers and support staff with an opportunity to get to know and be part of the social support system that a community of homeless people depended upon. Ebor House provided basic shelter, showers, food and a place to sober up off the street between nights in the shelter or sleeping rough, visits to the clinic for detox, or further short prison sentences.

We came to know our 'clients' (remember when that word disappeared in the 90s?) well, and would often start the day by meeting them in the cells at Oxford City Magistrates' Court where we went each morning to see who had been picked up overnight. The atmosphere was convivial. Relationships between the regulars, the small group of police officers that staffed the cells, the defence solicitors and day centre staff was warm and relaxed. After smokes had been distributed (does this still happen?), we would go into court and make helpful suggestions as to what might be done. In many respects, this was to be the precursor of bail information. What I recall was the relief of the bench that someone was trying to take in hand and assist defendants who were mostly seen as a nuisance rather than in need of punishment.

This cosy picture of interdisciplinary co-operation was to be dealt a severe blow by the politically inspired 'Operation Major', which was intended to send a clear message from the Thatcher Government that benefit fraud would not be tolerated, and that the scrounging culture would be stamped out. In September 1982, the DHSS conspired with the police, the prison service and the courts to set up a 'sting' for bed and breakfast claimants who were alleged to be claiming fraudulently whilst sleeping at the shelter or sleeping rough. Over 130 claimants had been told to sign on in a specially commissioned port-a-cabin from which they were immediately arrested and taken into custody. Special courts were already on standby, and it was only when the process was already in full swing that we first heard what was happening. Although we knew the majority of the defendants, we were denied access to the cells, as indeed were defence lawyers. I vividly remember Chris Brown, the Oxfordshire CPO, storming down to the magistrates' court to remonstrate, but he was no more effective in gaining access for probation staff than we had been ourselves. Most of those picked up in the sting received short prison sentences. Everyone who pleaded 'not guilty' was subsequently acquitted, though I recall they were held in custody on remand. The exercise achieved what it was intended to achieve: banner headlines in the tabloid press denouncing them as scroungers off the State.

I like to think that the emphasis on housing development within the Probation Service was partly rooted in the Operation Major experience. The B B and O Branch (later to become Thames Valley) took several motions to the NAPO AGM that year. One called for local Probation Services to establish Housing Development Officers as a key provision for offenders caught in the homelessness trap. Of course, the Branch denounced the rough justice so clearly at play in Operation Major. My abiding memory is of James Sandham, seconding the motion at conference, screaming over the ever increasing applause fearing that his three minutes would run out before he had completed his speech. He ended with a standing ovation with the conference pumped up with passion, outrage and moral indignation!

The Oxford Day Centre would have no place in the modern Probation Service, and I suspect, even at the time, it was an expensive resource working with a group of disadvantaged people whose offending behaviour was mostly of a relatively low order. The voluntary sector has now filled the gap that was left when the Day Centre closed. Those of us that worked there are just left with a warm feeling of nostalgia!

L' organisation européenne
de la probation

Can the *Conférence Permanente Européenne de la Probation* (CEP) Change the World?

Margareta Lindholm, Director,
Gotland Probation Service, Sweden

I worked as probation officer for many years and thereafter as manager of the Gotland Probation Service. I found that in a little country like Sweden it is essential to broaden the perspective about probation in order to do a good enough job with the clients. When I got an opportunity to become a board member of the CEP at the General Assembly (GA) in Lugano in 2004, I was very proud to take on the work for the next three years on the run up to the GA 2007. The board that is elected in the CEP consists of ten persons from different countries. The task is to work in line with the decisions made at the general assembly.

CEP is a private association according to Dutch law. Its secretariat is accommodated by the Dutch Probation Service, the Reclassering Nederland. The members are statutory and voluntary organisations working in the field of probation as well as a number of interested individuals. The members consist, at the moment, of 26 countries and 37 organisations and the CEP is looked upon as a respected contributor to the Council of Europe, the European Union and the criminal justice world.

The CEP organises seminars, conferences and workshops to bring together both managers and practitioners from probation services across Europe with the academics and others working in criminal justice. We are simply connecting people. One of the most important tasks is to identify opportunities in countries that are developing a Probation Service and to safeguard those services that have already been achieved in other countries.

Do the following concepts concern you?

* Running programs

* Tackling drug abuse

* Working in the community

* Good practice highlighted

* Opportunity to reflect objectively on used methods

- Safer society

- New crime patterns

These are only some of the things discussed during our workshops and conferences arranged by the CEP, and we would like all people involved in probation to be part of the discussion. Other important areas are research and practice, new technology, personnel and partnerships.

As a director for a local Prison and Probation Service on an island outside the Swedish mainland, I often lack the opportunity to meet colleagues with similar problems in managing probation or guiding probation officers to the best possible practice. Through the CEP, I meet experienced probation personnel from all over Europe who often give me new insights and knowledge. The Swedish Prison and Probation Service also benefits from the knowledge I gain from the conferences and workshops. It gives the Director General and the Division of Development at Head Office new input to better our services and routines.

Can CEP change the world?

Maybe it cannot change the whole world, but certainly it can change probation in Europe. With our observer status in the Council of Europe we can pick up important issues and prepare our members for changes and future developments. As a Board member of the CEP, I am responsible for transforming the members' outspoken wishes from the General Assembly in Lugano into practice. Examples of our work abound. A GA was held in Tallinn in September 2007. The conference in connection with the GA was called *Probation in Europe – Unity and Diversity*. The conference had two themes: old and new alternatives in probation, and how probation officers convey the basic values and aims of the probation system while carrying out their work. Perhaps we met there to develop probation to an important alternative to prison all over Europe? You are always more than welcome to join our activities!

End Note

Please read more about the Conférence Permanente Européenne de la Probation at www.cep-probation.org

---

Is It Any Easier to Find Offenders Somewhere to Live? – A Reflection on the Last 30 Years of Work in this Area

Len Cheston, Head of Community Commissioning,
London Area Offender Management Office, UK

When I joined the Service in the late 70s, probation staff led on a number of initiatives. It was not unusual to find staff and managers working with a range of partners in taking the lead in finding potential houses or establishing committees and applying for funding. It was a time of expansion, driven in part by the Hostel's Initiative led by the Department of the Environment. For front-line staff, accommodation always loomed as an issue, although there were often short-term but poor quality solutions available through the large church run hostels, local Rowton houses, the nearest 'spike' and a large range of private landlords. On the legislative front, the Homeless Persons Act 1977 had been implemented. The Act has been a remarkably resilient piece of legislation and its structure is still in place today.

The 80s continued as a phase of growth. I was working for North West London Housing Association (NWLHA) that had grown from the initiative of a range of staff in the former Middlesex Area Probation Service. NWLHA was an example of growth of the housing professional in the world of offender accommodation. Funding systems were becoming more complex, tenure laws had to be followed, and there was an expectation of higher quality staff providing an improved service. Whilst moving people from hostels was an increasing problem, I still thought we could accommodate the majority of referrals and, for front-line staff, the other options with private landlords and church-based agencies continued to exist.

It was in the late 80s and into the 90s that there was a sea change that made finding accommodation more difficult: the expansion money stopped; revenue funding became more difficult; there were housing benefit changes; there was a growth in NIMBYism, the Camberwell Replacement Scheme took out many of the poor quality large resettlement centres and replaced them with higher quality provision but lesser number of bed spaces; the expansion of house purchasing started to reduce the number of houses in the private rented sector; and finally, the sale of council houses and, more importantly, the Government refusal to allow the money from the sales to be re-invested in new public housing, started to drastically reduce the amount of public sector stock.

My career in the 90s was heavily immersed in this world. It was difficult to get other government departments interested in the housing needs of offenders, local authority interest was sporadic and private sector schemes could be established but often proved difficult to maintain. By the mid-90s the government decided to close a number of approved premises due to cost and under occupancy. It needed the reinvention of approved premises as places for high-risk offenders to help turn around that situation as it tuned into the growing drive for the surveillance and assessment of high risk of harm offenders.

The devolution of the Probation Accommodation Grant Scheme and the national redistribution of money coincided with the introduction of the funding changes brought on by the community care system leading to the loss of many drug residential services.

The pendulum swung back with the publication of the *Social Exclusion Report* on released prisoners and the introduction of 'Supporting People'.

Supporting People has given probation a seat at the commissioning table, although it is not clear to me whether this has resulted in an increase in access to services. The Social Exclusion Unit work coincided with the Homelessness Act 2002, which gave released prisoners an opportunity to access housing through the vulnerability route although, again, early evidence is that has not worked in favour of many prisoners and there is renewed work on offender housing through initiatives being piloted in the South West of England.

Today, however, whilst the policy environment is positive for offender housing, it coincides with a period where house prices and rent values are out of reach for many working people, leading to the potential for poverty trapping offenders in high-rent properties. In some parts of the country, the amount of housing stock is in decline with an increasing demand for it. Whilst the wider interest is welcome, life for front-line staff with homeless offenders seems no easier than in previous eras.

From Probation Hostels to Approved Premises: A Rehabilitative Thermometer – Where Next?

Dr Francis Cowe, Head of Newport Centre for Criminal and Community Justice, University of Wales, Newport, Wales, UK

Hostels have been a key feature of the last quarter of probation's first century. They arrived at a time when rehabilitative scepticism was in the ascendancy and when probations' clientele were changing. The 1960s may be seen as a high point of optimism on behalf of government to invest in penal reform. Hostels may be seen to 'arrive' on the political radar as a possible sentencing option at the high watermark of welfarism. Various potential purposes were predicated, all of which had in common a rehabilitative and transformative optimism. In their early years, hostels were variously used for homeless offenders, substance misusers, and specific offender groups, and in the 80s flirted with the concept of bail and alternatives to custodial remands.

By the early 80s, it was argued by Bill Jordan that probation, in general, was at risk of becoming a modified form of imprisonment as opposed to a modified form of liberty. If this was true of probation, then hostels today may be at risk of becoming community prisons or semi-penal institutions. The disentanglement of welfare from control tended to assume that welfare was not a form of control and has encouraged apparently mutually exclusive discourses. There were just a few dozen hostels in the 70s, peaking at around 116 in the early 90s. Today, there are around 100 approved premises in England and Wales. As probation has become more centralised and has highlighted punitive elements, hostels have increasingly become associated with public protection agendas and risk in the eyes of policy makers and the public. 1991 saw probation become a punishment and the removal of the requirement of 'offenders' consent.

This shift in policy did eventually lead to real shifts in practice within National Standards (1992) and other practice guides, moving the focus of the Service away from the welfare and needs of the individuals it supervised, to being a deliverer of community punishments with a sharper focus on victims and public protection. Hostels for the most part were relatively untouched by these developments and, initially, were not seen as part of the social control agenda. They did not begin to feel the policy and practice implications of such shifts until the late 90s, when the rise of public protection concerns saw hostels being seen as offering new sites of control in a risk averse service.

Hostels in the late 90s and early 2000s began to be reserved for those who required an enhanced level of supervision and were no longer meant to simply meet the accommodation or developmental needs of offenders. The purpose of probation hostels became, for the first time, more set against a background of changes in the wider criminal justice system. Hostels may risk losing their rehabilitative and reintegrative purposes and become redefined and remoulded into something quite different.

Approved premises today sit manifestly within the NOMS vision. A real shift in the nature of the modern hostel is clearly evident with CCTV, tagging, 24-hour staff cover and, in many cases, refusal to take residents below MAPPA Level 3. Risk has triumphed over need in deciding who hostels are for. However, a visit to a hostel today reveals that despite their residents risk status, many of the same staff skills and regime focuses are required. Substance misuse, poor literacy and numeracy, mental health problems, social discomfort, and lack of support and belonging continue to iterate with offenders needs and risks. In order to protect the public, the hostel needs to work towards reintegrating offenders back into society as useful and less risky citizens. Needs and risk may not be useful to juxtapose.

Hostels as alternatives to punishment, pre-1991, could to some extent avoid the panoptic gaze of the larger justice system. Hostels post-2007 may find their identities and rationale are shifting from being primarily a route back into the community or a tool to avoid exclusion from the community, to being seen as another punitive force in the penal bureaucracy that is 'community punishment', though residents still value its rehabilitative origins:

> 'I see my key worker once a week, talk over changes in my life, feelings, he keeps me aware of my limits. He took me on the jubilee challenge working with special needs kids on an assault course ... I would like to do more like that…being here has helped me stop offending ... I could do with more support though to get a flat and things together ...'

Hostel Resident (2002)

What Next?

Dr Kevin Downing, City University of Hong Kong

In the mid-1990s, the Probation Services of England and Wales faced the prospect of a complete restructuring, threatening to abandon its traditional alliance with a social work value base. Was this part of a wider historical trend? This Moment identifies a pattern which can be traced back to the 1830s.

Since the early 1950s, a sequence of schools of psychological thought have been used to explain why people engage in offending behaviour and to suggest how this behaviour might be addressed by the criminal justice system. In the 50s and 60s, psychoanalytic theories were used to provide an insight into potential motivations for crime. These were seen as the result of insufficient unification of the individual's ego with the demands of society and relied very heavily on consensus about the existence of the unconscious mind.

In the 70s and early 80s, psychological models for intervention in criminal justice turned towards behavioural theory which, on the surface, answered many of the criticisms made of psycho-analysis. Behaviour modification could concern itself directly with offending behaviour, its successes and failures were (in the short term) measurable, and it appealed to popular notions of punishment and rehabilitation. The simplicity of behaviour modification was one of the reasons it proved so attractive. It offered the possibility of controlling offending through shaping an individuals behaviour.

Psycho-analytic and behaviourist approaches were alike in one important way. Both theoretical viewpoints allowed for an offender who was not always rational in his or her decision-making. This made possible explanations of offending behaviour, which stressed the role of either complex internal factors affecting the make-up of an offender's personality, or environmental correlates that might significantly influence the route of an individual's behaviour. These were fruitful areas for probation officers attempting to rehabilitate offenders and reintegrate them into their communities, and a whole area of casework developed. Behaviourist descriptions also ensured that the individual offender was not seen as uninfluenced by the environment in which he lived. On the contrary, failure or success within the community might significantly affect the propensity for crime. Therefore, what society provided in the way of opportunities through education and employment, would encourage or reinforce the potential offender to more desirable forms of behaviour.

Towards the end of the 80s, behavioural approaches to offending began to be questioned at a conceptual level. In other words, criminologists, psychologists and practitioners began to query whether behaviour was determined by environmental contingencies or whether the focus of attention should be shifted to the role of free will for a more complete explanation. This shift in critical focus allowed the combination of cognitive social learning approaches with behaviourist explanations for offending and the rise in the use of cognitive-behavioural methods in the work of the Probation Service. Whilst the application of cognitive theories to offending behaviour was not a new phenomenon, it was only now that cognitive or cognitive-behavioural approaches to managing offending behaviour began to work their way into the vocabulary of the criminal justice system. The argument is both simple and attractive, stating that if offenders make rational choices after weighing up the costs and benefits of a particular course of action through 'social decision making', controlling and preventing crime, this merely requires agents of punishment and deterrence rather than professional probation officers who are skilled in interventions which relate to more complex views of offending and rehabilitation.

This pattern has repeated itself since the 1830s in one guise or another. More alarmingly, what has followed each time is a rise in biological or genetic explanations for crime. Each time, these 'explanations' have become more subtle and sophisticated as science has developed, and they have often been isolated, sometimes through conflict, to particular areas of the world. As long ago as the 1970s, Yochelson & Samenow were asserting that cognitive variations between offenders and non-offenders are such that criminals are like a different breed of person. More recently, Moir and Jessel (1997) referenced nearly 800 research reports over three decades to present what they contend is solid evidence that physiological problems involving the brain require biological, not psychological, solutions. In their discussions about the inter-relationships between hormones, neurotransmitters, alcohol, drugs, epilepsy, family violence, and rape, they assert that there are genes that predispose some to non-violent property crime and others to violent behaviour.

Whilst these neo-Lombrosian explanations are dangerous, resurrecting the spectre of Cesare Lombroso who in late 19th-century Italy was convinced that criminality was largely inherited and that the criminal personality revealed itself in physical appearance, surely they cannot gain ground amongst today's better educated population?

History suggests that, sadly, they might.

Coffee, Marxism and Systems Theory
– Probation in the Late 70s

*Charlie Watson, Director, Charlie Watson Staff
Development & Training, UK*

Imagine the scene. Collecting in the staffroom for start of the day drinks, the usual uniform of leather jackets, fair isle jumpers, maxi skirts, and long hair, the car park full of 2CVs, Beetles, Renault 4s, and the odd posh Escort or two. The only thing to ruffle the calm being the odd desultory call from court, capably dealt with by the duty officer, Michael Lucas, using his cattle prod to liven things up a bit in the waiting room, and Royce White fitting in the corner. But this was Friday and we had a team meeting to attend. And they were important. Everyone expected to be there on time. The allocation meeting to start.

Allocation meeting? Yep, we sat around having esoteric professional discussions about who in the team was best placed to take on a particular piece of work, the result being a series of vaguely democratic, but incredibly well-informed, decisions that took us comfortably up to the next coffee break, where any undercurrents and complaints would surface in hushed tones. Then back into the meeting to pursue our radical agenda. Oh yes, we were radical. And committed. And political. And, quite possibly, up ourselves.

The context …

Hot foot from a management training course some months before, our manager and her colleague arrived back at the office armed with a form of working called 'Systems Theory', formulated and promulgated by Peter Leonard, Professor of Social Work at Leicester University. This theory suggested that, whilst it remained important to try and work with people through the medium of the relationship in order to try and effect change (call it social work), it was as, if not more, important to analyse what social constraints and systems were increasing the potential for offending.

Having undertaken that analysis, it was necessary (and a legitimate part of the job) to identify targets for intervention in order to improve the life chances and choices of our clients (notice the avoidance of that term offender – in those days such an epithet produced a sharpish intake of breath). So this was some really radical thinking, helped by whispers that this could be seen as a Marxist approach. As a bunch of (mainly) action group members working in the north Nottinghamshire coalfields, this was music to our ears and heady stuff indeed.

And this is what we did …

We trawled for data from agencies in the area, we surveyed census information, we researched what community facilities were available, we investigated access to services by clients, we researched client views, we inspected council policies, and we interviewed key agency personnel. From there we were able to identify gaps in provision and subsequently able to agitate for those gaps to be filled.

Examples …

*   No provision for young school-age people on a particular mining estate. The estate was blighted by the bored antics of these young people who would often end up in court for criminal damage, public order offences, or car crime. We talked to the Youth Service, we talked to Social Services, we talked to the Colliery, we talked to the Miners Welfare. End result, we got some provision put in place, which reduced local criminality.

*   People coming out of prison were not deemed in need of housing. That was our job. Off we went to Housing Committee meetings, stood up and argued our case. Result – a change in policy, which helped homelessness.

*   Persuaded the council to pay the rent on a disused shop in a prime position, so we and other agencies could increase access to services for the public and make efficient referrals regarding need.

In a way, all this (dare I say it?) political activity predated that well-known dictum 'tough on crime, tough on the causes of crime'. We all spent a lot of time out there in the communities. We home visited a lot. We talked to other workers a lot. We worked individually. We worked in groups. We genuinely believed that we were doing something that, in the round, made sense. And if you want a measure for effectiveness, we looked at enforcement. The need to do it was low – very low. The old equation was proved right: high contact = high compliance.

And, bless him, Peter Leonard kept in touch, came to see us, reviewed it all with us, suggested tweaks here and there. Direct academic involvement in practice was rather a rarity then, but vital in its pioneering way. Because this was before the days of measurement, its effectiveness was never really 'proved', and it became yet another good idea consigned to the dustbin of probation history.

The Think First Programme Pre-Accreditation: A Lost Opportunity?

Simon Feasey, Deputy Director,
Hallam Centre for Community Justice,
Sheffield Hallam University, Sheffield, UK

During the 1990s, I was working as a probation officer in Manchester and, after 15 years of practice, I was looking for a fresh challenge. This materialised when I secured a post as a group worker at Victoria Park Day Centre in Longsight. Like most group work teams pre-What Works, we delivered a range of programmes that were largely determined by the knowledge, understanding, experience and specific interests of staff members; there was much scope for creative innovation but the phrases 'ad hoc' and 'on the hoof' also rang bells. Attendance rates were poor and there was a constant struggle to secure sufficient referrals.

During the mid 90s the What Works Movement had yet to take hold. Conferences during the early years of the decade that sought to debate effective practice had begun to generate interest amongst some policy makers, practitioners, managers and academics, but most of us were fully occupied with responding to the particularly hostile political climate that had developed since the arrival of Michael Howard as Home Secretary in 1993. Engaging with the enforcement and punishment agenda dominated much of our thinking at a time when the future of the Probation Service was very much in doubt.

Within this environment the day centre SPO suggested at a routine team meeting that we agree to pilot a newly developed group work programme called 'Think First', which had been written by James McGuire and which was based on a cognitive-behavioural approach to working with offenders. Although this was new territory for all of us, the response was enthusiastic and supportive. Here was an opportunity to engage not only with a new programme based on a clearly articulated theoretical model, but also to take part in an in-house evaluation of the programme's impact and outcomes. An exciting initiative, properly resourced!

James McGuire arrived to train us both in the theory base and programme delivery. We were expertly introduced to a brave new world of psychometric testing, programme and treatment integrity, highly structured manual-based session content and the fundamentals of cognitive-behavioural interventions. The experience was challenging but also very motivating and exciting; most of the group work team were highly experienced with a good grounding in group work skills. We recognised that the programme would be difficult to deliver but at heart had the confidence that we could convert what felt like a 'classroom' teaching programme into an effective group work process.

From the start we sought to introduce tried and tested group work techniques to enable effective communication and the development of a healthy group culture within which learning and change could take place. Offenders spent a day at the centre, before session one started, engaging in trust and challenge games with staff; this was recorded on video and used to generate discussion and debates around team building, group roles, leadership and relationship building. Pretty effective ice-breaking and group forming! Delivery of the programme itself was initially rather stilted and awkward, a combination of our lack of familiarity both with the content and also the need to maintain a highly-focused and structured environment, which was necessary to progress the content, whilst trying to ensure that process issues were properly managed. Many of us experienced the group as the most difficult intervention to deliver well, because of the tension between content and process. Nevertheless, we developed greater confidence over time and began to feel that the approach had value; offender feedback was positive, many stating that this was quite unlike any other probation experience but was significantly impacting on the way they were thinking about themselves and others. In different ways, most of us involved became champions of the programme, aware of its problems and failings but also convinced that the approach had much to offer.

Subsequently, the 'What Works' movement took a hold; the first Pathfinders were established and the accreditation of programmes and their national roll-out became the primary focus of the Service. Groupworkers became tutors, new staff – with little experience of working with offenders and no groupwork knowledge – were appointed and targets were set for completion that drove the accredited programmes agenda relentlessly on, resulting in huge numbers of unsuitable offenders embarking on poorly delivered programmes. I left the Service.

The Professional Qualification

Mike Worthington, Former Chair of NAPO Training Committee

I joined the Probation Service during a period of expansion in the mid-60s. The Service had recently taken on responsibility for prison after-care work from NADPAS (the National Association of Discharged Prisoners Aid Society), a voluntary organisation which became NACRO. The name of the Service changed to the Probation & After-care Service. In the next six years, parole, community service, probation hostels and day centres were added to the Service's statutory responsibilities, setting the framework for its work up to 2001. This expansion of the Service's role within the criminal and civil justice systems also saw the appointment of the first ancillary-grade staff and the recruitment of volunteers, who undertook particular responsibilities in the supervision of offenders in the community – particularly with those released from prison, who were not subject to statutory supervision.

Increasingly, probation officers entering the Service at this time held a professional qualification. Most were 'second career' entrants, who undertook the one year Home Office training course at Rainer House or Leeds University, leading to the award of the Letter of Recognition. However, an increasing number of graduate entrants were joining the Service having completed postgraduate qualifying training courses in social work. Throughout the 50s and 60s, the social work value base of the Service developed and these values became increasingly apparent in both Service policy and practice.

Not all probation officer entrants possessed a relevant pre-entry qualification, however, and there was no requirement for them to do so. With the expansion that the Service was experiencing, numbers of qualified entrants did not keep pace with recruitment needs. Consequently, local area services had little option other than to recruit untrained people – direct entrants, as they were known. It was always argued at the time that, within five years, it was difficult to distinguish a trained officer from a direct entrant. However, the pressures created for both direct entrants and their qualified colleagues during these five years led me to the clear view that this means of entry to the Service was not tolerable. The Home Office required direct entrants to achieve the Letter of Recognition, following 'on the job' training and occasional residential courses, which they provided. Within two years of joining the Service, I was both teaching and tutoring direct entrants, on top of an already heavy workload.

In 1974, I was elected Chair of NAPO's National Training Committee. Within my first year in office and with the support of NAPO, I proposed to the Home Office that it should be a requirement that probation officers, on appointment, should hold a recognised qualification and that this qualification should be the Certificate of Qualification in Social Work (later the Diploma in Social Work). At that time, matters relating to crime and justice were not the political and media obsession that they are today. Across the political parties, there was a broad consensus on criminal justice policy, which enabled sensible legislation and policy making. An age of enlightenment indeed!

Home Office officials thought that the NAPO proposal eminently sensible, as did the Conference of Chief Probation Officers (many of whom were still NAPO members) and the Central Council of Probation Committees. Consequently, in 1975, the requirement that probation officers hold the CQSW on appointment was written into Probation Rules. All holders of the Home Office Letter of Recognition were 'blanketed in', and therefore deemed to hold the equivalent of the CQSW. Some Probation Areas, who had relied on direct entry in their recruitment of probation officers were faced with a difficult few years. However, under the auspices of the Central Council for Education and Training in Social Work, increasing numbers of two-year CQSW courses were being established in universities across England and Wales. This led to a period of productive partnerships between local area services and universities, which had many spin-off benefits for both parties.

The requirement that probation officers hold the CQSW on appointment remained in Probation Rules for the next 20 years. It is my contention that it underpinned perhaps the most effective and professionally coherent period in the 100-year history of the Probation Service.

From CQSW to DipPS

*Mike Worthington, Former Chair of ACOP
Training Committee, UK*

In yesterday's Moment, I referred to the requirement written into Probation Rules in 1975 that probation officers hold the CQSW. I also referred to the political consensus on criminal justice policy ensuring that legislation and policy was, for the most part, sensible and took account of the considered views of professionals. Throughout the 80s, this became difficult to maintain, as an increasingly reactionary Conservative Government, under Margaret Thatcher, introduced legislation and policies and took decisions which were both abrasive and divisive. However, in spite of ever louder calls for more punitive penal policies from an unleashed Conservative Party and a less and less responsible tabloid press, the consensus on criminal justice held – thanks almost entirely to two remarkable Home Secretaries, Willie Whitelaw and Douglas Hurd, whose wisdom, intellect and political nous enabled them to keep the hawks at bay.

With hindsight, it was probably inevitable that the rightward political tide would eventually prevail. For those working in criminal justice, the point of change in philosophy and direction happened spectacularly with the appointment of Michael Howard as Home Secretary in 1993. Let us not forget that his 'John the Baptist' was one Kenneth Clarke, who in his brief time at the Home Office, clearly flagged up this change in direction. Over the next decade and up until today, criminal justice policy in this country has become ever more reactionary, has pandered to the lowest common denominator, ignored sane professional voices, has believed that toughness and punishment are the way to deal with offenders, has responded to every sensational tabloid story (which would have us believe that crime in this country is out of control) and enacted mountains of legislation 'on the hoof'. The incoherent mess that is today's criminal justice policy, with a prison population of over 80,000, is the direct result of this politicising of criminal justice and the ill-conceived decisions it has led to. The tragedy is that this has happened over a decade when crime is actually falling, due in large part to a favourable economic climate.

From the outset of this change of direction, a criminal justice agency based on social work values, whose primary responsibility since 1907 was to 'advise, assist and befriend' offenders under its supervision, was never going to be left alone to continue this role, however integral it had become within our criminal justice system. Michael Howard acted swiftly and ruthlessly. He did two things which started the process of undermining the Probation Service. Firstly, he cut resources. After another period of expansion, to enable the Service to implement the forward looking 1991 Criminal Justice Act, in the first two years of Michael Howard's time at the Home Office, we in Northumbria – where I was Chief Probation Officer – had to lose 100 posts from a total staff complement of 600.

Secondly, he announced that he was to remove the requirement that probation officers hold a social work qualification. To starve the Service of resources and to remove its professional base was, to say the least, draconian. His intention was clear. At this time, I was Chair of the National Training Committee of the Association of Chief Officers of Probation. It occurred to me that, if we were to save the now well-established and sophisticated qualifying training arrangements for probation officers, the Service, through its representative organisations and its partners in higher education, needed to act together and develop a coherent strategy to resist what the Home Secretary was planning. It proved to be a long and difficult five-year struggle. The alliance held firm and qualifying training was saved, albeit in a new form – but there were losses and serious wounds inflicted along the way, from which the Service has not recovered.

Perhaps my saddest moment came in 1995, in a House of Commons Committee room, when I witnessed the vote to remove the requirement that probation officers hold a social work qualification from Probation Rules. One of my proudest moments came in July 1997, when, two months after a Labour Government had been elected, Jack Straw, as Home Secretary, made a statement in the House of Commons setting out plans for a new qualification for probation officers. We were not able to persuade the Home Secretary that a social work qualification should be restored (sadly, I do not believe we had a clear mandate from the Service to argue for that), but the new Diploma in Probation Studies, when it was implemented in 1999, did retain the best of the old DipSW qualification and was, in my view, 'fit for purpose'.

However, that victory has proved to be short-lived. Professional bodies are not amenable to the kind of political control now exerted by central government and their power therefore needs to be diminished. Not only is there now a new moratorium on probation officer qualifying training, but this sits alongside plans to effectively dismantle the Probation Service as we have known it and seen it develop over a century. In 2004, *The*

Guardian stated that the Probation Service in England & Wales had gone from 'world leader to chaos' in the three years since it moved from being a locally accountable service to a nationally controlled one. Things have only got worse since then and from where I stand, the future for the Service is bleak.

The Introduction of Competences to the Probation Service

Lesley Thompson, Director,
North West Training Consortium, UK

It was in 1990 that I received a telephone call from the then Deputy Chief Probation Officer in Lancashire, David Rudland, asking me to attend a three-day training course on National Vocational Qualifications being run by CCETSW.[1] He told me that he didn't really know what it was about but that it was being promoted as something that might be useful for probation volunteers and auxiliaries (as PSOs were known then). As I was interested in working with these staff groups, he asked if I would I go along and find out what I could. I didn't know anything about NVQs at that time and those three days introduced a whole new world to me. I was confronted with language that I had never encountered before, for example, competences, performance criteria, portfolios of evidence. I was introduced to roles that were outside of my experience – assessor, internal verifier, external verifier, and I had to get to grips with the concept that candidates did not pass or fail but were assessed as 'competent' or 'not yet competent'. The only comfort during those three days was that all the other participants on the course, mostly from Social Services, were also struggling with both the concept and the terminology of these new and bewildering qualifications.

NVQs were developed in the late 80s in order to address the UK skills shortage and widen the range of employer led vocational qualifications. Based on National Occupational Standards, they are designed to enable candidates to demonstrate their competence in the workplace. The concept of people being assessed for what they could do rather than just on what they knew was one that I found attractive. At the same time, a key lesson I learnt in those early days was that good assessment practice also includes the assessment of knowledge and understanding that underpins competent practice. Thus, the assessment of performance against specified criteria should involve more than just a 'tick box' approach and, used properly, should be a developmental tool as well as an affirmation of competence.

I was appointed as an External Verifier by CCETSW before there were any Occupational Standards in place for the Probation Service and so was initially given two Assessment Centres in Social Services residential homes. Although this was outside my area of experience, it gave me an excellent grounding in the NVQ principles of assessing evidence against criteria as I wasn't able to make assumptions or take anything for granted. In 1993, following the introduction of the Criminal Justice Standards, I was appointed External Verifier to the West Yorkshire NVQ Assessment Centre, one of the few based in the Probation Service. I was finally able to put into practice, within my own professional setting, all that I had learnt about NVQs and competences. It was a real privilege to work with enthusiastic and motivated staff and, in particular, to see PSO candidates achieving nationally recognised qualifications.

However, despite the introduction of the Criminal Justice Occupational Standards along with standards for other staff including managers and administrators, and not withstanding the enthusiasm of those involved in NVQ Assessment Centres, there was still only limited use made of competences within the Probation Service. It wasn't until the introduction of the Diploma in Probation Studies in 1998, which incorporated an NVQ with an academic degree, that a competency-based approach started to become more acceptable and has gained more widespread credibility.

We have come a long way since the introduction of competences in the early 1990s, and there is an increasing acknowledgement that Occupational Standards do not just mean NVQs. The challenge facing us now is whether we can recognise how these can be more fully integrated into all of our working practices and thus be an effective tool in the way that we manage, develop and qualify people at all levels of the organisation.

End Note

[1]   Central Council for Training and Education in Social Work.

The Criminal Justice Act 1991 and the 'Risk of Serious Harm to the Public'

Hazel Kemshall, Professor of Community and Criminal Justice, De Montfort University, Leicester, UK

The Criminal Justice Act 1991 marked something of a 'watershed', both in terms of penal policy and the work of the Probation Service. Whilst extended sentences for certain categories of offenders already existed, the CJA 1991 introduced two important concepts: risk based sentencing based upon 'serious harm to the public' and a greater emphasis upon preventative sentencing for those deemed a high risk to the public. Within Probation Services the initial focus tended to be on the 'just deserts' sentencing aspect of the Act, and attention to the consequent changes in the content and format of court reports. Recognition of the importance of section 2(2)(b) was slower and, in the early years of the Act, probation policy and practice tended to conflate risk of re-offending with risk of harm. However, the move from 'just deserts' to risk had begun.

The CJA 1991 also ushered in a Service-wide and nationally-steered approach to in-service training, with attention to the practice changes required by the Act. This too created a change in how in-service training was later to be structured and used, playing a greater responsibility on in-service training for ensuring consistency and quality in practice – a tactic which continues to this day and is currently being applied to the assessment and management of risk of harm.

In the intervening years the risk agenda has gathered pace, with subsequent legislation such as the CJA 2003 strengthening risk-based sentencing and justifying special measures, including indeterminate public protection sentences for high-risk offenders. Both in policy and legislative terms, 'risk' has been eclipsed by the broader term 'pubic protection', encompassing community-based risk management as well as longer custodial terms. A significant 're-balancing' between public safety and offender rights is currently under way, with extensive debate about the appropriate balance between privacy and disclosure, and restrictive community conditions and personal freedoms for offenders. The tension between predominantly English and Welsh penal policy and subsequent legislation emphasising community protection on the one hand, and the European Convention on Human Rights emphasising individual freedoms on the other is very real.

For practitioners, the world of probation has changed considerably in the intervening 15 years or so. Risk management is certainly in the ascendancy, with an emphasis upon victim protection, community safety, restrictive conditions, surveillance and monitoring, and enforcement as a mechanism for ensuring compliance. Specialist public protection teams have developed and tiering to ensure that resources follow risk has ensued. Intensive risk-management strategies have required closer inter-agency working culminating in the Multi-Agency Public Protection Arrangements (MAPPA), and in some instances a blurring of role and responsibility between police and probation.

On a more personal note, at the time of the CJA 1991 implementation I was an in-service trainer with the West Midlands Probation Service. At the time I felt that the Act was going to exert considerable influence over the future of the Probation Service. Little did I know that the Act would also open up a considerable area of research and policy interest for me, or that it would start my long and exciting journey with risk and public protection.

Probation – A Social Service?

Brian Fellowes, retired Probation Officer, now involved in developing Circles of Support and Accountability and a trustee of Circles UK

The time was about 1967/68. *The Seebohm Report* had recommended setting up new Social Service Departments to avoid the perceived overlap/underlap between different social welfare bodies (Children's Departments, Mental Health Departments, etc.).

Should we in probation become part of the new combined structures?

I was a newish probation officer working in the old West Riding Service (Principal Probation Officer the Pickwickian, Mr Mostyn-Hughes). In addition to being a member of the NAPO local branch, I was also a member of the newly formed British Association of Social Workers (BASW). Why? Because I felt strongly that probation should be seen as a social work service.

It seemed obvious to me that in most cases the crime was evidence of a disturbed relationship between the perpetrator and his/her social milieu. Some young people (and we were mainly talking about youngsters then) showed their disturbance through behaviour which could be described as mental illness and thus would come to the attention of the Child Guidance Service or the Mental Health Departments; some could come to the attention of the Children's Department as in need of protection. It was surely right that there should be a merging of these departments and that probation should be part of the shiny new combined Social Service Department – the one-stop-shop for social and familial breakdown/disruption. Here the odd/strange/anti-social/criminal behaviour could be addressed without blame or stigma. Here the appropriate 'treatments' of counselling/psycho-therapy could be applied.

Seebohm was not, however, greeted with such enthusiasm by many of our probation colleagues; the question of whether probation should be 'in' or 'out' became a hot topic wherever probation officers met. Those against the Report cited the relatively good salaries and better conditions of service enjoyed by probation officers and the fear of being sidelined in a multi-purpose department. The West Riding branch of NAPO came out against, much to the disappointment of some of us. However, those of us in favour found a respite from the sceptics in the NAPO branch in the welcoming arms of the local branch of BASW. In these meetings, our colleagues from the other departments confirmed our views that probation's presence in the new departments was essential. It would provide a stiffening of culture and of the 'professionalism' which was seen to have been established in probation through its longer history and especially since the Criminal Justice Act 1948. No longer would 'treatment' for 'clients' be subject to the lottery of which 'door' they happened to be presented at. Referral between agencies which already had a poor record of success (one of the main problems identified by Seebohm) would become a thing of the past.

'Social work' probation officers were thus defeated. Social Services Departments were set up and probation remained separate, reinforcing the criminal justice nature of its rationale rather than its social work leanings. In Scotland, the equivalent of the *Seebohm Report*, the *Kilbrandon Report*, did lead to the integration of probation in their new Social Work Departments.

It only took me a short while to appreciate how wrong I had been and how right my colleagues were to oppose integration! Only months after the creation of the new departments, a series of legislative measures appeared, of which, I think, the Children and Young Person's Act of 1969 was the first. Each of these Acts gave Social Services Departments further tasks to perform without any apparent reference to resources. Our BASW colleagues were overwhelmed and, as far as I can see, remain so.

For years afterwards, Scottish colleagues would complain that probation had been sidelined in the face of new and urgent responsibilities. Meanwhile in England, probation was to be driven further down the criminal justice/ punishment route, eventually losing contact with 'social work' altogether. Who knows what would have happened if the 'social workers' had won?

Volunteerism as a Profession?

*Jenny Ögren, Lay Supervisor and Project
Co-Ordinator, Sweden*

Can you teach compassion? Can you learn empathy? Of course you need some basic skills, like interest in other people and the capacity to see other people's problems and situations in life but do you need more?

I have arranged courses for lay supervisors through the Swedish organisation, Voluntary Community Workers. As an employee in an organisation for lay supervisors, I taught and instructed both people who wanted to become lay supervisors[1] and people who have had several tasks as supervisors. During these courses and seminars we discussed different subjects relating to supervision but, in particular, one subject: how to create a good relationship with your client. I think I did a good job and that I had some experience to lean on since I had previously been a probation officer for the Swedish Prison and Probation Services. Of course, I supervised and recruited lay supervisors as a probation officer as well and when I changed jobs and no longer worked for the Swedish Prison and Probation Services, I continued as a lay supervisor myself – and what a difference from being an employee!

As an employed probation officer I would never have dreamt of seeing a client in my own home, but of course as a lay supervisor I did. I learnt Spanish during evenings for a term with an ex-cannabis-addict, something I certainly would not have done as an employee, but as a lay supervisor I found the language sessions to be very stimulating and I developed alongside my client. I recently became a mum, and I supervised an ex-addict and ex-prostitute woman who was expecting her first child alone. I supported and comforted her during the last months of pregnancy and the first months as a mum. In that process I allowed myself to be much more personally involved than I ever would have been (or could have been, for that matter) as a probation officer. I am very proud of what we achieved together; she has now moved to a safer and calmer little town close to her own mum and thereby gets more help in her daily life than she could have had in an anonymous capital city like Stockholm where she hardly knew anyone outside her former criminal world. As a benefit from that, she increased her self-esteem in a remarkable way and I can only wish her good luck in the future.

Recently, I have more consciously co-operated with the probation officer, responsible for my client, to agree what role models we 'play' towards them. The probation officer is able to be the authority figure pointing out rules and legislation, while I continue to be the 'alright mate' figure that can translate the difficult rules of probation into reality. Of course, there is not always a complete understanding anyway, but I have managed to continue having a good relationship with the client and the probation officer has been the 'bad guy' to blame, not me. Remember that this was an agreement beforehand between me and the probation officer. My experience is that this 'play' has made the probation easier for my client in the sense that he or she can trust me and count on me, knowing that I am not responsible for all the rules concerning probation. The probation officers have been very professional and humble letting me do the easy part as good guy. On the other hand, it's their profession, isn't it? Representing the authority and thereby applying the rules, whilst I am only representing myself and am more like a friend helping another.

So, my answers to the questions in the beginning are: by reflecting upon what you are doing as a lay supervisor and preferably why you are doing it, both individually and together with other lay supervisors and officials from the Probation Service, I think you can achieve results in the probation area you had not thought of before and not only 'do' a sentence of probation. In such a way you are able to develop (and keep?) your empathy and interest in other people and situations of life. The aim is to help the client to become a better person in some sense through probation, isn't it?

End Note

[1]   Lay supervisors are unpaid volunteers who work with clients of the Swedish probation service to support their welfare needs.

The New Careers Project

Malcolm Thomson, Project Manager, Clinks, UK

Ex-offenders as social workers? It might sound like a run-of-the-mill concept now, but when NACRO brought the idea over from the USA 30 or more years ago, they initially had their work cut out getting the funds needed to pioneer the idea. I was lucky enough to experience the project in its formative days as it trod the fine line between innovation and disaster.

With funding from the Home Office, the Bristol branch of NACRO established The New Careers Project, a residential facility for young offenders at risk of a Borstal sentence, which opened in 1973. The Project was based on an approach developed in America during the late 60s which sought to recruit the experience and skills of ex-offenders into provision for offenders and those at risk of offending. The project had a number of unique features including: the employment of ex-offenders as 'link workers' offering day-to-day support; the targeting of persistent young offenders who also, crucially, had the potential to undertake social work training; providing residents' income from the Home Office in a similar form to a regular student grant thus reinforcing the educational focus of the regime; and an independent, self-catering regime which was unusual in those days. Residents undertook placements in a variety of social work environments including a day centre for homeless people, a hospital for adults with severe learning difficulties and a number of adventure playgrounds. Tutors from a local college delivered courses in sociology and social work theory on one day while another was occupied with personal development activities.

I attended the facility on a residential placement while I was on my CQSW course in 1977. I shared a room with one of the residents and participated in all the project activities for a four-week period. Most memorable was the ability of the link workers to confront and engage with the residents. They brought a level of credibility and authority to the work which was probably unavailable to even the most experienced worker.

Almost as remarkable was the empathy and commitment of the residents in their work with other vulnerable individuals. 'Allan' was a young man from Swansea who had devoted the previous four years to stealing as many cars as he could between court and custodial sentences. He formed a relationship with 'Wilf', an individual with profound learning difficulties, literally through constructing objects using Lego. Allan's patience and humour was remarkable. The placement was only for four weeks and I was there when 'Wilf' and 'Allan' said their final goodbyes – it would be difficult to imagine a more genuine expression of mutual sorrow and loss. 'Kevin' seemed at times absolutely dedicated to violence and had to be diverted on more than one occasion from deliberately engineering confrontations. However, he also completed a highly successful placement at a day centre for homeless people.

The Project was not without its problems. Residents often found it difficult to deal with the issues raised from their offending and it was a constant battle to challenge destructive attitudes and behaviours. Rules were broken but just about anything short of physical violence was dealt with through negotiation rather than immediate exclusion. Weekly residents' meetings were lively affairs.

The link workers battled with their own demons at times. A previous staff member had carried on with his criminal activities and was arrested from the hostel. However, the outcomes for about three quarters of the link workers employed by the Project ranged from good to exceptional. About 25% of the staff went on to careers in the criminal justice system, with an equal proportion unable to manage the pressures of residential work. The rest usually remained at the Project for about 18 months.

There were remarkable outcomes for some residents as well. At least three went on to successful careers within the criminal justice system, and another was employed as a residential worker in the voluntary sector

The New Careers Project had struggled to maintain a sufficient occupancy level due to the narrow age criteria (18–22). It was difficult to identify enough offenders who had the maturity and insight to benefit from this unusual provision. My own experience confirmed for me the potential for change in some of the most difficult and persistent offenders. However, it clearly was not right for everyone. The degree of intelligence and insight in the resident group was exceptional.

The atmosphere was often highly charged but also incredibly warm and funny. More than anything else, this was an initiative that focused not on deficits and weaknesses, but on drawing out positive qualities in ex-offenders and improving their capacity to form powerful and worthwhile relationships with each other and with those that have also struggled to succeed in the world.

The Project lasted about five years before Avon Probation Service took over and subsequently it became a probation hostel.

Un-Natural Acts:[1] Pushing the Boundaries in the 1970s

Bruce Hugman, PO and SPO, SYPACS during 1970s, currently Medical Communications Writer and Consultant, based in Thailand

Sheffield was a lively and exciting city in the 70s, and its dynamism was evident even in its magistracy and probation leadership and committees; optimism and experiment were in the air. There was a degree of panic about the mushrooming of drug use among young people but, on the whole, it was met with agonised concern rather than punitive suppression. The liberating revolutions of the 60s came late to this great city, but they had their benign and bewildering effects in some of the most unlikely circles, even in the behaviour of some members of the judiciary.

The Probation Service was in a ferment of debate about its purpose and its future, its values and its politics, and it was a great time to be part of it. The Detached Project was one of the expressions of the contemporary spirit of adventurousness, and it opened new doors of insight and experience for workers and clients alike. For me, it exemplified an ideal model of effective response to the personal and social needs of a wide range of people who had become tangled with the criminal justice system.

In those days, Broomhall, where the project was located, was a physically dilapidated and superficially depressing area; one of the notorious red light districts of the city, home to dropouts, hippies, prostitutes, minor and major felons, as well as a number of long-term residents and immigrant families. Here, in the midst of this rich social mix, we believed a probation officer might be seen to be more approachable and useful than one stuck in a smart, city-centre tower block.

It was also a time when rather pretentious notions of professionalism were beginning to sweep probation and social work circles and, it seemed to me, helpers were at risk of becoming more and more detached from the people they served, and more and more cocooned in rituals and bureaucracy. If our job was, as I believed it to be, to help people to achieve some freedom and self-determination in life (not least reducing the chances of arrest and prosecution), then I wondered how much I could achieve distanced from the day-to-day context in which their lives were influenced and shaped, and with resources largely limited to talk.

Clients came to the flat (which was home and workplace) for regular meetings, but also at any time of the day or night when they felt the need: to talk, to avoid risky situations, to recover from crisis, to eat or take a bath, to seek company and sanctuary. Clients were often neighbours as well, but even those who didn't live nearby were very comfortable in coming to such a homely kind of place in such an ordinary kind of location. It was possible to offer much more than talk, though talk – and the search for meaning and choice and purpose – was often what was most sought. Such talk also took place in other places where probation officers were rarely seen: pubs where Hells Angels met, or dark clubs where the air was thick with marijuana smoke and Pink Floyd.

The whole experience challenged so many of the assumptions of professional practice that one seemed always to be on the edge, but it was at that edge that I believed it was possible to get closer to the truth of people's lives, and that their perception of that process as it happened deeply enriched the possibility of a probation officer being useful to them, and to society.

After I left, the project continued for some years, in a larger house in the area with more staff, and it continued to be a beacon of good practice for clients and probation officers alike, though there were those, of course, who felt it was an extravagant and dubious setup. It was eventually closed down, against considerable but unsuccessful resistance, at a time when national policy was starting to shift the Probation Service inexorably along the road from helping towards control and punishment.

The lasting legacy of the project, for me, is set out below. To be useful, we must:

- get close to those whom we are serving;
- have a genuine understanding of their lives as whole people;
- not relate to them only through the distanced rules and perspectives of role;
- expose and share our common humanity, uncertainties and dilemmas;
- provide our service and ourselves in ways which make real, explicit sense in our clients' terms; and
- have a driving vision of what we are trying to achieve.

End Note

[1] Bruce's book about the project was called *Act Natural*. For more info, e-mail mail@brucehugman.net

---

A New Frilly Nightie – Boundaries and Helping

*Bruce Hugman, PO and SPO, SYPACS during
1970s, currently Medical Communications Writer and
Consultant, based in Thailand*

The Detached Probation Project, like all true outreach work, provided a succession of both exhilarating and frightening events and experiences. One of my favourite moments is as follows:

I was providing coffee in my hovel of a home and probation workplace to two of the magistrates who were members of the large-hearted committee responsible for the project, along with my wonderful supervising APPO, Jack Porter. There was a knock at the front door, and the visitor turned out to be Elisabeth, a neighbour from across the street. She was a homely, cheerful and endearing woman with a cuddly figure, about thirty years old and a single mother with a healthy, exuberant child. She ran a pretty brisk business in her house where she entertained, mothered, listened to and satisfied a succession of men of all ages, of all ranks and backgrounds, for very modest fees. She was occasionally picked up and taken to court for soliciting and was usually fined (putting more financial pressure on her) but on the last occasion she had been put on probation, and I was assigned as her supervising officer. (She claimed that she had once appeared in court before one of her clients.)

Here she was, now, at my front door, excitedly wearing her latest gift from a grateful customer and wanting to share her delight with me: an extravagant pink nightie with as many frilly bows and as much frothy lace as it is possible to imagine. I congratulated her on her ravishing appearance and invited her to come and show my friends, without telling her who they were. She shyly did a quick pirouette and said she needed to get home.

At the time I felt excited by this improbable and extraordinary meeting (I still sense the thrill of the moment): here were magistrates, not only risking visiting me in one of the most disreputable areas of the city, but coming face to face with one of those mysterious beings whom they would normally see only in the dock and about whose life most would have not the slightest inkling: furthermore, she was a neighbour and friend of a probation officer. We talked long about her and what she represented;

about the couple of occasions she had been able to seek refuge in the flat from abusive clients; and about the usefulness of what she did.

(A kind of reverse sartorial exposure happened when clients woke me in the middle of the night, and I received them in my pyjamas – a professional depravity which caused some sharp drawing-in of breath among my more regular colleagues.)

This was a sample of the wonderful upside of being close to where people lived their lives, but there was also a darker side too. Knocks on the front door were just as often an individual in distress or a group of lads bringing a mate who had been slashed in a fight or who was out of his mind on some substance or other. There were a lot of mishaps, especially amongst youngsters experimenting with drugs, and I sometimes had no idea if I was facing a transient intoxication or an imminent death. Fortunately, I had an emergency line to a wonderful consultant physician (Ralph Edwards) who could be called at any time of the day or night and would come round if there seemed to be any hint of danger. He and I spent many hours in the deep of the night talking about the meaning of life over the prone and unconscious bodies of youngsters who had gone just too far.

I was very clear what the project was about: it was to be available in locations and at times which were comfortable and accessible; to provide tough, realistic, compassionate, temporary support to those who were struggling to make it on their own; to walk with people through the bad times and hope to help them find their own way and a life which fulfilled them; to offer food and sanctuary as much as therapy or behaviour modification or control; to try and help them make choices in the full knowledge of what the consequences would be. For some I know it helped; for some, much, much later – I know this, because some have flourished, and they have told me so.

End Note

E-mail: mail@brucehugman.net

Introducing the STOP Programme in Mid Glamorgan

Christine Knott CBE, former National Offender Manager, NOMS, UK

My reflection stretches from November 1990 to the summer of 1991 and centres on the first of the accredited programmes, known as the Reasoning and Rehabilitation programme. I was an ACPO in Mid Glamorgan and first heard about the R&R programme when I came into work, having just come back from holiday. My flight had been delayed for over 24 hours, I was horrendously jetlagged and had popped into the office. I had only been there a few minutes when Dave Sutton, my Chief, caught me, dragged me off to the pub (anybody who knew him will know that was where he was most comfortable), and proceeded to tell me all about this programme from Canada. I could hardly keep my eyes open by this stage, but even then I knew this was something exciting.

Over the next few days, the enormity of what we were about to embark on began to dawn on me. We had been able to obtain the R&R manual. Even that was something of a culture shock, we had never had to pay for a group work programme before and we had never had anything that needed a manual, all we had ever worked to before was a series of headlines and outcomes for each session. Everybody was pretty sceptical. Would our offenders be as compliant as they appeared to be in Canada? Could we get our offenders to do that kind of thing ... sit in a 'classroom' and be taught? Most had done everything they could to avoid school. Before we started investing a lot of money, we got a group of offenders together for a day and tried out some sessions. We were upfront about what we were doing, we wanted to know what they thought. Despite our lack of experience at running the sessions, the feedback was overwhelmingly positive! They had given us a really strong steer; get on with it, we like it and we think it could make a difference.

We needed to get everybody on board – staff, magistrates and the powers that be, and that was never going to be easy. We held a staff conference to discuss the idea, used some end-of-year savings to pay James McGuire and Phillip Priestley to provide training for all staff. If this was going to work it had to be available to every team and we needed everyone in the organisation to know what their contribution was going to be. Then it was down to the really hard graft of getting ourselves organised to deliver the groups. We had to video each of the sessions (completely new ground for us) and pay attention to programme integrity (not a term that was in everyday use in the UK). Our groupwork model was heavily based on using the group dynamics to challenge behaviour rather than teach thinking skills.

One of our first challenges was to get sentencers lined up, if they didn't like it, then we would never get the orders that we wanted. We used one of the programme sessions, based on distinguishing between a fact and an opinion, and ran it for groups of magistrates. They were enthusiastic about the idea and gave us their seal of approval. For the first time, they really had some clarity about what would happen to somebody on Probation.

The first group was run in Merthyr Tydfil, probably an unlikely place to play such an important part in probation history. John Merriman, who was the senior there at the time, was determined to get the first group off the ground. Peter Raynor and colleagues were involved in doing the research and evaluation. It was a very small beginning to what has since become a range of accredited programmes that are now available to offenders. We never thought it would be the panacea; it was always only going to be part of the overall armoury to tackle re-offending. Dealing with social exclusion, drug treatment and all the other practical services were still going to be an essential part of any community or prison sentence. Whatever structures are there for probation intervention in the future, I cannot forget that some (although not all) of the best initiatives have come from the bottom up. Mid Glamorgan was a small organisation that would struggle to compete in today's world, but we helped lay a foundation stone for accredited programmes and that was a great achievement.

Becoming a Practice Development Assessor: October 1998

Sue Parkinson, Senior Lecturer, Hallam Centre for Community Justice, Sheffield, UK

Becoming a Practice Development Assessor in October 1998 felt different, more purposeful. During the preceding four years, I had worked as a practice teacher, facilitating learning in the workplace with DipSW students. During this time both the students and I had experienced elation and frustration. The Practice Teacher's Award had prepared me for working with students' 'barriers to learning'. I saw joy in students when, after grappling with key competing demands of the professional role – power, control, rehabilitation and fairness – they developed an ability to observe and reshape their belief systems. However, I also saw this newly acquired ability to self-reflect degenerate into self-justification or self-pity when their reformed self had not transformed their practice.

Similarly, I had observed the enthusiasm of students when they achieved a level of competence in the routine activity of preparing Pre-sentence Reports. They had learned to apply their hastily acquired basic understanding of the assessment of 'offence seriousness' and 'offender suitability' by using those ubiquitous sentencing matrices that had been strewn around the probation office since the implementation of the CJA 1991. Nonetheless I also became familiar with their frustration in understanding the uniqueness of each PSR. They struggled in assessing the impact that a particular offence committed by a particular offender may have had on a particular community or victim. They had difficulty in knowing how to engage different offenders on issues of motivation to change and how to recognise the unique dynamics of an interview when offenders presented differing levels of denial. They continued to wrestle with the formulation of a sentencing proposal, which was required to flow logically from their initial assessments.

It became apparent to me that these more opaque concepts (and, importantly, their interconnectedness), which are based upon a knowledge of psychology, victimology, criminology and sentencing theory and comprise a deep understanding of the meaning of community and criminal justice, were not accessible to DipSW students through their academic curriculum. Their barriers to learning were difficult to dismantle.

With the DipPS came a curriculum that established a range of core content areas drawn from the probation officer occupational standards. This, combined with a set of assessment principles, which required the academic accreditation of practice, provided a framework for the integration of 'theory' and 'practice'. Academic learning was now geared towards an understanding of the link between academic research and professional knowledge, related legislative and policy frameworks, as well as the key ethical and value issues in probation practice. Trainee probation officers and I now had an explicit body of 'probation knowledge' that we could use to enhance the reflective learning process. In other words, I now had the apparatus to promote conceptual development in the workplace by helping trainees to avoid the knowledge impasse experienced by the DipSW students. Trainees had the opportunity to use 'theories' as tools to help develop their own private suppositions in order to translate and transform practice.

It would be naive to believe that either the original or the newly revised Core Curriculum alone can bring about a learning process that would generate effective, critically reflective probation officers who are, in essence, sufficiently motivated to continually strive towards change and improve practice.

Continued success relies upon the skill of academic tutors to present 'theory' in a way that trainees can recognise and enthuse over its relevance to the practice situation and context. In turn, the successful transfer of this learning from the academic to the vocational arena depends upon the trainees developing an ability to use 'theory' to read between lines of the complex dialogues, intentions and actions of themselves, their clients and their colleagues. From the early days of the DipPS, I remember clearly the messages from the professional literature about the pivotal role of the PDA in closing the 'theory-practice gap'. In order to achieve this, a PDA must work in collaboration with academics to encourage trainees to develop a network of deep understandings about protecting the public and reducing crime through effective work with offenders. A PDA then needs to enable trainees to apply these understandings in order to interpret their experience and work out a series of further terms of reference appropriate to the many practice situations and dilemmas they will face. This is an extraordinary task that requires an expertise beyond their professional capabilities as probation officers and NVQ assessors. An expertise that I believe should be acknowledged and nurtured through a specialist, professional awards framework.

Creative Probation Practice

Rita Richmond, Practice Development Assessor,
West Midlands Probation Area, UK

One of the most satisfying aspects of working as a probation officer is when you find the key to helping someone to make some positive changes to his or her life – especially if this is the first time this has been achieved while the person has been subject to probation supervision, or perhaps ever. I am thinking of one particular man who everybody in the office used to dread coming in. Peter (not his real name) had a chronic alcohol problem and there was always a fuss when he came in to report. Alcohol consumption had become a major issue – previous officers had tried to get him to come in to the office sober, but this had not proved possible so little work was being undertaken with him.

Peter was allocated to me, a newly-qualified probation officer, in the autumn of 2000. A number of stays in hospital indicated that his physical addiction to alcohol was such that he suffered blackouts when alcohol-free for any length of time, and so it was unrealistic to expect him to always be sober when he reported. I made up my mind that, although I would look at his level of alcohol consumption with him (because it is not possible to work at any depth with somebody who has been drinking), I would always speak to him when he reported – drunk or sober – and would accept that there were going to be times when he was going to ramble on and not be very coherent. It seemed more important to see him regularly than to insist that he control his drinking. I felt that once I could get him in and engage with him then other things would follow. I was right. Peter said himself that he might not be able to give up drink completely, but he would try to cut down. Once he achieved this, we were able to start looking at the problems it caused him, including his offending. A key moment for me was when the Aquarius worker, from the local alcohol partnership agency, left me a note saying that Peter had been lucid and articulate in one of his sessions.

Peter was imprisoned again for shoplifting, but remained subject to supervision on release and seemed more determined than ever to make some changes to his life. In our work together, a critical session was one in which he was talking about his personal circumstances and was drawing with his fingers on the desk. I remembered that he had worked with charts and diagrams in a previous job as an electrician. So I gave him paper and a pen and said, 'Just draw for me what you are describing' and, with some prompting, he did this. I kept the drawing in his file and over the next few sessions he added various squiggles and circles and arrows and things that made sense to him, if not to anyone else. He said himself that the more he looked at it, the more embarrassed he felt about it. However, it provided a focal point for our supervision and I used to say to him, 'I'm going to frame this and give it to you when your Order is finished'. Looking back now, I think that diagram was central to him being able to see me as someone who was trying to understand him and help him make sense of his life. It also matched the way he learned, and recalling that he worked to diagrams in his job was an important link between his former and current self. I also think it helped give him some control over the experiences he was explaining to me.

I am not saying Peter changed totally, but there was a noticeable amount of movement and, through a softly, softly approach, he made tremendous progress in sorting out his life. He moved into a 'Damp House', run by the local alcohol agency, where he was able to drink safely outside, but not in the house. For the first time in many years he felt accepted into the community there and did not, to my knowledge, re-offend.

The damage sustained over many years of abuse often prevents a happy ending. Peter was no exception and died of head injuries sustained through falling off an outside staircase when returning home one night. Nevertheless, I remain confident that the work we undertook together helped him restore some of the self-esteem he lost through years of drinking and offending, and gave him several months of a very different kind of life experience.

Throughcare, Aftercare, Resettlement: The Work of the Probation Service with Released Prisoners

David Pidwell, former National Resettlement Manager,
Offending Behaviour Programmes Unit, HM Prison Service, UK

Until 2006, the probation office in Worksop had above its door a sign proclaiming, 'Nottinghamshire Probation and Aftercare Service', although the Service was only so named for a very short period (1967–1982) of its 100 years. I never found out whether the sign hung there negligently, in praise of a bygone era or in defiance of modern trends.

1967 saw a major reorganisation of existing aftercare services with the major provider, the Discharged Prisoners Aid Society, disbanded and its work taken over by Probation; seconded officers were introduced to all prisons; and discretional early release on parole was legislated for. Probation embarked on its new responsibilities ably aided by Mark Monger's book, I think called, *Casework in Aftercare*. Mark deserves a wider mention in any celebration of probation. During the 1960s and 70s he was a key figure in establishing probation officer training at higher education establishments as well as publishing a number of landmark books on practice.

So how has resettlement fared under probation these past 40 years?

1. Officers took their responsibilities under the new Parole process extremely seriously and it was their endeavour that gave the system its public credibility and success. It always struck me that officers put more into this area of throughcare work because prisoners had to apply for Parole and thereby signalled their wish to engage and be under supervision in much the same way as a probationer would by agreeing to a probation order. In contrast, many officers found the compulsory and automatic nature of Borstal, Young Prisoner and Detention Centre Licences off-putting.

2. Meeting the basic resettlement needs of prisoners was never straightforward. I marvelled at the speed at which accommodation officers, working with case managers and duty officers, somehow housed homeless offenders before close of business, magicking a new address, squaring the move with 'Social' and often needing to convince landlords that they were taking on a good bet. I do hope accommodation officers are rightly honoured in this centenary year. It only slowly dawned on the Service that housing people should

not be part of its core business but more properly belonged to local authorities.

3.   In the 1980s, many areas established pre-release groups for those about to be released on YOI licence. South Yorkshire, for instance, ran about a dozen such groups annually. The four or five days were spent on a mixture of offending behaviour work, family work and meeting various community resources. Governors at Young Offender Institutions were usually very supportive. However, such groups disappeared suddenly after 1994 when the Government considerably tightened the temporary release criteria.

And the down sides?

On reflection, it seemed neither prison nor Probation Service grasped the strategic issues arising if resettlement was to work properly. In many respects the Probation Service gave low priority to resettlement work: to prisons, probation officers were seen as subversively sympathetic to the prisoners' cause. No-one identified the common interests between the two and, indeed, there were many on both sides of the wall keen to accentuate the differences. The rather promising sentence planning structure put into place by the 1991 Criminal Justice Act – and I am sure that oft-talked-about end-to-end offender management – withered for want of leadership.

The lack of strategic thinking was no more apparent than in the deployment of seconded staff to prisons. Although they did extremely good work, it was in spite of any thinking at a national level about how they could be deployed. Their work was against a background of a long-running and occasionally acrimonious debate about whether the Service should second its staff to prisons at all. The debate secured resolution only as late as the 1990s.

Furthermore, and perhaps fundamentally, the Service never answered the question: what was the purpose of all this throughcare and after-care work? It never resolved whether resettlement work was a kind of social service – an apology to the prisoner for State incarceration with them passive recipients of help – or whether it was about empowering prisoners to take responsibility for their criminogenic and resettlement needs and motivating them to address both in a structured and directed manner.

Care and Control: Taking Stock

*Iolo Madoc Jones, Principal Lecturer, North East
Wales Institute of Higher Education, UK*

Dedicated to Dafydd and Grace.

My first and last applied jobs in the Probation Service were in approved premises. In this piece I wish to share my reflections on how things changed in the twenty years that separated these jobs and in so doing draw some implications for contemporary practice.

My first job was at a hostel managed by a senior probation officer and a deputy who, from fifty years of combined practice experience, had developed their own practice wisdom. Such wisdom, as Scott (2006) identifies, is all too often dismissed as a source of valid knowledge. In the hostel, staff were encouraged to spend time with residents, to live with them and explore their ideas, hopes and dreams. 'Advise, assist and befriend' was the mantra of the Service in those days. Staff did things for residents and with them, advocated on their behalf, helped them find and move into new accommodation and work; all the time, however, gently talking to them about the pain offending often caused to themselves, their families and their communities. In today's parlance it might be said that we were engaging in pro-social modelling but, at the time, guided by the hostel managers, staff just cared for the residents and let them know that they were respected as human beings. The residents appreciated this. Many returned for months after leaving because, for some, it was the only home they had known.

At about the time when crime became politicised in the mid-1990s the Probation Service came to embrace a more authoritarian, punitive philosophy. 'Assisting' and 'befriending' became words to be avoided and treatment became the new goal of practice. In my last posting as senior probation officer at a bail hostel, I spent my time completing returns. Doing things for or with residents (now rebranded as offenders) came to be considered soft or irrelevant. Controlling, monitoring and protecting the public were the new buzz words. Staff monitored CCTV screens from their offices and, following the Wintercomfort incident, watched out for illicit drug use. The tendency of hostel staff under this new philosophy was to breach and condemn rather than understand or empathise, to refer to policy forms rather than principles of care, and to dismiss people rather than embrace them.

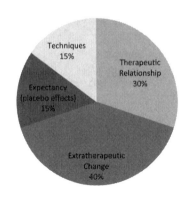

The Service now manages very serious offenders and numerous public enquiries attest to the fact that policies and procedures on risk assessment, management and supervision can make the difference between good and bad outcomes. However, recent literature on the non-specific or common factors responsible for 'what works in therapy' by Hubble *et al* indicates the ongoing importance of the human dimension in the therapeutic process. In relation to explaining variation in outcomes between different treatment modalities the relational and extra-therapeutic factors figure prominently. Vennard (1997) too has found that 45% of the variance in outcomes between intervention programmes can be attributed to whether the workers involved expressed empathy and positive regard for their clients. System studies of encounters between individuals and Probation staff (Bottoms, 2001) also suggest that people are generally more concerned about issues of procedural fairness and the manner of their treatment than with the outcome of their contact. In summary, what is important is less what therapies and programmes we use, than how we do things, how we help address the extra-therapeutic, environmental problems people face and how we treat people.

My original mentors knew that kindness and empathy mattered and used this as a platform to inform their practice. Fortunately, as the poet Frost has noted, most of the changes in the world are largely due to truths revolving in and out of favour. Therefore, the centenary celebrations present an apposite time to take stock of how we balance the responsibility we have to care and control.

Restorative Justice – The Development of the Early Programmes in the United Kingdom

*John Harding, Visiting Professor of Criminal Justice,
Hertfordshire University, UK*

Students of restorative justice often mistakenly think that the practice model was borrowed by youth offending teams in England and Wales from the experience of aboriginal style family group conferences in New Zealand and Australia that emerged in the early 90s. While the Australasian experience had a direct influence on the Home Office funded restorative cautioning arrangements for young offenders, pioneered by the Thames Valley Police Force in the late 90s, probation played a key role in the development of restorative justice in the UK, particularly in the early 80s.

The first recorded scheme in England emerged in 1980 under the auspices of the Exeter Youth Support Team, made up of probation officers, police officers and social workers (some 18 years before the official introduction of multi-disciplinary teams as a result of the introduction of the Criminal Justice Act 1998). After a caution was administered by the police to juvenile offenders, crime victims were asked if they would be willing to meet with the offender to discuss the impact of crime on themselves and agree, if appropriate, some form of reparation, either directly for the victim or through the medium of a community-based agency in Exeter. A full account of this experiment has been written up by June Veevers.[1]

The first adult probation experiment in victim/offender mediation was led by Peter Dixon, a senior probation officer in South Yorkshire, and a team of probation officers, bringing together the victims and offenders on defined housing estates in part of the Sheffield area. Following mediation between the parties, the probation officers entered their findings in social inquiry reports for the Sheffield Magistrates, together with recommendations that addressed key issues of reparative activity and compensation to the crime victims.

Running parallel to these developments, both Martin Wright, a former Director of the Howard League, and John Harding, then a Deputy Chief Probation Officer with the West Midlands area (who had made separate factfinding visits to the United States in 1980), advocated a different approach to criminal justice that focused on victims' needs and offenders' responsibilities. Both these commentators were deeply influenced by the work of Mennonite communities in Indiana, whereby volunteer mediators with the agreement of local judges and courts placed victims and offenders face-to-face, so that the former could confront the latter with their sense of loss, pain and bewilderment that often accompanies a house burglary or an unprovoked assault. At a different level, too, they reported on the experience of neighbourhood dispute centres in deprived parts of Boston, Massachusetts and Columbus, Ohio, where neighbours in conflict with each other over matters of theft, vandalism, etc. were encouraged to seek the help of locally trained mediators.

Early in 1983, Harding secured money from the Cadbury Barrow Foundation for Martin Wright to undertake a feasibility study of reparation by offenders linked to the courts in Coventry but the plans lacked money for implementation and research.

In July of that year at an ACOP conference held at Durham University, David Mellor – then Parliamentary under Secretary of State at the Home Office – sat in on a workshop at which Harding spelt out the benefits of a reparative approach whereby the offender took responsibility for his crime and began to acknowledge the victim's right for explanation of his predatory behaviour, and the need for some redress. Mellor, in a subsequent interview with the criminologist, Paul Rock, said he was sympathetic to what had been said in the workshop and promised to give the matter further attention. On his return to London he let it be known to officials that he was impressed by what he had heard and the potential represented by restorative justice, saying that funding applications would be treated sympathetically. Funding applications duly arrived from probation areas and the politics of reparation jumped forward at Mellor's initiative, following the Durham conference.

After a short delay in January 1985, the Home Office sponsored four demonstration projects in restorative justice: in Cumbria, designed to divert offenders from the courts; in Coventry, which allowed reparation to become an order of the court for conviction; in Leeds, an alternative to imprisonment in serious cases; and in Wolverhampton, to be administered by the Wolverhampton Crypt Association, a voluntary body, in conjunction with the West Midlands Probation Service. The schemes were called experimental, and they were all evaluated by Tony Marshall and Susan Merry in a Home Office publication called *Crime and Accountability* (1990).

End Note

[1]   Veevers, June. *Pre Court Diversion for Juvenile Offenders in Mediation and Criminal Justice.* Wright, M. and Galaway, B. (eds) (1989: Sage: London).

Sex Offenders: After-Care for Life

Mary Anne Zammit, Probation Officer,
Probation Services of Malta

The heavy caseload which we face day by day is overbearing, so the weekend comes as a relief: a special time which temporarily takes us away from the workday routine and which feels good. Without doubt our clients need their relief too from the heavy conditions of the order imposed on them by the court. Some of them really succeed in doing this.

Can you imagine this scenario? One afternoon while relaxing in the park with the rest of the family members, a man gets your attention. You may think you know the man but for some reason you cannot place him and choose to keep enjoying the afternoon embracing the warm rays of the sun rather than worry about why he is familiar to you. The man is walking in the park, alone but steadily along his path. A little girl strays away from the rest of the family and crosses his path.

The next day all the papers contain news of a man assaulting a young girl and it suddenly dawns on you that the man was one of your clients who was under supervision for three years. Despite your work with other professionals, exerting all your pooled resources to control the man, he is back again facing the same charges. The client went back to where he started from. Suddenly, your head is buzzing with questions. What happened to all of your efforts? Is everything lost?

As the years roll by, the number of sex offenders is continually increasing, presenting us with various problems.

Having worked for almost nine years as a probation officer within the Probation Services in Malta, I have come across sex offenders. Most often, these offenders are given a supervision order from court which enables the tools of treatment and psychotherapy to be well combined with the conditions of the order. We all know that the most important goal of treatment for sex offenders is that they refrain from committing another sex offence.

This proved to be quite successful where clients lived by these conditions and followed treatment. In such cases, there was considerable support from family members and, in some cases, their relationships have even become stronger. Such cases made me feel warmer inside than the Mediterranean sun has ever made me.

A period under intensive supervision can prove extremely positive, as offenders are shown the way to recover their self-restraint. However, one day, I learned about another case that had formed part of my heavy pile of files: one of my clients who had stopped the treatment had relapsed again, six months away from the termination of the supervision order. All the collective work other professionals and I had done went down the drain again.

Therefore, I dare to ask: do we have the absolute reassurance that sex offenders will not relapse after the three-year supervision period? Most often, they will re-offend. After the termination of the supervision order, the offender is not obliged to follow treatment. This creates a serious risk, as the position of the client and the community is endangered.

With the increasing rate of re-offending and recidivism, I am compelled to question whether these high-risk offenders should be coerced to undergo treatment for an extensive period of time, preferably on permanent basis. I am fully aware that this would entail a lot of detailed studies and amendments in law but it does seem to be one of the measures which could be adopted. If these offenders could comply for a three-year period under supervision, they can do it for a lifetime.

Only then may we be able to enjoy the weekends without fretting about a man crossing the path of our children.

Biography

Mary Anne Zammit is from Malta. She is a Graduate from University in Social Work and Probation Services and has been employed as a probation officer within the Probation Services Malta since 1997. She paints and writes poetry, novels and articles both in Maltese and in English. Mary Anne is the author of three fiction books in Maltese. The latest was a fiction novel about rape. Following its success, Mary Anne is currently working on the English version.

Services and Structures for an Almost-Forgotten Group: Whither or Wither the AURs?

Paul Douglas, Senior Probation Officer and CARD Project Manager, Exeter, UK

Let's go back in time …

In 1982 a callow probation officer co-led what we called a Survival Group in Exeter prison. The initiative was within the blanket category of voluntary after-care and so pitched at those on automatic unconditional release (AUR). A mixed and lively gathering – as I recall – of men who had been in and out a few times, not usually drawing a sentence long enough to trigger licence supervision. The common refrain usually included: "I've got nowhere to live …", "my wife is giving up on me …", "I'm no example to my kids …", "I got the sack after coming in here …"

"The Probation Service is missing a trick here," I thought. Here was a nucleus of men for whom offending had become a way of life, but the Probation Service was not involved in their future because there was no statutory responsibility for it to be involved. Was this group not vulnerable to re-offending, and therefore should not the Service be involved?

Fast-forward aeons …

In 2003 the CARD (Closing a Revolving Door) Project was launched. CARD is a mentoring support service for unlicensed men, to assist their resettlement back into local communities from Exeter prison. The same, but now not so young, probation officer has been seconded as project manager for CARD, based in a charity which champions social inclusion and community development. We demonstrated that within the AUR population there is a significant core of almost lost and wandering souls, who do not do sufficiently heinous things to attract the interest of the Probation Service but do become increasingly dissociated from mainstream life and, as a group, create much damage and distress to victims. We can now assert that the AUR group are the most likely to re-offend (apart from the youngsters). They still do not trigger supervision on licence.

A committed group of volunteer mentors has been recruited, trained and supported to provide the direct contact with selected men who have developed a pattern of criminal behaviour and short prison sentences.

Mentoring begins within the prison and comes into real effect post-release. It re-creates the principle of continuity of contact, which is so well received by prisoners, and has more recently been re-branded as end-to-end management.

Compare and contrast …

The language has changed. Drugs are, of course, now near the top of the list of problems but in most respects the practical and emotional backcloth remains the same. Probation has increasingly moved towards those more heavily convicted and has long since only delivered any support and supervision within a statutory framework. The new provision of Custody Plus came tantalisingly close to providing formal intervention for short-sentenced prisoners but alas dropped away, again, last November. This has left short-sentence prisoners still largely ignored and yet very vulnerable to re-offending.

The NOMS commissioning framework specifically adverts to the voluntary and community sector as the provider of complementary services with a pledge of 10% budget spend imminent. This sector will need to demonstrate real worth and value added, which is right and proper, but reflects the application of a more rigorous slide rule than in ages past.

Probation has historically marginalised this group and it would be a bitter irony if the commissioning crucible should unleash a negative, competitive process between probation and the community sector. Structures are more complex for sure, but short-sentence prisoners do deserve proper oversight and support which will soon be possible and, I would hope, likely. This would of course be to the advantage of us all. Mentoring support is beginning to prove its worth in a number of criminal justice settings so I do hope CARD will become mainstreamed and not remain a joker in the pack.

At last, we are nearly there …

Hey! Wasn't there once something called the Discharged Prisoners' Aid Society? Bring it on.

Desistance – Focused Probation Practice?

*Paula Hamilton, Senior Lecturer in
Criminology and Community Justice,
Sheffield Hallam University, Sheffield, UK*

Despite the recent emergence of a growing body of literature and research which focuses on the process of desistance from crime, probation policy and practice remains relatively untouched by the insights afforded by this work. This would appear to be somewhat curious given the Service's focus on – and responsibility for – reducing re-offending. However, perhaps this is not as curious as it might first appear, given that much of literature around desistance has tended to stress the 'spontaneous' (Maruna, *Making Good* (2001) and 'self-motivated' nature of desistance, i.e. that it is something that happens 'outside of' and separate from criminal justice interventions. Furthermore, as Maruna points out elsewhere, much of the general desistance literature and theorising has not been very helpful in terms of offering practical guidance to practitioners in terms of what they can actually do. The most well-known and referenced theories of desistance stress either the importance of maturational reform or 'growing out of' crime and social bonds theory.

Maturational reform theories date back to the 1930s and the work of the Gluecks and engage with the long and well-observed 'age-crime curve', i.e. that the majority of young offenders do not go on to become adult offenders and therefore desist from crime after a period of involvement. The Gluecks suggested that an intrinsic criminal impulse naturally declines after the age of 25. More recent proponents of this school of thought include Gottfredson and Hirschi's *A General Theory of Crime* (1990), which similarly suggests that desistance is largely due to the ageing process. Unsurprisingly, this type of theorising has been criticised for implicitly assuming that physiological changes associated with ageing simply and directly affect behaviour and behaviour change and also for failing to 'unpack' the 'meaning of age' (Sampson and Laub, *Crime in the Making* (1993) and the complex social and institutional processes associated with ageing. Age therefore may be better understood as a mediator for factors associated with desistance as opposed to a direct influence in and of itself.

This brings us the second influential and well-known theory of desistance, that of social bonds theory. This theory suggests that the process of desistance is associated with offenders gaining a 'stake in conformity' or having 'something to lose' in terms of informal ties to family, relationships, employment, parenting and so on.

This brief overview perhaps highlights why the desistance literature has had such a limited impact to date in probation practice. As Maruna points out, they suggest that practitioners either wait for their clients to simply 'grow out of crime' or for them to get a 'steady job and the love of a good woman' (2001: p.30). Neither of these courses of action (or inaction) would appear very credible in the current criminal justice climate!

However, more recent theorising around desistance, for example Maruna (2001), has stressed the importance of understanding the role of internal, subjective changes in the persons sense of self and identity and in how they interpret 'external' factors and experiences in the process of desistance. Giordano *et al* (2002), in their study of female desisters, similarly stressed the role of cognitions, outlining a four-part 'theory of cognitive transformations' that they argue the desistance process involves. Similarly, Gove, in *The Effect of Age and Gender on Deviant Behaviour* (1985), linked desistance to a range of internal changes including a shift from self-absorption to concern for others, increasing concern for others in the community and increasing acceptance of societal values and behaving in socially appropriate ways.

There is obvious resonance here with contemporary probation practice which is now, based on the 'What Works' research, also heavily influenced by cognitive theories of criminal decision-making. Indeed, Maruna (2000) proposes a marriage of the two research agendas where lessons from 'What Works' research at the 'macro' level of offender rehabilitation are integrated with 'individual level' accounts of change processes involved in desistance.

Perhaps then an understanding of the process of desistance which stresses the importance of the interplay between social context/structural factors and internal cognitive changes offers more in terms of guidance to practitioners about what they can *do* in terms of developing desistance focused practice. Practice informed not only by 'What Works' principles but by an understanding from offenders themselves about the internal change processes involved in desistance may allow practitioners to develop interventions which complement, promote and accelerate 'spontaneous' change efforts. Maybe for probation practice the moment is coming for desistance ideas to have impact!

Working as a Volunteer

David Phillips, Senior Lecturer in Probation Studies, Sheffield Hallam University, Sheffield, UK

In 1981 I was between jobs and casting around for something different. I had given up school teaching after a decade of working in London, Bristol and Norwich.

I considered a number of options, including psychiatric nursing and becoming a careers advisor. While I was searching I saw, and answered, an advertisement from the Norfolk Probation Service that asked for volunteers in Norwich. At that time, the Service used a large number of volunteers. Those who applied were invited to a meeting which brought together a wide variety of individuals from different walks of life. All were united in a common concern for and interest in people, together with a desire to help in some undefined way.

Following this meeting, we were assigned to a probation officer who would select individuals for us to work with and would introduce us to them, explain our role and support us with regular meetings. We were made aware of the work of a probation officer and what 'advise, assist and befriend' meant. The work that we did was very much centred on the 'befriend' part of the remit with some advice thrown in. Of course, probation was then an alternative to a sentence and offenders gave their assurance that they would be of good behaviour and lead an industrious life. In terms of the actual process of intervention we were left to our own devices, drawing on our experience and life skills.

I was assigned two people, one of whom lived nearby. He had a history of depression, petty offending and drink-related issues. In these days, I suppose, he would fit into the 'low risk' tier and be offered 'punishment'. He might, in time, have progressed to the next tier and have been offered some intervention for his criminogenic need.

At that time, I remember we did talk about his behaviour in a very informal way. The boundaries of befriending were very broad. We visited each other's homes and got to know each other's families. I also helped to run a club for young men who were on probation. This provided contact time on neutral territory for talking with their probation officer. Again, this was very informal but the probation officer seemed to know the young men and their families. He had built up knowledge of the local community and was aware of the problems on this particular estate. The club was also visited by various officials who could help the young men too. The men who attended the club were able to enjoy the facilities, such as snooker, which should not be thought of as 'treats for naughty boys' but instead as part of the general ethos of 'inclusiveness' that was prevalent. These days we might talk about 'building up social capital' and helping 'the disaffected' and alienated to become more a part of the community and therefore eventually 'grow out' of offending.

Other volunteers worked with 'prostitutes' (the accepted terminology for the time). Again, this was a befriending role. The Service also offered 'shadowing' so that we could experience the full range of the work that a probation officer did. I remember the terror of my first visit to a magistrates' court when the officer left me alone for a while.

It was difficult to evaluate the work that we did. I know that the particular individuals with whom I worked seemed to value a friendship that helped them to feel less alienated. We would accompany people to the Social Security office, to hospital or to visit the doctor. We would also help sort out finances and help with job seeking. I also used my teaching skills to help with literacy. All of this was conducted in a very informal way.

We were unfocused I suppose, certainly lacking boundaries and had little awareness of health and safety. In those terms matters have changed considerably. The Service is now very different and concentrates on risk, both in assessment and management. I have enjoyed previous Moments related in this book, when Bruce Hugman, for example, talked about his detached 'outreach' work and also the use of volunteers in other countries. There is, I think, something to be learned in terms of helping individuals to build up 'social capital' and in becoming familiar with a particular geographical area, its families and the issues that concern the inhabitants. The Service has lost this 'connectivity' and has been in danger of becoming detached from the everyday experiences of individuals, offenders, victims and the wider community by working in large centralised offices and in individual specialisms.

I value the experience that I gained as a volunteer and I was enthused to apply for training in 1981.

The Non-Treatment Paradigm

*Dr Fergus McNeill, Glasgow School of Social Work
and the Scottish Centre for Crime and Justice
Research, University of Glasgow*

Back in the late 1970s, Tony Bottoms (by then already an eminent Professor of Criminology) and Bill McWilliams (a research officer in the South Yorkshire Probation Service) wrote a classic paper that set out a 'Non Treatment Paradigm for Probation Practice' (British Journal of Social Work, 1979, 9(2): 159–201). Tony Bottoms recounts that the paradigm emerged from informal evening conversations between the two friends. Essentially, the gist of their discussions was that when Tony presented Bill with the research evidence of the time that 'nothing works', Bill's reaction (aside from initial resistance and scepticism) was to suggest that they had better work out the implications for the Service, or risk its demise. In one sense, the most important legacy of the paradigm is summed up in this determination not to ignore or marginalise inconvenient evidence, but to creatively and constructively confront its implications.

Though their 42-page paper defies any serious attempt to summarise the argument here, the central thrust is that the treatment model of probation practice had been discredited empirically, theoretically and ethically. Not only was there little evidence of treatment effectiveness, its conceptual basis was flawed. First, crime is voluntary whereas most 'treatable' conditions are not; secondly, crime is not pathological in any straightforward sense; and thirdly, individual treatment models neglect the social causes of crime. Worse still, neglect of these flaws produced ethical problems: over-confidence in treatment had permitted its advocates both to coerce offenders into interventions (because the treatment provider was an expert who knew best) and to ignore offenders' views of their own situations (because offenders were victims of their own lack of insight). Perhaps most insidiously of all, within this ideology coerced treatment could be justified *in offenders' own best interests.*

Far from destroying it, however, these devastating criticisms cleared the ground for a reconstruction of probation practice around its traditional core values of hope and respect for persons. Bottoms and McWilliams (1979: 173) suggested that in their paradigm treatment would be reconceived as help, diagnosis would become 'shared assessment' and the 'Client's

Dependent Need' as the basis for action would become 'Collaboratively Defined Tasks' as the basis for action.

In this formulation, 'help' included but was not limited to material help: probation could continue to address emotional or psychological difficulties, but this would no longer be its *raison d'être*. Critically, the test of any proposed intervention technique would be that it must help the client. Bottoms and McWilliams went on to explore the implicit tensions between help and surveillance. Accepting that probation officers were 'law enforcement' agents as well as helpers, they drew on an earlier article by Peter Raynor in which he argued for a crucial distinction between coercion and constraint; 'choice under constraint is morally acceptable; manipulative coercion is not'. Their paradigm therefore invoked a distinction between the compulsory requirements imposed by the court (with the offender's constrained consent) and the substantive content of the helping process. In the latter connection, the 'client' should be free to choose to accept or reject help without fear of further sanctions. Put another way, the authority for *supervision* derives from the court but the authority for *help* resides in the offender. For Bottoms and McWilliams this required that the (then) legal requirement of consent by defendants to probation and community service should be taken much more seriously.

Though the paradigm succeeded in giving the Service a strong conceptual basis around which to reconstruct its identity, much has changed since 1979. New evidence about 'what works?' and about supporting desistance from offending has revived confidence in rehabilitation (if not treatment, *per se*) and provoked subsequent writers to revise the paradigm (notably Raynor and Vanstone in 1994 and McNeill in 2006). It seems to me to be telling however, that while the empirical arguments have moved on, Bottoms and McWilliams' attention to theoretical and normative questions about the ethical basis for coerced or constrained interventions in offenders' lives remains unsurpassed and more relevant than ever. Sadly, these crucial arguments have been neglected in a contemporary climate where the practices of compulsory 'offender management' seem increasingly prepared to cast offenders precisely as the objects on whom practitioners work in the interests of others. Now might just be the moment to return to those questions.

Youth Justice – Probation Joins the Multi-Agency Experiment

Anne Robinson, Senior Lecturer, Hallam Centre for Community Justice, Sheffield Hallam University, UK

Starting work as a new probation officer in the Easton office in Bristol in 1993, I quickly found myself pushed into taking on the youth justice specialism for the team. This was not initially because I had a huge enthusiasm for working with young people, but largely because most of my more experienced colleagues were distinctly unenthusiastic! Admittedly, young people can be a challenge to engage and need a flexible approach, as well as a readiness to acknowledge that young people cannot be seen in isolation from their families, schools and other support networks.

I had not at first envisaged my career taking this turn, but I found working with young people incredibly satisfying, if demanding, and was constantly amazed to see how they grew and developed during the time I was in contact with them. I also enjoyed the more proactive (or frenetic?) approach to supervision, visiting schools, children's homes, family centres, the local motor project and becoming a regular presence in youth court. However, when my Probation Service moved into specialisms and I joined a youth justice team, I was really faced with how marginal young people and youth justice were becoming to an agency that once would have seen work with juveniles as part of core business!

The creation of Youth Offending Teams under the Crime and Disorder Act 1998 helped us to cement relationships locally with our long-term partners in Social Services and NCH. However, it did mean breaking away more decisively from the mainstream Probation Service and it was a strange feeling moving out of the agency where I had felt so comfortable into definitely uncharted multi-agency waters.

My secondment to Bristol YOT began from January 2000, three months before the statutory deadline for YOTs to be established. It was certainly a strange three months, with my team based in the old NCH youth justice centre doing case management and throughcare, the court team back in the Social Services office and the Diversions team (mainly, at that stage, four officers from Avon and Somerset police) camping out at what would eventually become the YOT offices. It took months before we all moved in together and had telephones, computers and all the necessaries to do the job. In the meantime, the young people still needed our help. It really tested our ingenuity to find places where we could meet and perform supervision sessions in the midst of personal change and challenges to professional attitudes and practices that had become just too comfortable.

In order to prepare practitioners for the new youth justice environment, the Youth Justice Board provided us with a six-day training package, 'Working Together', which we agreed to deliver in conjunction with the nearby local authority secure unit at Vinney Green. As with so many things at this time, this requirement was thrust upon us with practically no notice and, within 48 hours of being asked to be part of the training team, I was delivering the first tranche of training in rooms rented from the YHA to a very mixed audience indeed. It was a question of getting up and doing, with no time for reflective practice. It was this process that was more dominated by the 'suck it and see' mentality that took us through the initial stages of the YOT!

Looking back on this period, I have mixed emotions. It felt like being part of a hugely exciting enterprise, with access to health, education and other services that had been so hard for me to access as a probation officer. On the other hand, it was sad not to see our old colleagues and it was tough to be fighting battles to establish norms about care versus control, ways of engaging young people, standards of recording (did social services ever do any?) and the old bugbear of enforcement.

From my perspective, I am also sad to see current YOTs so tied up with managerial concerns and positions on performance tables, because that is so far from the spirit of the early days, which were developmental and experimental in a way I don't think I will experience again in my career. Furthermore, it is regrettable that the Probation Service has engaged so little with YOTs when they had so much to contribute in terms of a long and proud history of work with young people, a much more thought-out position on how most appropriately to balance welfare and offending concerns, and how to bring social work values into the criminal justice system.

The Henry Asplin Day Centre
Circa 1979

Professor Paul Senior, Director of Hallam Centre for Community Justice, Sheffield Hallam University, Sheffield, UK

Henry Asplen was the first probation officer in Doncaster to give his name to a charitable fund – the Henry Asplin Fund Association. You may think I made a spelling error in the name of the Association, but when it first started out, a letterhead was prepared at great expense and 500 sheets were printed. When it was pointed out that the 'e' had become an 'i', the secretary decreed that the name of the Association would have to change because it would be far too wasteful to throw the letterheaded paper away.

In 1979 the Association supported the Henry Asplin Day Centre (almost named after Henry!) A group of us were charged with looking at a provision for homeless and rootless clients who were the classic 'revolving door' type, drifting in and out of prison with great regularity and unable to break that cycle because conventional support did not offer sufficient time to maintain them in the community. The notion of a drop-in day centre was proposed. We put a proposal to a Home Office Voluntary Grants Unit and with 25K we were able to buy a house in the bedsits area of town, a prime location for attracting our clients. The Centre was to be open door, though the expectation was that there would be referrals and targeted support offered to those individuals who could benefit from more than 'tea and sympathy'.

Two features of this centre were clearly innovative and helped shape the style of the Centre. Alongside the Day Centre Manager we engaged two ex-offenders as Day Centre Supervisors under an MSC (Manpower Services Commission) Scheme, which was targeted at ex-offenders to give them employment as a stepping stone to permanent work. This was an unusual move for the Service in Doncaster. It was my first opportunity to work alongside ex-offenders. Three lessons emerged. Firstly, the Centre staff observed how different and positive the engagement with clients was when staff had had similar experiences and could use that in a productive way. Secondly, many probation officers, despite their job with clients being to encourage employment for their clients, could not cope with having the same ex-offenders as colleagues. Thus some officers never referred a client to the Centre at all and others refused to sit in on case conferences if the Day Centre Supervisors were present. The prejudice was alarming and I note with sadness that, working in the past few years with a Peer Support Project for resettling women, these attitudes have not entirely disappeared. The third insight relates to the experience for the supervisors themselves. The transition to a new non-offending persona was not easy. It meant giving up things as well as gaining a new direction. One supervisor, who had been a heavy drug user, found himself drawn back to using drugs. Ultimately, with our support, he reverted to a non-drug taking lifestyle.

The second feature of the centre came about through industry via companies which were looking to give experiences to executives who were nearing the end of their career, part of a drive to encourage companies to have social responsibility. So instead of early retirement, the skills of a senior executive could be brought into organisations – for nothing! As a result of this, in the first year of the Day Centre we were introduced to Steve, who brought his executive experience. It was clearly a clash of cultures in many ways and both ourselves and Steve struggled to find an understanding. On a practical level he was able to access resources very easily: the house had to be decorated and furniture provided. His contacts managed to do that without cost. We used to cook for the clients every day and Steve sourced very cheap suppliers for that. Steve simply opened doors we had no experience in opening. He approached our issues from a very different perspective and encouraged us to think about things in a new way. Equally, it was a culture shock for him and the fact that he was now working with offenders took a long time for him to accept!

This sort of provision sprung up in many towns, offering an environment to reach a client group we had previously struggled to service. Maybe it is a client group we would not provide a service to today but I doubt those individuals have disappeared. The Centre changed and moved with the times and groupwork programmes developed following the 1982 Act alongside the open provision which continued certainly into the 1990s. I hope Henry Asplen and his cousin Henry Asplin would be proud of what we achieved in his name.

Memories of the Broadwater Farm Riot and the Death of PC Blakelock

Simon Feasey, Deputy Director, Hallam Centre for Community Justice, Sheffield Hallam University, Sheffield, UK

My first job as a probation officer, following qualification in 1981, was at the Lordship Lane office in Tottenham, Middlesex, located at a short distance from the Broadwater Farm Estate. The relationship between the black community and the police was on a downward spiral: the Brixton riots in 1981 had resulted in the Scarman report which had been critical of policing approaches to the black community and a more recent disturbance in Brixton, during September 1985, clearly indicated that little progress, if any, had been made during the intervening years.

As a probation officer working with young offenders I had become involved in helping to set up a probation football team consisting of a combination of both black and white offenders and ex-offenders which took part in occasional games with other probation teams. A recent disturbing experience of taking our team to an away fixture at which our black players were verbally and physically abused by 'spectators' that had assembled on an all-white housing estate outside London had raised my awareness of the racial tensions that were prevalent within the south of England during the 1980s.

Following the death of Cynthia Jarret, who experienced a fatal heart attack when a disturbance ensued between her family and police officers who were investigating a minor motoring matter, a demonstration against the police action was organised which later precipitated the onset of violent disturbances between younger members of the black community and the Metropolitan Police. During the course of the day, the violence escalated: bricks, petrol bombs, barricades and gunfire ensued and, in the late evening, PC Blakelock was attacked by a group of youths and died of multiple injuries in shocking circumstances.

Coming to work the next day it was immediately apparent that the tension between the black community and the police had gone beyond breaking point: mutual suspicion, distrust and even hatred epitomised the heightened emotional atmosphere; the police were intent on mass arrests and both adults and juveniles were being held in police cells with little regard for due process. As a probation officer with an interest and commitment to civil and human rights, it was frustrating to be denied access to defendants in police custody and rumours of police brutality were rife within the community. My overall feeling was one of a complete loss of power, a sense shared by colleagues and other criminal justice workers, including some local solicitors who were similarly unable to see their clients in police cells. Moreover, as a white probation officer, it was apparent that within the context of a breakdown in the relationship between white authority and the black community, some of the suspicion and distrust was aimed at my colleagues and I. Like others, I shared the revulsion at the terrible death of a police officer and had huge sympathy for his immediate family, relatives and friends. However, it was also apparent that the police response was doing nothing but damage both to specific young individuals and to community relations generally. There was an inevitable polarisation of opinion and the pressure to 'take sides' was considerable.

The repercussions for the Probation Service locally were far-reaching. Some of those arrested were charged and the Service prioritised resources targeted at a group of defendants who were reported as dangerous pariahs by the press but who were in fact particularly vulnerable within the criminal justice system. If anything, the riot and its aftermath highlighted the extent to which the Probation Service was relatively disengaged from the local black population. Significant efforts were made to develop a far greater degree of community involvement: engaging with local leaders, building relationships with community groups and pro-actively responding to issues of racism and discrimination within the criminal justice system. At the same time it was alarmingly clear that the Probation Service at that time was a white organisation and that without determined and effective strategies to address that issue, our usefulness and contribution within the community cohesion agenda was always going to be marginal. It has subsequently taken many years of institutional transformation to open up the Service to non-white entrants and managers but, without risking complacency, there is much evidence that this particular change agenda has had positive outcomes.

18 Months on the Old Town Estate in Hartlepool, 1979[1]

Roger Kennington, Senior Probation Officer,
Northumbria Probation Area, UK

Hartlepool (a rundown industrial town in the North East) in 1979, the Labour Government is waning fast. A social worker and probation officer qualified in 1977 (Newcastle Poly, radical social work, etc.) become frustrated working on Old Town Estate, an isolated, badly designed 'damp, decaying, squalid, neglected' enclave of 106 houses with higher-than-average rent arrears, delinquency, care admissions, and 'inadequate, aggressive clientèle'. These were perceived as emanating from environmental, economic and social causes.

A council 'community development strategy' was proceeding frustratingly slowly. Probation and Social Services transferred all cases to one worker/ team to focus on the community (whilst retaining statutory responsibilities). They called a 'public' meeting. One woman turned up! She gave advice and offered the use of her house. Attendance at weekly meetings between April 1980 and July 1981 ranged from 3 to 20 (average 5–10).

Outsiders under-estimated the severity of environmental problems vociferously illustrated by the residents. Tensions between the 'community action' and statutory roles of the workers were exposed (but continued to be worked with). The (unelected) 'Old Town Action Group' (OTAG) formed and pressed the Council into a demolition strategy by objecting to houses being re-let. Without consultation with workers, they picketed the house of a couple moving in. 'Hangers on' became violent. OTAG moved their protest to the Civic Centre, attracting front-page newspaper headlines and photographs. Workers decided not to intervene.

OTAG were embarrassed and therefore focused on local authority services, benefits for residents and improving services from the workers' agencies. They undertook a study by residents and students which was presented to the Council. They attended a 'liaison committee' (housing director, ward councillors housing chair). The Council took concerns seriously. A decision to demolish Old Town by 1985 was changed. All residents moved by September 1982. During this phase the welfare of remaining residents was addressed.

OTAG organised events to raise money and provide resources. It was expected that these activities would also promote group cohesion and develop organisational skills for the future. However, difficult dynamics (around jealousy, status, etc.) persisted, inhibiting wider progress. Improvement of service provision by the workers' agencies seemed (impressionistically) to occur. Workers felt closer to 'difficult to reach' clients although some groups, notably young men, remained wary. Indeed, they were initially hostile and burgled a short-lived office base. Conventional probation and social services work continued, including breach and care proceedings.

During the final demolition period, representations to the Council continued, the project finishing with a flurry of activity. Residents resorted to previous unsuccessful strategies (individual letters, phone calls), complaining about the demolition contractor. A press release written by residual members of OTAG (initiated by the workers) resulted in the termination of the firm's contract.

Reflections

Old Town would not have been cleared as quickly without OTAG's intervention and some activities were beneficial but a number of issues were not addressed. Tensions were never addressed, leaving aims unclear and workers exposed. No management group was ever appointed to retain focus on longer term aims, and indeed potentially hold the group to account.

Membership of OTAG was all women. There was no liaison with other groups (e. g. Labour Party, Women's Aid, etc.). There would have been a debate about whether that would have drawn the group into wider (albeit relevant) issues and diluted the focus on their chosen aim. Similarly, the workers had ideas about influencing 'local power relationships'. Little formal evaluation of the project was undertaken, membership and structure of the group was never clarified and some issues of group dynamics remained unaddressed.

However, these later critical reflections were from the workers themselves and academics who published the paper. In retrospect, one might ask what right these people have to question the aims of the local people who only wanted out of their awful surroundings. In contrast, the workers had private houses, good jobs, pensions, etc. This is an ongoing tension in such projects.

Would such a project be considered in today's Probation Service? No.

End Note

[1] Published in *Going Local In Probation* by Duncan Scott, Nigel Stone and Paul Falkingham (1985: University of East Anglia).

Bulldog Manpower Services Ltd

Steve Cosgrove, Director, Yorkshire & Humberside,
Probation Training Consortium, UK

'Bulldog' was a supported work project established by the Inner London Probation Service in 1975. Its aims were:

> 'to concentrate on solving one problem: that of unemployability, by creating a realistic work situation in which regular and graded demands are made upon employees. The demands are intended to secure regular attendance, to improve performance and to engender a more realistic and reasonable attitude to authority at the work site. For employees, there is also a clear objective – placement in more remunerative work outside of Bulldog and to achieve this within a time span of six months.'

Referrals to Bulldog were made directly by probation officers and clients had to be on statutory supervision of one kind or another. In its simplest form, Bulldog had to generate income to cover 70% of its total running costs. There was always a real commercial pressure to survive.

At its peak in 1979 there were Bulldog offices in each of the four London Divisions, each of them employing approximately 30–40 clients together with a workshop in Kennington employing 10. Bulldog had to compete in the open market for its work against other companies and deliver work to a standard required by its customers. The main work provided was centred around painting and decorating and general house improvements; gardening and landscaping and the workshop-manufactured wrought iron and metalwork goods. Local Authorities and Housing Associations provided the bulk of the contracts, although there was also a substantial amount of work for private companies and individuals.

Bulldog's staffing was a mixture of probation and technical staff with experience in the building and allied trades – site foremen were employed at a ration of about one to every five employees. Many of the foremen themselves were ex-offenders. An officer from the Department of Employment was seconded to Bulldog and he dealt with DHSS issues and assisted in the placement of employees into work. All employees were members of the Transport and General Workers Union.

Running Bulldog was always challenging and never easy: finding the right volume and type of work, and delivering a quality product and maintaining health and safety was difficult enough but, for some staff, remembering that the work provided was actually only the means to the end of helping the employees move on to permanent jobs was sometimes easy to forget. Like any other business, Bulldog was subject to changes in the general economy: from 1975 until 1979, unemployment was relatively low in London and Bulldog's employees were genuinely long-term unemployed/unemployable clients, usually with little ability. Work generally was in reasonable supply.

From 1979 onwards, as unemployment rose rapidly in London, referrals began to be for more able clients who were unable to find a job. There was also a slump in the building trade and on more than one occasion we ended up bidding for painting and decorating work against national building companies who were trying to maintain their workforces. One solution was to bid for and take on more complicated contracts which stretched the technical competency of the company to deliver them.

Bulldog was eventually wound up over the course of 1984, the project had run its course and the Home Office research project came to an end, though I never did discover why the decision was made and who actually made it.

The question is: did Bulldog deliver what it was set up to do? In general terms, from 1975 until 1980, Bulldog succeeded in placing about 25% of its workers into long-term employment when they left, a creditable result given the calibre of referral. From 1980 onwards it became more difficult to sustain this number. The final research which reflected a time of harsh national economic recession showed that we succeeded in placing only 10% into work – but that we had equipped large numbers of our employees with skills to supplement their state benefits with private work and reduce their offending. To assess the link between employment and a reduction in offending by its employees would require a revisit of the Home Office research papers.

I was at Bulldog from 1979 until 1984 and, as a personal experience, it was absolutely excellent: the staff were totally dedicated to the task and believed that getting clients into work contributed to their reduction of offending and an improvement in their life opportunities. Charles Crockford, John Longhurst, Liz Dixon, Pat Beresford, Syd Foggarty, Philip Moorland, George Cole, Joe Jenvey and many others made substantial contributions to this special project.

The Introduction of the 'Ancillary'

Lol Burke, Senior Lecturer in Criminal Justice,
Liverpool John Moores University, UK

In 1968 the Home Office introduced the post of 'ancillary worker' on an experimental basis. This move was, in part, to address the ongoing discontent over probation officer's salaries, which together with staff shortages, recruitment problems and heavy workloads, had contributed to low morale. Anticipating concerns over role boundaries, the circular outlining the scheme had been careful to allay fears that the use of ancillaries would threaten the casework responsibility of probation officers, and the employment of ancillaries to assist probation officers working in prisons was not permitted. It was envisaged that tasks that an ancillary could undertake would include escort and court duty, visiting families on behalf of the probation officer, helping to recruit employers and landladies, supervising repayment of fines, and those tasks not thought to need the skills of a qualified officer. From these modest intentions the role of the ancillary has morphed into the probation service assistant and officer – each reflecting the increased responsibilities inherent to the role.

Between 1985 and 1988, I worked as a probation service assistant in a probation team in inner-city Liverpool. My role was largely ill-defined and in many ways reflected the ad hoc way in which the grade had developed (and indeed there has never been, to my knowledge, a generic job description at a national level). The post had come about because a number of the team probation officers had been influenced by the 'going local' ideas in the 1970s which had tried to move probation practice away from the formalised setting of the probation office and into local-based community facilities such as youth clubs, citizen advice bureaux, tenants' associations, etc. Through establishing links with community groups, my role was to assist the work of the probation officer and utilise what in contemporary discourses is often referred to as the potential 'social capital' mechanisms to assist desistance from crime (although we would not have recognised it as such at the time!). This involved liaison with neighbourhood groups to explain the work of the Probation Service and to relay the concerns of the local community back to the team. The work was underpinned by the belief that offenders were part of the community rather than 'outsiders' to which they have been re-cast in post-modernity.

Looking back now, it feels like another world – I guess that in many ways it was. In the spirit of casework supervision, I was supported but largely unaccountable and much of the work was not solely based on those under statutory supervision. For example, we established a welfare rights surgery which was open to the general public on a drop-in basis. Such work now seems somewhat incongruous with an organisation driven by public protection and risk assessment and overburdened by performance targets and paperwork. I still travel through the same area, which despite claims to the contrary shows little visible signs of benefiting from the large-scale regeneration of the inner city. My old probation office now lies disused and the staff moved to one of the remote call centre type buildings that are so favoured by contemporary probation managers – so much for 'going local'!

On a personal level, the creation of the ancillary grade gave me an introduction into an area of work where previously I had no knowledge. Like others, it provided a route to qualifying training and a career in the Probation Service. Perhaps, more importantly, it was as a somewhat young, and naïve probation service assistant that I began to appreciate the value of probation work and develop my beliefs, values and understanding of what constitutes good probation practice in working with offenders – long before academic training enabled me to contextualise and label my actions. Perhaps most of all I remember the sense of camaraderie in what was a time of opportunity and experimentation; also the enduring threat from central government policies that sought to exert greater control over the direction of the Probation Service and reform the public sector through the marketisation of its services – the beginnings of a long and incessant process which has culminated in the Offender Management Bill.

The introduction of the ancillary grade represents a largely unheralded moment in probation history. There would seem to have been little academic discussion or research into its contribution despite the fact that it has fundamentally altered the staff demographics of the organisation. Today the probation service officer accounts for the largest percentage of staff in the Service, outstripping in growth that of the probation officer and made significant encroachments into the supervisory responsibilities of that grade. The Offender Management Model takes this process further by seemingly conflating the two roles based upon risk classifications. In recent years, probation service officers have been at the forefront of the delivery of accredited programmes and continue to contribute to the achievement of service delivery. It may well be that the development of this grade was, and continues to be, driven by financial concerns to reduce staff costs but – as a moment in probation history – it is extremely significant nonetheless.

Jarvis

*Professor Paul Senior, Hallam Centre for
Community Justice, Sheffield Hallam
University, Sheffield, UK*

When I started work in 1976 I asked my supervisor a question about MPSOs. Her reply was to 'look it up in *Jarvis*'. Between the 1960s and 1990s, most would have understood this injunction. *Jarvis* was the probation officer's bible. The preface to the first edition states:

> 'the ethos of the Probation Service extends beyond the statutory and administrative provisions which structure its work. An undue concern with the latter might kill the spirit, but properly used the letter creates and defines the setting in which the spirit can develop. It was in this belief that the manual was conceived'.

The first edition was the work of the late Fred Jarvis, Chief Probation Officer of Leicestershire until 1984. When Alan Sanders and I were commissioned to produce the fifth edition, we visited Fred and the photo above illustrates that moment. When we asked him what had inspired him to produce that first edition in 1969 he replied as follows:

> "There was a stream, indeed a torrent of statutory instruments, blue books, white papers, circulars, circular instructions, bulletins, notes and memoranda extending, elaborating and commenting on the work of the Probation Service. It was to help Probation Officers find their way through this welter of words, that this plethora of print that the *Probation Officer's Manual* was produced."

His efforts were repeated in the 1974 and 1977 editions. These regularly updated editions established the manual as the one volume you had to have to hand. It was THE reference point for probation officers, plus it contained a good deal of Fred's own interpretations of the job. The more obscure the information needed, the more *Jarvis* would deliver. Upon retirement, Fred's legacy was perpetrated by Bill Weston – the former General Secretary of the Association of Chief Officers of Probation – who produced the fourth edition in 1987 under the name of *Jarvis's Probation Officers Manual*, in recognition of the *de facto* acceptance that this manual was known simply as *Jarvis*.

Ten years between editions was manageable in the 1980s – change was still slow and the torrent that Fred had referred to was actually more like a babbling brook than the tsunami of legislation which has occurred in the previous decade. Towards the end of the decade it became clear that change was nigh and that a new version of *Jarvis* was needed to reflect the quickly changing landscape of probation. In 1990 Alan Sanders and I were engaged as the new editors. The preface highlighted significant changes to the format: it was to be a looseleaf edition; become a 'one stop' reference guide and to have editorial provision which was properly underpinned instead of relying on the editor's spare time. This was thus a modernised *Jarvis* which had now become *Jarvis's Probation Service Manual* (1993), given that many staff were not probation officers. Publication coincided with the 1991 Act which fundamentally changed legislation for probation practice and which promised to be the blueprint for future practice.

A little daunted by the task, we undertook the work in three stages: assessing the accuracy of the original editions, developing a format which was capable of being updated and producing a referencing style which was user-friendly. I recall finding what looked like authoritative interpretations but with no link to any verifiable source. We decided to take out any material which had no verifiable audit trail. However, on certain areas of more obscure practice we thought there would be authoritative voices in the Home Office. Alan was invited to a meeting at the Home Office on the supervision arrangements for those on probation elsewhere in the world. He expected that his knowledge would be corrected. Disconcertingly, he found that the meeting had been called to pick his brains as none of the civil servants present had any knowledge of practice in this area! It was on the more obscure end of practice that *Jarvis* really scored.

We updated three times in the 1990s but, as the pace of change increased, it was increasingly recognised that *Jarvis* in written form was not flexible enough to provide a verified resource for the Service. Accordingly we began conversations about creating a new online version which could be more instantly updated. This has lain fallow as the National Probation Service came into being in 2001 and since. There is a project for the Centenary year – the creation of a *Jarvis Probation Wikipedia* which can be owned by the community of probation and developed as a user-friendly resource. Watch this space!

Jarvis felt to us like '*painting the Forth Bridge*'. Even in the relative calm of 1992, tracing all references and keeping up with changes was a tiring, almost endless task. I booked a month's holiday to the USA as the volume was on its way to the publisher. I settled down to read a novel denied to me in the months spent, day and night, writing Jarvis. The novel was *Solomon's Carpet* by Barbara Vine. I opened the first page and discovered the name of the chief character – Jarvis. It was a long journey to the USA!

Ordinary Cases: the Day-to-Day Work of a Team of Probation Officers

David Pidwell, Senior Probation Officer,
South Yorkshire Probation Area, UK

2000

I received a phone call from the hostel SPO. Excitedly, he asked me, "Do you remember a Harold PXXX?" I did indeed – I was surprised how quickly this character came back to me. My SPO colleague told me that he had seen him the night before. He had driven his son, who had been remanded on bail, over to the hostel. Harold had told my colleague that he was glad that his son was here, as probation had helped him when he was a kid. Intrigued, my colleague had made further conversation and out of that came the link with myself.

1980

Harold was typical of our caseload: 19, unemployed, a bit of a drinker, impulsive, occasionally committing burglary or minor violence, trying to make his way independently but unsuccessfully through lack of personal and social capital. His girlfriend was also on probation for shoplifting. They were a transfer from the sub office, whose workers were heavily involved in the community. The work I did was nothing outstanding. I saw them fortnightly but often they just called in – sometimes twice a week, occasionally bypassing reception and coming straight to my door. The visits usually coincided with a crisis – accommodation, benefits, failure to perform Community Service, pregnancy scares, family and often relational problems. You knew if it was relational because one would always arrive ten minutes before the other to tell you who was to blame. A phone call to the Social or the landlord usually sufficed. The relationship thing tended to sort itself out after a chat. Once Harold was remanded in custody and I argued strongly for the non-custodial disposal. I firmly believed that young offenders grew out of crime and that keeping them in the community accelerated that 'maturing process'. Probation work to me was that simple then. Not only simple but credible, possessing integrity.

At the twice-weekly allocation meeting our SPO would 'market' the cases and reports that needed attention. We argued that it was imperative to match client need with officer interest. Whilst that was undoubtedly true, if you didn't attend, you got the unattractive cases no-one else wanted! One day a drug user became a new case. It was 1980 and it was the first drug user case we had ever had. We fought like crazy for him. Liz, the psycho-analytical expert, who was in therapy herself as a prelude to becoming a qualified therapist, argued she could get to the underlying root cause. There was Maggie, a keen family therapy worker, who made a bid, as did Arnold, the second careerist, whose clients could benefit from his contacts with former employers, his community and Church.

Another team member was Pat. Psycho-dynamic to the core, she specialised in the first time offender – some as young as 13. I always recall how envious I was about her organisation skills; she had her young clients report on a Tuesday after school; remarkably, they all came in. She kept immaculate records. How she did it always puzzled me as my practice, like many, was to blitz out of date files only when some event, like confirmation, annual appraisal or case termination beckoned. There was supportive, wise Ted, and Frank, a working Franciscan monk. He struggled with the tension between care and control. I recall that once he tried to get a Borstal licensee recalled because he was offending. Frank was met with incredulity by the Governor. Referred to the Home Office, Frank spent a fruitless afternoon trying to find the right department. He never did: the Home Office were seemingly disinterested in public protection in those days. The rest of the team were scruffy sociology types, keen to pursue community work and not interested in this case because it was out of their patch.

I got the drug user. I did not have him for long as he went to rehab (that being the only intervention we had to offer). I do recall doing a home visit, not to him but to his parents' house to discuss their son's progress. It was an unusual case as I had to turn right out of the office to get there. All our clients lived to the left so, if you went right, you knew you had either a mentally ill member of a dysfunctional bourgeois family or the occasional bent professional who had just done his 12 months in the nearest open prison for embezzlement. Sure enough, this drug user was from a middle class background who blamed the drug-taking on being part of the wrong crowd at university. How different from our drug-using offenders on today's caseloads!

Evidence Based Practice – If I Had Known Then What I Know Now

Tim Chapman, CTC Associates, Northern Ireland

I still remember the 'What Works' conferences in the 90s as a revelation. After many years of debate and confusion, I was fascinated by the conviction and clarity of speakers about research which virtually guaranteed reducing re-offending through structured programmes. They spoke a new language of criminogenic need, cognitive deficits, responsivity and programme integrity. I liked the focus on practice. This approach promised a clear and transparent practice supported by evidence rather than good intentions or political ideology. It seemed a more empowering model of practice.

When I was invited by the HMIP to write, with Michael Hough, *Evidence Based Practice*, it was clear that Home Office officials found it difficult to understand what probation officers did, how they did it and what they were trying to achieve. They distrusted the Probation Service and were pessimistic about its ability to adapt to the modern world. There existed a strong belief that 'effective practice' would provide answers and save the Service. I shared this faith and was pleased to contribute. I was responsible for practice and management and Michael covered evaluation. There followed a process of drafts, meetings at the Home Office, redrafts and a final edit by Jane Furniss. It was strange experience. Like a Hollywood scriptwriter, I sat as important people discussed and changed my words as if I was not present. Obviously it had to be written in a style acceptable to government and when I read the outcome I recognised most of it.

Evidence Based Practice: A Guide to Effective Practice was published in 1998. I left the Service in 1999 when the effective practice strategy was being launched. Since then a huge amount of financial, intellectual, human and organisational capital has been invested. I hoped that a transparent practice based upon what works in North America would yield evidence of what works in Britain and Ireland and would result in a strong Service confident in its knowledge base and ability as a provider of effective community interventions. Re-offending rates would be reducing, the public would value the Service, more people who were persistently offending would be supervised in the community and the prison population would shrink.

What happened?

Since 1999 I have not been closely involved in the Service. I do know that there have been many changes. There seems to be low completion rates for many of the accredited programmes. There is little evidence of substantial reductions of offending. The prison population is rising steadily. The legislation to establish the NOMS is passing through parliament.

What went wrong?

A populist criminal justice policy has been more anxious to be perceived as 'tough' than effective. The strategy became a means of defining, controlling and measuring probation staff's behaviour rather than a concerted effort to change offending behaviour. Assessment, accredited programmes, rigorous standards of enforcement and performance targets all served to impose discipline on a Service perceived as out of control. Longstanding skills in engaging with people who offend and in enabling them to improve their personal and social circumstances have been treated with suspicion and neglected. This is a practice in which people are held responsible for their past behaviour, are viewed negatively and not considered capable of change without enforced re-education. Most people who offend tend to resist such an approach.

If I had known then what I know now

I would have:

- used research into desistance;

- stressed motivation and agency in a process of change;

- made it clear that it is 'tougher' to engage than to enforce;

- made it clear that assessments and programmes do not change people. People change their lives with the support of programmes and individual work;

- made one-to-one work the core of the process;

- made it clear that it should be measured by achieving community reintegration not programme completion;

- included victims, families and communities;

- stopped calling the people – whose self perception we seek to change – offenders;

- integrated restorative justice with effective practice to engender real personal responsibility.

However, I lacked the necessary knowledge, courage and power in 1998. I hope that the Probation Service – in whatever form – can use such qualities in the next 100 years to deliver a truly effective practice which will satisfy victims, protect the public and enable people who offend to transform their lives.

Remember the Four Departmental Committees

Dr Philip Whitehead, Senior Lecturer in Criminology, University of Teesside, UK

Since the Probation of Offenders Act 1907, the probation system has periodically been reviewed. In fact on four occasions, separated by 53 years, different Home Secretaries appointed Departmental Committees which culminated in reports in 1909, 1922, 1936, and 1962. The first and briefest examined whether full advantage had been taken of the 1907 Act during its first year. The next was a more substantive report on training, appointment and payment of probation officers appeared in 1922. By 1936 a comprehensive review had been undertaken during the previous two years into matrimonial jurisdiction, law and practice, other social services of the courts, and its developing organisation. Finally it was not until the 27th May 1959 that the last Departmental Committee was appointed under the chairmanship of R.P. Morison QC. All aspects of probation work became the business of this Committee, which presented its findings in March 1962.

Even though these reports address numerous issues of increasing complexity as the system expanded from slow beginnings after 1907, to its location at the heart of government penal policy during the 1960s, there is one specific feature which binds them together. This is illustrated by paragraph 28 of the 1909 report which drew attention to the probation officer's personality and qualities of sympathy, tact, and firmness. By 1922 it was reinforced that the relationship between probation officer and probationer was important. Furthermore, if the developing system aspired to professionalism then it required a body of trained staff, which implied knowledge of academic disciplines relevant at that time. However, aspirations to professionalism via training after 1930 did not imply the creation of a body of officialdom, but rather people who were equipped to work with, engage, and provide advice, assistance and friendship through a professional relationship. The 1936 report at paragraph 83 reinforced yet again the importance of the probation officer's personality and then, by the early 1960s, the Service had become a profession replete with the training arrangements, knowledge and skills to undertake casework through the medium of a relationship. In fact, at the heart of the probation enterprise people – in the form of probation officers – were working with people with many personal and social problems (clients/offenders).

The first 53 years of probation produced four Departmental Committee Reports; the last 45 years since Morison in 1962 have not produced any. It is not possible to explore the significance of this omission, except to say that by the time the Service arrived at SNOP in 1984 (Statement of National Objectives and Priorities), this was a very different document to the aforementioned reports. Nevertheless, only a few years earlier, Fred Jarvis continued to remind the organisation of the significance of the people who were required in the Probation Service:

> "The quality looked for in potential probation officers, in addition to a wish to work with people, is above all else a resilient personality. Good intelligence, a good general education, some varied life experience, some experience of other forms of social work; all these are valuable too, together with flexibility of mind and a capacity for listening to and understanding others. People with these attributes are well suited to go forward to acquire in training the specific knowledge and skills required of a probation officer."

Accordingly he echoes a significant theme contained in the Departmental Committees.

Therefore, from the beginnings of the system, continuing throughout the period of the four Departmental Committee Reports and into the 1970s, the *modus operandi* of probation work was a people-based relationship. Through a relationship the rationale of probation was given expression: advise, assist and befriend; reduction of re-offending; public protection. By contrast, since the 1980s, a process of modernisation and cultural change has created organisational structures which have undermined the efficacy of relationships. New Public Management, bureaucratic developments, computerisation, audits and targets and a greater focus on policies, procedures, and processes have transformed the personal into something impersonal. What was acknowledged by the Reports as significant over many decades has become discernibly less so now. The Probation Service cannot do its job unless staff are enabled to build relationships of trust with people who offend. This used to be understood better than it is now.

Thank You, Probation Staff

Jane Watt, Writer and Coach, with long Probation Service Career

Brought up in a strangely unemotional and dysfunctional family, educated in the blinkered confines of a rural direct grant girls' grammar school, bewildered by three years following a conventional English Literature degree in a large industrial city while trying to understand the wildly differing early life experiences of fellow students, I fell by chance into the unknown world of the Probation Service in 1975.

There I stayed as Ancillary, Home Office sponsored student on a two-year postgraduate CQSW course, probation officer, trainer, lecturer, senior probation officer. In the world of the Probation Service, I was enabled to grow up. I believe that probation workers took me responsibly through the stages of learning, development and emotional maturing that one normally experiences in a family.

My curiosity and need to learn was encouraged, but guided, advised and directed, without stifling the essential interest on which creativity is based. There were clear rules and laws, which made sense because they were based upon respect for the individual human being and upon the wider needs of a well-functioning society. I had to learn these rules, was encouraged to question and examine them and then to function within them. It was OK to disagree and to act for change, but whilst the rules existed, one maintained them and helped others to work within them.

I saw probation officers operating that 'tough love' which we are told is so sadly lacking in today's society. It is never easy and workers struggled with it but were always supported in the knowledge that colleagues were consistently there to debate and help clarify dilemmas and provide emotional and practical support. Colleagues offered encouragement when 'failures' occurred and empowered persistence, repetition and creativity.

Creativity was in evidence all around as probation workers sought out innovative and practical ways to work constructively on an individual offender's most important issues. Groups were created to deal with diverse particular issues that were seen to arise from time to time (car crime, glue sniffing and so on). Workers also responded to the needs of localised issues and this responsiveness was often greatly appreciated by offenders, their families and neighbourhoods. Groups created in this way were researched, practical responses to need and were followed up and re-examined continually and thus changed or ended at appropriate times. I learned a very professional approach which was always based upon need and financial accountability.

Giving and receiving constructive criticism, learning to be patient and mark time and even accepting two steps backward for three steps forward were more valuable experiences. Valuable lessons were in accepting that everyone is unique and that therefore reactions will vary, and realising that different approaches are necessary for different people as we appreciate that prejudices and learning styles can make unimagined life paths.

Of course I also learned about emotions: about giving and receiving acceptance, discussion and action planning for dealing with emotions. This was very new to me and fascinating to come out into the real world rather than that of books. I still believe that there is much to be learned from fiction, autobiography and poetry which cannot always be easily assimilated from psychology or sociology texts. My plan to create a complete probation training course with 'alternative' reading lists for each part listing only poetry and novels was limited to the course I ran on sex offenders but remains an interest.

Incidentally, my writing skills were developed and honed within the Probation Service. The constant challenge of old-fashioned court reports – to display something of the character, background and development of an offender, as well as addressing their criminality and future within a limited space and in a way that is accessible to a widely varied audience – was a daily challenge. Working to deadlines creates a stress all of its own and skills in time management developed in the Probation Service stand us all in good stead throughout life.

The Probation Service's generous, strong, intelligent and wise staff provided a wonderful place for me to grow up and learn basic life skills. I went on to learn a wide range of other skills too (business management, budget creation and management, mentoring, assessing, inspecting and so on) which have been invaluable in my working and personal life ever since.

I thank the many probation workers who have taught and given me so much over the years.

Probation's Work with Estranged Families

Professor Rob Canton, School of Applied Social Sciences, De Montfort University, Leicester, UK

It is rather alarming how quickly many people are starting to forget probation's work with estranged parents and their children. Narrative histories of probation refer to it in passing and as a peculiarity of marginal significance to probation's main business. Yet until 2001, when separating parents unable to agree about residence or contact took their dispute to court, the agency with the responsibility to offer impartial advice and conciliation was the Family Court Welfare Service, a part of the Probation Service. This accounted for up to 10% of probation's workload.

When I joined the Probation Service, our standard Court referral sheet recognised reconciliation as a task that the magistrates might refer. Although we increasingly passed on such work to organisations like Marriage Guidance, it was still seen that relationship advice was a legitimate part of probation's work. In those days, most officers did some civil work and I undertook five or six civil court reports in the course of each of my first years. These included guardian *ad litem* assignments, in which I prepared information relevant to an adoption application, and what were then known (before the Children Act 1989) as custody/access disputes.

In 1997, I was working as a Senior Family Court Welfare Officer. A new government had a Minister in the Lord Chancellor's Department for this work. It was Geoff Hoon, MP in our locality. The Chief suggested that we should invite him to the office to demonstrate the quality of our civil work. So it was that Mr Hoon came, where he was welcomed by the CPO, members of the Probation Committee and our team. I had asked two particularly skilled officers to talk about how they worked with children, helping them to make some sense of the confusing and painful events around them, and involving them appropriately in the decisions that were going to be taken about them such as where they would live and how and how often they would have contact with their absent parent. Mr Hoon was plainly very impressed with the quality and care that staff showed and at first we were feeling pleased, satisfied that we had done ourselves justice. We felt less comfortable when he remarked:

'The work that you do is excellent and really important. Why, then, do you want this work to remain among the functions of an organisation charged with implementing punishment in the community?'

The answer was plainly insufficiently persuasive because the Government created CAFCASS under the 2000 Act. I am not wanting to suggest that Mr Hoon's morning at our office influenced subsequent developments (it wasn't my fault, honestly!), but I have sometimes wondered how we should have responded.

This work exposed officers to an appreciation of the significance of family and upbringing in children's development and the implication that this had for them later. Skills of mediation and conciliation, now applied to other circumstances of conflict (victim/offender mediation) were originally honed in Family Court work, and challenges of diversity and difference of culture too. Inter-agency work – especially child protection – developed here, as was work around domestic violence and the ways in which (most usually) fathers could harass and undermine their former partners. Whether or not the insights from 'civil work' were *sufficiently* applied to criminal work, the work enriched officers' repertoire of skills. An holistic appreciation in the context of people's personal lives and relationships – working with people not just with regard to their offences – afforded insights that offered a more rounded understanding. It also offered an enhanced appreciation of the ways in which relationships can influence desistance.

Family Court work appeared an oddity – a strange thing for a 'criminal justice organisation' to undertake, as Mr Hoon noted. Yet the historical contingencies which influenced the development of this work – the recognition that traditional adversarial approaches may not be the best way to resolve conflicts, that a welfare service might have a role in working directly with parents and in advising the court, that the court already had such a service in probation – could be taken to represent a sensible and pragmatic organisational development. By contrast, beginning with precept and principle in a rational blueprint rather than out of any perception of need, the Government decided to create a distinct agency. It is by no means self-evident, however, at least in the early years of CAFCASS, that contemporary arrangements represent an improvement. What lessons are to be drawn for the theory of organisations?

We Did More Than Crime

Alan Sanders, Probation Officer 1966–1975

A standard feature of working life as a probation officer in the 1960s and 1970s was office duty – a day a week or fortnight on which you were chained to your desk in order to deal with anyone and anything that you could not legitimately palm off to a colleague. In days when welfare services were not so well-developed, you could have a waiting room full of casual callers presenting a wide range of personal troubles. This aspect of probation work was significant enough to have its own category in Home Office statistics as Kindred Social Work.

Amongst the callers, you could guarantee to pick up at least one – sometimes many more – matrimonial cases. These consisted, for the most part, of women coming to complain about an errant husband (the term partner had not yet been invented and co-habitation was relatively rare). The history often included domestic violence, something that had not yet really been problematised and was not taken that seriously. The woman's aim was usually to get the probation officer to write to the husband inviting him to come in and discuss the problems and, implicitly at least, to fire a warning shot over his bows. Letters were often sent but it was rare for there to be any response.

We were also rota-ed to cover the weekly Magistrates' Matrimonial Courts. The breakdown of a relationship often led not to divorce but to an application by an aggrieved partner in the magistrates' court for either a separation order or a maintenance order. Most applicants were women. Reduced to statutory benefits as a result of the husband's desertion, they had often been forced to seek an order as the price of financial assistance. Magistrates would often pressurise the women to 'give it another go'. If a woman weakened under this pressure, the case would be adjourned for the Probation Service to try reconciliation. This was viewed cynically by most probation officers, who went through the motions of writing to the parties to invite them to an interview. They neither expected nor received any response usually. Most adjournments ended with a brief probation report to the court that 'unfortunately, reconciliation has not been achieved'.

At a local level, many Services took their involvement in 'keeping marriages together' very seriously and some were greatly involved in the setting up of local Marriage Guidance Councils. At a national level, the Home Office supported this work through its link with the Institute of Marital Studies at the Tavistock Clinic. I was one of those privileged to spend three weeks at the Institute being worked over by such luminaries as Dr Pierre Turquet, Doug Woodhouse and the wonderful Janet Mattinson. We were sent out to offices in the Inner London Service to sit in on their duty systems and pick up any matrimonial work that came in, and these cases became the material for our learning. At that stage, any theorising of practice tended – whether it be work with offenders or these other aspects of practice – to have its roots in psychoanalytic thinking. For me, the net result was to deepen my understanding of human motivation, but it left me with few tools to actually help people change. The field was open for more focused interventions such as task centred work and, later, cognitive behavioural therapies.

Whilst the Probation Service is clearly associated primarily with crime, we should not forget its wider social work role in the post-war period and, in particular, this pioneering work which would eventually become the remit of organisations such as Relate and CAFCASS.

Researching the Impact of Training: What it Meant Then and What it Means Now

Professor Gwyneth Boswell, University of East Anglia, UK

In 1988, I was seconded for a year to the University of East Anglia as a Research Fellow from my post as Senior Probation Officer (Training) in a student training unit in Liverpool. The Home Office-commissioned UEA research on the relevance of CQSW probation training to probation practice, which became known as *Skills, Knowledge and Qualities in Probation Practice* (Davies, M. Boswell, G. & Wright, A. (1989) UEA Monographs), and often 'the Martin Davies Report', constituted the first and arguably the only comprehensive investigation of qualifying probation training ever to take place. Unlike its successors (notably, the Coleman and Dews Reports), it contained no hidden agendas and was properly funded by the Home Office so that a piece of work which could genuinely be called research, as opposed to a 'quickie review', could be conducted over an 18-month period.

Our research team comprised Professors Martin Davies and Peter Wedge (both former probation officers and long-term academic friends of probation), Andrew Wright (a seconded Norfolk Probation Officer), and myself. Through questionnaire and interview, we canvassed the views and experiences of over 1,350 probation staff. To cut a very long story short, we found strong support for retaining the social work base of Probation training, but a consistent view that it needed to be much more practice-relevant.

Recently-qualified probation officers identified the following tasks as most important in rank order: PSRs; workload management; counselling individuals; court work; record-keeping; working with other professionals; group work; and family therapy. However, these levels of importance were not reflected in the amount of attention paid to them by training courses, with counselling, PSRs and group work appearing most prominently.

Probation officers with over five years of experience identified their unique role as 'holding the balance between court and client'. This was, of course, expressed in a range of ways, one of which included 'taking the gravel out of life's vaseline', which I never quite understood until last weekend when I heard the expression used in a song by Jake Thackeray, who used to appear on *That's Life*!

What these findings meant then was that probation streams of the generic CQSW courses needed to become much more focused on the Probation task. A follow-up study showed that, four years later, this had effectively been done (*Contemporary Probation Practice*, Boswell, Davies & Wright (1993). Aldershot: Avebury). It was, of course, spurred on by the developing requirements to implement CCETSW[1] Paper 26.3 on practice teaching and learning (1989) and Paper 30 on the arrangements for the new Diploma in Social Work (1991).

It is instructive to reflect upon the meaning of these findings 15 or so years on from a period when social work and probation training matters were largely left in the hands of the professionals, who had reached their decisions based upon a deep knowledge of their subject and a healthy debate process. With the appointment of Michael Howard as Home Secretary in 1993, criminal justice shamefully became (and under New Labour has remained) a political pawn. The expression 'social work' in connection with the probation task very quickly became a 'no-no'. In relation to the experienced probation officers' identification of their unique role of 'holding the balance between court and client', probation officers ceased to do court work, clients became 'offenders' – a label which all the good anti-discriminatory teaching of the time would have been at pains to counsel against – and balance-holding has 'morphed' into enforcement.

The new Diploma in Probation Studies qualification, starting in 1998, required programmes to focus upon the so-called 'What Works' agenda, though the one on which I was employed for six and a half years was at pains to include a question mark at the end of this expression! Thinking now of the training topic rankings by our study's newly-qualified probation officers, it is salutary to realise that counselling and family therapy would be most unlikely to feature in any form within the DipPS. Ironically, however, Trainee Probation Officers (TPOs) whose training I have been involved in over the last nine years have frequently expressed a wish that their training had included some of the traditional social work skills so that they would better be able to identify the factors associated with 'criminogenic need'. You can take the TPO out of social work training but perhaps you cannot take the social work out of the TPO!

End Note

[1]   Central Council for Education and Training in Social Work. This has now been superceded by other bodies in recent years.

1st April 2003: The Dawn of 'Supporting People'

Louise Gartland, Reducing Re-Offending Manager, NOMS, UK

As the date approached for financial control of offender supported accommodation to pass from Probation Boards to Local Authorities, the government named the run-in period as 'Sunset'.

In my role as the Housing Services Manager for West Yorkshire Probation Board, I wondered whether this term defined the future for offender housing.

Supporting People was a joint commissioning arrangement where probation areas would sit alongside health and local authorities. Offender needs were thrown into the pot, along with those of older people and a range of other vulnerable groups.

When the digits turned past midnight, there was no fanfare or fireworks, perhaps most of the thousands of offenders affected were asleep, and the local authority staff responsible for the smooth transition had reached exhaustion many hours earlier.

Often I was asked, "What did offender housing organisations ever do for probation areas?". My response was always, "Apart from employing a dedicated workforce, highly trained in risk assessment and management; apart from offering intelligence straight from offenders homes and communities; apart from offering around three contacts per week all of which could be taken into account for national standards; and apart from representing the voice of the Voluntary Sector, making the case for offender inclusion within all local communities?"

This was a high business risk for Probation Boards. There was much to lose, bearing in mind, as the Social Exclusion Unit reported in 2002, that 'settled and suitable accommodation reduces the risk of re-offending by 20%'. How could offenders address substance misuse issues and complete offending behaviour programmes, and even keep out of custody, without having somewhere to live?

West Yorkshire Probation Board had also seen a tremendous business opportunity, and invested staff time in addressing the legal aspects of transfer of responsibilities, in supporting providers, and in maintaining and building relationships in preparation for the commissioning role. The Board grant funded the development of new supported housing services for offenders, and almost doubled the level of provision in accordance with local need.

This was a huge leap of faith, and come 1st April, would we be proved foolish for our belief? As we stepped out into the brave new world, reborn as joint service commissioners, what challenges lay ahead?

Certainly the stakes were high, in West Yorkshire alone we were playing for a share of around £100 million, and nationally the pot stood at over £1.2 billion.

In the Supporting People casinos, were we equipped as cool, sophisticated players, or would we be turned away at the doors for not meeting the dress code? After all, the arena of local politics had not always been welcoming to those seen as 'banging the offender drum', and in a lottery with vulnerable members of local communities, the dice were weighted against the citizens whose cards we held.

Three years later, I believe investment has resulted in the payback we looked for. If we continue to support our commissioners, to evidence unmet offender needs, and make a strong business case based on achieving safer communities, then most local authorities are receptive partners.

The role of NOMS in joint service commissioning now stretches across the drugs, health and offender learning and skills arenas, and there are increased opportunities through these arrangements too.

By 2009, Supporting People will rest within Local Area Agreements, and work is in hand to secure offender housing and other outcomes within these.

We must seize these opportunities now to ensure the best deal possible for offenders into the future.

Offender housing win or lose?

We decide.

The Befriending Fund and Allan

Paul Senior, Probation Officer,
Doncaster (South Yorkshire Probation
Service) 1977–1982

I don't know whether this was unique to Doncaster but if we considered a client worthy of some small monetary support, we could try and get money from the so-called Befriending Fund. This was run, when I first started in 1977, by someone we shall call Jayne, whom you did not cross if you wanted any money. The fact that I was just trained was not sufficient for me to decide who was worthy. The money was carefully managed as if too high an allocation would severely disturb the balance sheet of the whole Service. There was a maximum of £5 on any money Jayne was willing to grant and that outcome was no foregone conclusion. Above that, a senior probation officer had to countersign the decision which made it even more daunting to access.

Bus fares, a good meal, a phone call or a taxi were some of the requests made. Needless to say I rarely accessed this fund. I just could not bring myself to go through this process for the sake of only a few pounds. They were also meant to be repaid which left another hurdle and the wrath of Jayne if you failed to recoup the money. I tended to dip my hand into my own pocket for such small amounts. This was frowned upon by older hands.

One of my early clients was Allan. He was the archetypal example of what my course had taught me was the 'revolving-door syndrome'. These were people whose criminal behaviour led them into and out of prison at an alarmingly consistent and repetitious rate. Allan was due out from prison and I had been to see him a few times and corresponded with him as was encouraged to do in 'voluntary after-care'. He was a fascinating character. Extremely well-read, a model prisoner and I had had deep conversations with him about crime, prison and society. I calculated once that he had spent over 70% of his adult life in prison though never for more than 12 months and most often two-, three-, and six-month stints. He had never received probation and the length of time he stayed on the outside would be as little as a day sometimes and rarely more than few weeks.

He did not arrive in the office. I had no power to command him to be there (soft policing was a few generations away); my duty was to '*advise, assist and befriend*. I told myself he was self-determining whilst wondering why my pro-social modelling (though I did not know it as that then) had failed. I did not have to wait long as a phone call revealed he had got arrested and was in police cells. I visited him and he seemed both crestfallen and realistic. "Blown it," he said, "Get three months for this ..." (assaulting a police officer). In court the next day I pleaded for bail. He had told me he was meeting a girlfriend and wanted to set up house (well, caravan) and had got frustrated but really wanted to make a go of it. I believed him. He was 43 and seemed ready, somewhat belatedly, to make a change. I pleaded to the court and he was bailed. The first occasion in over 20 years he had not gone straight back to prison. I met him and his girlfriend at the police station and took him back to my office. He was not escaping this time! He told me they had a caravan ready and just needed to get there with his stuff. He needed £12. Images of the Befriending Fund and then Jayne drifted into my mind. I could not let him down. I gave him £15 and he went off happy and I think with hope.

Postscript: I did not see Allan for some weeks. He had rung me to thank me for the loan and said he would repay me. Nothing happened and I dreaded the court officer telling me he was on his way to Armley. His girlfriend arrived one day. The first thing she did was apologise for not returning the money. She then told me that last week Allan had had a heart attack and died. He was 43, about to start a relationship and maybe, just maybe, start to break that cycle. I still believe he would have succeeded. I never got the money!

R&R: A Brief Time in the Sun

John Deering, School of Health & Social Sciences,
University of Wales, Newport, Wales

I joined the Probation Service in 1991. This was a big year – obviously the Criminal Justice Act, supposed to bring the Service 'centre stage', would be passed in the October – but it was also the year that 'What Works?' (it had a question mark in those days) perhaps first manifested itself in practice. I worked for the Mid Glamorgan Probation Service in South Wales and its Chief Probation Officer, David Sutton, was a man of some innovation and very much a passionate believer in practice and its potential to improve the lives of probationers and to effect change in their behaviour which would benefit them, their families and the local community.

As a result, Mid Glamorgan closed its 4B Day Centre and invested the money in the Reasoning and Rehabilitation Programme (*Reasoning and Rehabilitation: A Handbook for Teaching Cognitive Skills.* Ross, R.R., Fabiano, E.A. & Ross, R.D. (1986) Ottawa: University of Ottawa), aiming to train all probation officers as group leaders/tutors. With R&R came a commitment to evaluation and emerging 'What Works?' principles around risk, need and responsivity. Swansea University were employed to evaluate a pilot programme, under the acronym S.T.O.P. (Straight Thinking on Probation), and the entire Service geared itself up to deliver a pilot programme to 130 'chosen' probationers.

In contrast to more recent issues of *targets*, the criteria for inclusion were based in *targeting*. In order to be considered for the STOP programme, probationers had to score highly on two actuarial assessment measures in use at that time: POROC (Prediction of Risk of Custody) and a risk of re-offending measure. STOP was thus reserved for that group of individuals identified as being of medium to high risk of re-offending. A more clinical approach to assessment was also intended to assess people for their suitability for the programme in other ways.

Eventually the first orders were completed and in due course, the evaluation delivered. The results were encouraging in some respects, e.g. in the first 12 months after completion, the completing group (a 75% completion rate was achieved) reconvicted at less than the predicted rate and below a comparison group that received custodial sentences. However, a complex picture emerged. For example, at 24 months, the STOP completers had reconvicted as predicted, but they were by now committing less serious offences and reporting a significant drop in self-reported problems in their lives (*Straight Thinking on Probation: The Mid Glamorgan Experiment.* Raynor, P. & Vanstone, M. (1997) Probation Studies Unit Report No. 4. University of Oxford, Centre for Criminological Research).

The things that distinguished the STOP pilot scheme for me was the commitment of the whole of the Service (or at least it seemed like it!) to a programme that did promise effective work with more persistent offenders. Field teams within Mid Glamorgan were completely restructured in some cases to enable probation officers to run STOP, with transfers of cases to other officers and other changes taking place. Although the whole cognitive-behavioural movement would be criticised as a pathological, one-size-fits-all model by some in the Service and beyond, I do not think it is entirely a rose-tinted spectacle view that I take when I recall those early R&R groups not fitting that profile in important respects. For example, participants were targeted and only accepted if seen as suitable on a range of measures; there were no targets in the way that for me cast a shadow over the Accredited Programmes Initiative. Secondly, participation on the programme was regarded as just one aspect of probation supervision and officers continued to work with individuals on other aspects of their lives, both structural and personal, that had an impact on their offending.

In the years that followed, for many reasons, enthusiasm for R&R seemed to dim and many programmes folded due to poor attendance. Nationally we now seem to be in a position where R&R is no longer run, seemingly due to high attrition. R&R (and cognitive behaviourism) was never a panacea, but perhaps that initial (if partial) success was never built upon in ways that might have helped it make a contribution.

Reflections on *Sparks Beneath the Ashes: Experiences of a London Probation Officer* by Mary Ellison, published 1933

† *Mark Harris, Head of Quality and Standards, Victim Support (on secondment from London Probation), UK*

The flyleaf in Mary Ellison's book, *Sparks Beneath the Ashes: Experiences of a London Probation Officer* states: "Probation Officers see life at its greyest and grimmest … mixed with the worst in human nature there are wonderful streaks of kindliness, pathos and humour". In the 1930s, female probation officers had women-only caseloads, which in Mary's case were predominantly prostitutes, and the book consists of a bunch of loosely-connected vignettes of some of the people she worked with.

As one might expect, there is quite a lot of judgmental thought in this book, and a strong but not overplayed sense of the redeeming nature of religion. Her use of authority sat uncomfortably for me as a probation practitioner in the 1970s – I suspect much less so for front-end staff nowadays. On the other hand, Mary's analysis of the triggers to prostitution is insightful and remains pertinent today. Further, her approach to the impact of poverty on crime, and to the double standards played out by the criminal justice system (not that there was such a concept in those days) with regard to the poor and the well-off, is hearteningly egalitarian.

The most shocking thing about this book, to her probation officer successors, is the fact that Mary routinely saw her clients (ah, I remember that term!) *at her home*! They knew where she lived, and she encouraged them to call at any time, including at the weekend. Some of them would raid her bookshelves for improving reading (always a good sign, it seems).

Nowadays we would undoubtedly be deeply perturbed were any of our staff to work in this way. We might worry about collusion (no sign of that in Mary's practice), or call her unboundaried. There is no doubt that for Mary, working as a probation officer was a vocation, and she would therefore give her time when it was needed. There are no accounts of her hospitality being abused, or of her offering accommodation to her clients, and little evidence of a scope for manipulation that we would undoubtedly anticipate today – and, of course, she had no supervision to explore or monitor any of this. The book is dedicated to her husband, who does not otherwise feature, and one wonders what his feelings might have been.

In an era when even home visits have all but dried up, this sort of approach is almost incomprehensible. Even in the 1980s, I was highly disconcerted when mowing the lawn one day, to have an offender of my acquaintance call out, "Hello Mark", over the garden fence, as he was visiting my next-door neighbour.

Set against this is a no-nonsense practicality in her approach. She was faced with a problem and used what resources were available to her to address it. Thinking back, there was not an enormous amount of that in my practice. One example stands out because of its rarity. Fred was a 23-year old tramp, who commuted between Finchley and Brighton. I was impressed the first time I met him because he had a copy of *The Times* under his arm. A gentleman of the road, I thought, only finding out later he couldn't read. In the summer Fred was smelly, and so we would give him a bit of money if he attended our drop-in clean-smelling as an incentive. If he was not clean-smelling, we insisted that he wash his feet before joining in, providing a bowl of hot water and towels. Mary Ellison with a touch of behaviour modification, I thought.

But not really. In Fred's case we barely touched the surface (literally). Mary would have had him spruced up, and sorted out, in double-quick time.

Yet beyond all that to Mary, her clients – and their welfare – mattered. I remember a rather dour probation officer, retiring in about 1974, saying to me, "They know if you care, that's what makes the difference". Mary cared passionately about the scope for improvement, for redemption, in those she worked with. In our current target-driven world, they can still know that we care; but I suspect it is more difficult.

End Note

Mark Harris died during 2007 and we thank his wife for permission to include his Moment. It is many years since I last came across Mark. We were both active in Napo and our paths crossed regularly during those wonderful conferences held at some seaside resort. He was always enthusiastic and committed at everything he did, up for an argument but also willing to listen and learn. He was an archetypal probation officer of the 1970s and 1980s and will be sorely missed by all who knew him.

Criminal Justice Administration Act 1914

Dr Emma Wincup, Senior Lecturer in Criminology and Criminal Justice, University of Leeds, UK

The Criminal Justice Administration Act 1914 aimed to 'diminish the number of cases committed to prison, to amend the Law with respect to the treatment and punishment of young offenders, and otherwise to improve the Administration of Criminal Justice'. Almost a century later, most of its provisions have been repealed by subsequent legislation but its legacy is important because it paved the way for the development of residential work with offenders.

The Act built upon the Probation of Offenders Act 1907 and allowed a condition of residence to be attached to a probation order. In direct response, a number of charities established hostels for young people, which aimed to offer a disciplined and character building experience for young offenders whose homes were considered unsuitable for successful rehabilitation. The first hostels were small, based on an extended family model and run without the support of the Home Office.

As a more professional criminal justice system emerged, the Home Office became concerned about this seemingly *ad hoc* and inconsistent provision and, in 1927, a Departmental Committee report recommended that that Home Office should approve (but not manage), inspect and fund hostels. These recommendations were enshrined in the Criminal Justice Act 1948 which empowered the Home Secretary to approve and regulate hostels for offenders aged between 15 and 21. Following the prohibition of probation orders for those under 17 in the Children and Young Persons Act 1969, hostels lost their original rationale of providing temporary accommodation for young petty offenders who went out to work during the day. As a consequence, they established themselves as a resource the courts could draw upon to accommodate defendants awaiting trial and, to a lesser extent, offenders on probation orders. By 1972, Probation Services were encouraged to develop bail hostels and probation committees were empowered to manage them. The Home Secretary was granted powers to approve them in 1973 and, in 1974, it was determined that bailees could also be accommodated in probation hostels.

In theory, hostels served as an alternative to custody, but a number of studies found evidence of net-widening: in other words, hostels were accommodating those who would previously have been allowed to remain in their own accommodation rather than diverting offenders from custody. The introduction of National Standards for the Supervision of Offenders in the Community in 1992 offered an opportunity to clarify the role of hostels. In the 2002 version, the role of approved premises (as they became known following the implementation of the Criminal Justice and Court Services Act 2000) was defined as follows:

"The purpose of approved premises is to provide an enhanced level of residential supervision with the aim of protecting the public by reducing the likelihood of offending."

In response to a recommendation in the Halliday Report to review the 'intermediate estate', an approved premises and offender housing strategy for higher risk offenders was published in 2004. This noted the need to ensure that in the interests of public protection, approved premises are predominantly used for offenders assessed as 'very high' and 'high' risk of harm. Approved premises were not mentioned in Carter's *Review of Correctional Services* or the Government's response to it but it can be surmised that approved premises will play an increasingly important role in the future because they are well-placed to support policies concerned reducing re-offending and protecting the public.

Current provision stands at 104 approved premises providing 2,300 bed spaces for offenders. Approved premises now accommodate a resident group whose characteristics stand in stark contrast to those they were originally set up to accommodate. Typical residents are now in their 20s or 30s, convicted of a sexual or violent offence and living in an approved premise as a condition of their licence. Approved premises managed by the voluntary sector are the exception rather than the norm: the remainder are managed by Probation Boards. The Offender Management Bill 2006, now progressing through the House of Lords, will almost certainly alter the way approved premises are funded and managed. In the new era of contestability, the private sector will be allowed to develop and manage approved premises which many will interpret as a culmination of a move towards privatisation which began with the contracting out of the facilities management role (catering, cleaning, maintenance, etc.) in 2002. Once more, residential work with offenders will be carried out by non-statutory agencies albeit in very different circumstances to the past.

How I Became a Předvstupni Poradce in the Probační a Mediacní Služba ČR

*Kevin Barry, International Projects Manager,
NOMS, UK*

I now spend more time in airport lounges than in senior management meetings because – for the past five years – I have been actively involved in the development of other European probation services.

It all began with a round-robin e-mail advertisement, entitled 'How would you like to live and work in Prague for a year?' This introduced me to the new world of European Union development projects as part of the enlargement process.

In 2003–4 I spent a year and a half working with the new probation and mediation service in the Czech Republic – seconded from the London Probation Area but employed by the Ministry of Justice in Prague as a pre-accession advisor. I managed the Czech end of a 1.2 million euro training and development project and also acted as advisor to the Director (Reditel) of the Czech Service and to my abiding delight, lived in the centre of Prague, that (for me) is the most beautiful of European cites.

The sharp end of the project was delivered by probation officers and seniors – mostly from the NPS but some from our sister services *NEUstart* in Austria and *Reclassering Nederland* in Holland. Together we delivered a range of requested training from equal opportunities to risk assessment and report writing. 25 of the 240 Czech probation and mediation officers visited the UK, Austria and Holland as part of the project and as a result of both the training and the visits built up close professional links between our two services.

The success of this project led to Foreign Office encouragement of the Home Office to bid for more projects and over the past three years we have bid for and won eight more EU projects in Romania, Estonia, Turkey, Bulgaria, Czech Republic and Croatia. In the newly acceded countries the focus has been on developing work with their young Probation Services (Romania, Estonia and Czech Republic) but in Bulgaria, Turkey and

Croatia it has been the exciting ground-breaking work of helping in the creation of a new service – with all the challenges and excitement that this involves.

There is no one European model for probation services. Each country has to develop their own model that suits their own needs, but inevitably look to the older, established services such as the UK and the Netherlands because of our experience and willingness to share knowledge and expertise. There is an ever-present danger of 'big sister knows best' combined with an understandable rush to catch up. However, the EU principle of partnership twinned with caution helps to reduce these risks. These programmes do not export a UK (or Dutch) model but rather a set of principles and concepts that then have to be applied and developed according to the culture, mores and legal framework of the beneficiary.

Managing the interplay between the core values and principles of modern probation practice and the local justice system is probably the most challenging part of the role of the resident twinning advisor. Five senior staff have taken up secondments to date and more will follow if we win further projects. Over 300 frontline staff have worked as short-term trainers and developers. While the work is demanding it is also exhilarating and encouraging. It is refreshing to work in countries where the English and Welsh probation and prison services are highly regarded and this is a counterweight to the often negative environment we work in here at home. While our colleagues in central and eastern Europe are keen to learn and study our methods, it is also a unique opportunity for us to learn that there are other ways of working. The Czech Service is based on principles of restorative justice and offers penal mediation as a standard intervention. The Turkish service has 'probation protection boards' that actively involve the local communities in the seeking of employment. So this work is very much a two-way process.

What better way could we find to celebrate our centenary than by participating in these most exciting of European projects.

28th February 2007

Harry Fletcher, Assistant General Secretary of Napo,
UK

Over three years ago the Government introduced its plans for the National Offender Management Service which would merge the prison and probation services. However, by 2004, these plans had vanished and what was on the agenda was effectively the abolition of the National Probation Service (NPS) and its replacement with a pseudo-market of multiple supervisors. The plans were astonishing. NPS was only created in 2001 and most organisations, including Napo, supported what the Government wanted. Previously there had been 54 probation areas, each relatively autonomous, there was no national plan and no national continuity. It was a sensible idea. Yet, without evaluation or even the production of a business plan, the Government by 2004 was planning to tear it all up.

Numerous blueprints were produced in the ensuing 30 months. The vast majority who responded said they were against breaking up the Service, found no case for separating programmes from interventions, and forecast that the whole thing would end up a terrible mess. Ignoring warnings, the Government ploughed on. It introduced a Bill in 2005 but abandoned it because of too much opposition. In November 2006 the Bill was re-introduced. Napo warned that if it was passed it would undermine public protection, erode local accountability and lead to more – not less – re-offending. The Bill went through the various stages reaching its Third Reading on 28th February 2007. I, along with many people in Napo, was involved in massive lobbying. Many MPs were seen, ministers were contacted, briefing papers were sent out to many parliamentarians. Both the Liberal Democrats and Conservatives pledged support. The number of Labour rebels grew as the Bill approached its final Reading on the momentous day of 28th February. It looked as if as many as 40 Labour MPs might rebel.

I attended the Third Reading together with colleagues and lobbied remorselessly. At one stage, a Whip told a BBC journalist that the vote was impossible to predict. Gerry Sutcliffe, the Probation Minister, said he thought the Government was going to lose a Bill for the first time in over

30 years. With a much reduced majority of 25, the Bill was passed. This was a major disappointment. I have never felt so professionally demoralised. At least 60 Labour backbenchers had expressed their opposition and the likelihood of them voting against or abstaining. The outcome of the vote might have been different on another day. Most Irish MPs were not in Westminster. Three Labour rebels mysteriously disappeared on foreign trips, and another three were unwell. In addition, 26 Conservative MPs were absent. The SNP voted against the Bill. Other Labour Members voted for the Bill or abstained because of Whips' pressure, personal promises, the intervention of Ministers, or because of genuine concessions. In the end, 24 Labour MPs voted against, 37 abstained, 27 on principle, and 18 of the sympathetic group surprisingly voted for the Bill. The Whips worked overtime. One MP was threatened with no support for his Private Members Bill; another that promotion would be withheld; others were told that the Government was going to lose the Bill by four and that it was therefore a vote of confidence.

Nevertheless the fight continued. The Government did retreat. They conceded that court reports would stay with the public sector, a promise was made that supervision of offenders would remain in-house for three years, a commitment was given to ensure local consultation about probation plans and that national collective bargaining would be retained. The Bill, however, was still flawed and leaves probation work open to privatisation, fragmentation and the chaos that will ensue. The Campaign, therefore, will accelerate into the Lords. Napo expects cross-Party support for amendments excluding supervision from the Bill, secure local commissioning, enable adequate resourcing, and place duties on agencies to co-operate. The key votes will be taken in mid-May. When it returns to the Commons, probably in June, opposition Labour MPs will be given the opportunity to think again. Many said that it is very hard to vote against a whole Bill and easier to support amendments. It remains to be seen, therefore, whether those who abstained or voted in favour will vote on principle. By the time you read this these decisions will have been taken.

I have been involved in hundreds of campaigns over a 20-year period on behalf of Napo. None of them was as vital as this represented the very essence of probation survival. It looks as if the campaign has been remarkably successful. The Government has made concessions, and there may be more to follow. What is now absolutely critical is that the Probation Service, its personnel and its friends, join together to campaign for a set of values that reflect what the Service should be all about:

effective supervision which maximises public protection, rehabilitation by challenging criminal behaviour, working in partnership with the public and others to reduce crime and ensuring that offenders are aware of the effect of crime on victims. The Probation Service has had a battering and been the subject of unfair criticism. If it is to survive then it must be based on a value system that its staff have total belief in.

When Heroin Hit the Streets of Bootle

Julian Buchanan, Professor of Criminal Justice,
North East Wales Institute of Higher Education, UK

I began work in 1980 as an 'Ancillary Officer' with the Merseyside Probation Service (MPS), before starting the CQSW at Liverpool University as a Home Office Sponsored student in 1981. Half of the two-year course involved four placements: a city centre probation team, a residential hostel for 'seriously disturbed' young adults, a psychiatric ward, and a final placement at the Home Office Student Training Unit (Old Swan). These were very challenging experiences which I still consider to be excellent preparation for work as a probation officer. I began work as a probation officer in Bootle, Merseyside, in 1983.

There had been no input concerning drug use on my course, hardly surprising as problem drug use amongst the probation caseload was very rare. Probation work concerned itself with reducing offending by directing offenders into life skills activities to support engagement in education, employment and the wider community. However, such opportunities became severely limited when the economic recession of the early 1980s, exacerbated by Thatcherist monetarist policies and deindustrialisation, left many working class areas ruthlessly blighted by mass long-term unemployment. In Bootle many parents who worked in factories and the docks lost jobs they thought they would have for life, while a new realisation dawned on their children – their hopes and aspirations for housing, employment and a better future were misplaced.

It was within this context that widespread heroin 'smack' use amongst youths (17–25 years old) appeared almost overnight in Bootle. It was one of the first areas in the UK to suffer a heroin problem. The local press labelled it 'Smack City' and people travelled from all over Merseyside for the opportunity to buy a 'bag' of heroin and 'chase heroin'. It wasn't long after that other Areas – with similar social and demographic backgrounds – witnessed a heroin epidemic. Looking back our ignorance as probation officers regarding illicit drugs was embarrassing. The perceived wisdom was that heroin addiction was the 'road to death' and my role as a probation officer was to persuade heroin 'addicts' to become drug free. I remember doing lots of drug-related Social Inquiry Reports (SIRs, now PSRs). In my

SIR interviews I tried to secure promises from offenders to become drug-free. Fearing prison, many offenders duly obliged and if given probation I would take them as agreed in court to residential detox, or sometimes direct to Therapeutic Communities (Chatterton Hey, Inward House, Phoenix House).

No sooner had I dropped them off than they would be back again in Bootle using drugs – and in even bigger trouble having breached a court order, broken a promise, upset relationships, and blown a chance from the court. It didn't take too long to realise that this abstinence-based approach was – for the majority – inappropriate. Even worse, I was setting up these young people to fail and adding to their problems. They accepted all that was on offer (abstinence) but most were either not ready, not able, or not willing to become drug-free. A different approach was needed.

In 1986 a group of us with specialist responsibility for drug services in Bootle began working together: Pat O'Hare (teacher), Andrew Bennett, Annie Spiers, Dave Halford-Smith (social services drug counsellors), Dr John Marks, Dr Tim Garvey (psychiatrists), Russell Newcombe (health promotions officer), Geoff Wyke and myself (probation officers). We devised and promoted a risk/harm reduction strategy and set up one of the largest multi-agency Community Drugs Teams in the UK. This innovative practice to engage more effectively with problem drug users arose from listening and learning from people who had problems with illicit drugs. It was enhanced by multi-disciplinary debate and exchanges. It was a 'bottom up' approach that was encouraged by MPS who appointed probation officers as drug specialists in 1986 and expected them to investigate, reflect and formulate policy and practice to meet local need. By 1988 MPS had approved a new policy document which promoted a risk/harm reduction approach for work with drug using offenders. This 'Mersey' approach to drugs subsequently had national/international impact.

When drugs hit the street of Bootle in 1985 many thought it would just be a passing phase. However, drugs have not gone away. Neither has unemployment and social exclusion, deep divisions and a lack of social mobility. Drugs are widespread and continue to dominate the lives of a significant proportion of people in prison and on probation supervision. That experience in my early years of probation has profoundly affected me. I am still engaged in the issue, still arguing that problem drug use is essentially a social problem, not a medical or physiological problem, and one that has its roots in social exclusion. Problem drug use disproportionately impacts upon those who start life damaged and disadvantaged, as Susanne McGregor observes, 'the impact of deindustrialisation and the rise of the consumer market society has created a class of losers and discarded youth who continue to provide new recruits to the ranks of problematic drug misusers' ('The Drugs Crime Nexus'. *Drugs Education Prevention and Policy*. Vol 7, No. 4. November 2000: p.315). The underlying causes of problem drug use remain.

Probation Journal: The Journal of Community and Criminal Justice

Hindpal Singh Bhui, Editor of Probation Journal
1997–2007

It is not straightforward to put an exact date on the establishment of the *Probation Journal*, as it has existed in different formats for much of the history of the Probation Service itself. Owned and, until a recent partnership with Sage Publications, also published by Napo, it started to look more like a modern journal in 1956, though it has existed since 1929. It currently has subscribers in 26 countries and a readership that extends well beyond the Probation Service.

This longevity and reach means that the *Journal* is an instructive source of information on probation history and its place in political thinking. The articles and commentaries that have appeared at different points say a great deal about the environment in which they were written. For example, the frequent publication, particularly in the Journal's early history, of speeches and articles by senior figures in the church, highlights the religious foundations of the Probation Service. A glance back at older editions also illustrates the comforting circularity of much criminal justice debate: for example, considerably in advance of recent announcements about a new Ministry of Justice, we find a paper in a 1934 edition entitled *The Archbishop of York Stresses the Need for a Department of Justice*. Current probation staff might also find it interesting to note the relevance to them of passages such as the following, taken from a speech in 1966 by Mr Noble, the Chairman of the Advisory Council for Probation and After-Care:

> 'There has been a period of uncertainty which came when there had been the stress of expansion of numbers, the development of new schemes of training and the anxieties of new functions and responsibilities.'
> (T.A.F. Noble, 'The Service Develops', in Probation 12 (2): 40, 1966)

His subsequent confidence that 'the uncertainty will soon be forgotten …' was clearly misplaced, but his 'confidence in the Service's professional capacity to shoulder its burdens' certainly was not. Forty years later, the

Service, like the *Journal* that has striven to reflect the vicissitudes of its long journey, is still here. The respect in which the Probation Service has been held by many influential people comes through strongly from the Journal's pages, which are littered with supportive speeches and articles by a variety of princes, lords, earls and other dignitaries. Notably, Prince George made time in 1933 to 'plead' for 'an efficient Probation Service' and followed this up in 1934 with a paper on 'Crime and Mental Health'. (Back issues can be accessed via the Sage Publications website: http://prb. sagepub.com/archive/.)

That the *Journal* continues to reflect the initiatives and thinking that come from practice is illustrated by more recent articles. For example, debates about 'What Works?' in criminal justice have featured on a regular basis. Published critiques have occasionally deviated from the conventions of academic formality, as when Kevin Gorman, then a senior probation practitioner in West Yorkshire, memorably described an attempt to identify key ingredients of offender programmes that 'work' as: 'an exercise reminiscent of the bizarre, scientifically futile experiment to extract sunbeams from cucumbers, observed by a bewildered Lemuel Gulliver at the Grand Academy of Lagado (Swift 1726)' ('Cognitive Behaviourism and the Holy Grail: The Quest for a Universal Means of Managing Offender Risk', *Probation Journal* 48, 1:3–9, 2001). Unsurprisingly, his paper helped to provoke much subsequent discussion.

The Journal's explicit commitment to developing debate about probation practice means that 'practitioner wisdom' has always been given some prominence in its pages, though all writers, whatever their background, are encouraged to aim for a synthesis between theory, research and practice relevance.

I am grateful to have been the editor of a journal that reflects the journey of an organisation which, for the moment, still symbolises inclusivity and optimism about the human condition. Like the Probation Service itself, the *Journal* has motivated much loyalty and passion, both from successive editorial teams, and from its readers. Whatever becomes of the Probation Service in the future, I remain confident that the *Journal* will survive to provide an outlet to the dedicated professionals who, through their research, their practice, or both, work to achieve the rehabilitation of offenders.

David Garland and Probation

Dr Philip Whitehead, Senior Lecturer in Criminology,
University of Teesside, UK

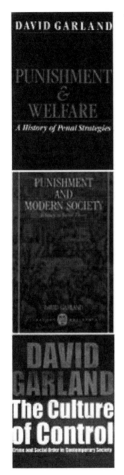

Throughout the history of probation, both practitioners and academics have been contributing to the literature which has grown up around the organisation. Practitioners – from the inside – have been reflecting on and writing about their experiences of doing the job. This is a significant area of work in its own right to which the Probation Journal, in addition to other publications, has been instrumental in disseminating forms of practice knowledge. By contrast academics – more on the outside looking in – have made distinctive contributions to probation work from the standpoint of political, socio-economic, cultural frameworks; exploring relationships between probation and the wider criminal justice system, penal and social policies; examining the changing nature of society influencing the changing nature of probation. One such contribution by an academic, since the 1980s, is the work of David Garland and I want to draw the reader's attention primarily to the following trilogy:

- *Punishment and Welfare: A History of Penal Strategies* (1985: Gower)

- *Punishment and Modern Society: A Study in Social Theory* (1990: Oxford)

- *The Culture of Control: Crime and Social Order in Contemporary Society* (2001: Oxford)

Firstly, *Punishment and Welfare* is a significant text when thinking about the emergence of the probation system in 1907 against the background of the re-ordering of the political, social, economic, and penal realms which occurred during those years towards the end of the Victorian period. The transition from Victorian penal politics to the emergence of what Garland describes as the penal-welfare system is analysed in detail and, of course, it was the latter system which found a place for probation within an emerging 20th-century social-democratic welfare state. In fact, the emergence of probation along with other forms of social work, social security, and particularly criminological positivism, constitute responses to escalating crises from the 1880s which focused on the role of the state in relation to social and economic issues and the regulation of problem populations under capitalism – the poor and offenders. Thus, Garland provides us with explanatory frameworks, including Marxism and Foucauldian theoretical concepts, which deepens our understanding of the beginnings of probation and its place in the penal-welfare system which existed from the 1900s before the crises of the 1970s caused certain disruptions.

Next, *Punishment and Modern Society* (1990) constitutes Garland's analysis and re-working of different traditions within the sociology of punishment. By addressing Durkheim, Weber, Marx, and Foucault, etc. … he builds up a multi-faceted picture of what is the complex phenomenon of punishment. By doing so he argues that penality is more than a simple instrumental means-to-end, response to crime because it encapsulates many other facets: coercion, power relations, legal procedures, symbolic and cultural effects, class domination, bureaucratic processes, a moral action reaffirming social solidarity, its expressive nature encapsulating outrage and vengeance. In fact, it is presented as a complex social institution that no one theoretical perspective can fully capture.

Finally, *The Culture of Control* (2001) brings the project began in 1985 into the present. In fact this book builds upon and extends the earlier text in terms of how penal-criminal justice transformations can be accounted for and theoretically explained. Therefore, within the context of analysing political, socio-economic, cultural changes since the 1960s – in addition to the profound effects associated with the decline of the rehabilitative ideal during the 1970s that had provided the space and ideological supports for probation to function – the conditions of existence and surface of emergence for contemporary penality are analysed. Consequently, the modernised and culturally transformed nature of probation, which can be plotted since the 1970s, fits more with the new political configurations which are a feature of contemporary criminal justice.

This is an important body of work which helps to situate probation work over the last 100 years, in addition to offering a body of theory for exploring the nature of profound change, particularly during the last two decades. I commend Garland's trilogy to readers of these *Moments*.

Memories of Working in Brixton

Michael Teague, Senior Lecturer in Criminology,
University of Teesside, UK

It was a sunny Brixton afternoon in 1987 when we were stopped by the police. I was driving my old Mini and my probation colleague Nick was in the passenger seat. We were Assistant Wardens at the Inner London Probation Service's Tulse Hill Bail Assessment Hostel (the Service had yet to embrace the more progressive label of 'Assistant Manager' for hostel staff). We had left the hostel in the midst of a lengthy shift to seek treatment for Nick at the local hospital.

Our car was stopped – unlikely as it sounds – by two police officers on horseback. They rode to the centre of the road and ordered us to halt. We were ordered out of the car, and questioned relentlessly, in a discourteous and disrespectful manner. Eventually, after more routine unpleasantness, we were asked where we had just come from. When we gave the hostel address, the officers immediately assumed that we were offenders. The imperatives of community policing had, it seemed, yet to permeate the lower echelons of Metropolitan Police. Their manner became even more challenging, as they interrogated us on the reasons for our stay. 'We are Assistant Wardens there,' we replied.

A miraculous and instantaneous change in the officers' demeanour occurred. They doubtless realised that the hostel liaised closely with Brixton Police and, as a consequence, we might enjoy a degree of credibility were we to complain about their discriminatory behaviour. Though our previous requests to know why we were stopped had been brushed off, we were now repeatedly addressed as 'sir' in a manner verging on the obsequious. The officers claimed that a car resembling mine, with occupants resembling Nick and I, had been spotted behaving suspiciously. This uncanny coincidence did not ring true. I am a white male, and had never been stopped in three years of working in Brixton. My colleague Nick, however, was black. The conclusion that a car with occupants of different races immediately attracted police suspicion in Brixton during that era was inescapable. It offered us a real insight into the daily experiences of some of our clients (we had yet to progress to labelling them as 'offenders').

What was the outcome? As a *Guardian*-reading liberal, I favoured a formal complaint. To my surprise, black co-workers counselled against this. It would, they felt, attract unwelcome attention and could render the daily act of commuting to work problematic. What I considered harassment was simply part of the territory. No-one had been charged and now it was over. All my male black hostel colleagues recounted their experiences of being stopped by the police, with little apparent reason other that what one colleague defined as '*that most culpable offence – being black in a public place*'.

Nowadays, the National Probation Service (NPS) has embraced the wider diversity agenda, pledging itself "to equal service for all our members, the offenders, victims of crime and our communities" (*The Heart of the Dance* (2003)). These are fine aspirations, but when HM Inspectorate of Probation's *Towards Race Equality* report (HMIP, 2000) explored the extent to which probation achieved race equality in its employment practices and in work with offenders, it was evident that service delivery for white offenders was better than for black and minority ethnic offenders. It raised extremely serious concerns about disparities in standards.

All this led the then Home Office Probation Minister Paul Boateng to summarise its conclusions as 'profoundly disturbing, deeply disappointing and deeply challenging'. Gurbux Singh, Chair of the Commission for Racial Equality, said it illuminated a Probation Service which was 'struggling to deal with all races and cultures in an equal and fair manner'.

When the *Macpherson Report* (1999) into the murder of Stephen Lawrence defined institutionalised racism as the "collective failure of an organisation to provide an appropriate and professional service to people because of their colour, culture or ethnic origin", many in probation felt that our professional culture would not tolerate such racism. Our complacency was shattered by *Towards Race Equality*. Its carefully evidenced pages reminded us that we should never underestimate institutionalised racism's resilience, or its tenacious capacity to survive. A follow-up report (HMIP, 2004) confirmed that aspects of work with white offenders were of a slightly better quality when compared to the standards achieved with minority ethnic offenders. In addition, the prevalent sense of disadvantage experienced by some minority ethnic probation staff members was explored.

In terms of promoting race equality, probation has much to celebrate. Probation leads other criminal justice agencies (not least the police and prison services) in best practice on diversity. The agency is focused and committed on diversity issues, and we should be proud of that. However, we still have a long way to go, and we should not lose sight of that.

Working with Racially Motivated Offenders

Andy Stelman, Assistant Chief Officer, Merseyside Probation Area, UK

History has been described in many ways: 'History is bunk' is what Henry Ford is alleged to have said when he sued the *Chicago Tribune*. Another American commentator said it was 'just one damn thing after another'. Thomas Carlyle (perhaps more famous for his only manuscript of his history of the French Revolution being thrown onto the fire by his servant) stated that 'history is the essence of innumerable biographies'. Voltaire described history in one of his plays as 'just the portrayal of crimes and misfortunes'.

Three short biographies follow, from 1955, 1993 and 2005, and all of which concerned a terrible crime.

Money, Mississippi does not have a great deal in common with Huyton, Merseyside. Except that both communities have witnessed the murder of a young black man in the most violent of circumstances. In 1955 Emmett Till, a 14-year old black youth from Chicago, went to visit relatives in Mississippi. One day, in the company of some friends, he entered a general store in Money. In a brash, 14-year old way but with the greater certainty of the 'liberated' northern black citizen, it is alleged that he wolf whistled at the young white woman looking after the store. Three days later, two men came to Emmett's uncle's cabin at night, and took Emmett away. Two days after that, his body was found in the local river with a cotton gin tied round his neck to weigh him down and a bullet hole in his temple. Some contemporary newspaper reports added that he had had his genitalia cut off and put into his mouth.

The trial of the young woman's husband and his half-brother for murder lasted less than a week and ended with their acquittal on all counts; they later told a reporter that they had committed the crime. Despite a national outcry from a nascent freedom movement for southern black people, the two accused remained free until their deaths. Emmett had been murdered because he had dared to step outside the rigid social expectations that still pervaded those states.

Nearly forty years after Emmett's murder and the 'trial' of the perpetrators, a slightly older Stephen Lawrence was murdered in Eltham, again, because he was black. The five young men quickly arrested for his murder escaped punishment because of technical issues to do with the laying of charges and the prosecution process. At least two significant outcomes emerged from the farce of the prosecution: first the *Daily Mail* published the pictures of the young men on its front page and simply stated 'MURDERERS'. It went on to challenge them to take the *Mail* to court. This did not happen. The second, much more important outcome was the publication of the *Macpherson Report* and its – uncomfortable – introduction of the term 'institutional racism'.

Furthermore, almost exactly 50 years to the day after Emmett's murder, Anthony Walker was killed in Huyton, Merseyside: again, because he was a young black man.

The response to Anthony's murder differed from the two previous tragedies in two major respects. First, Anthony's perpetrators were brought swiftly to justice and sentenced to long-life imprisonment tariffs extended precisely because of the racially aggravated aspect of his murder. The police and CPS acted decisively and thoroughly to ensure that no loopholes existed and therefore that justice was done.

The second response was that the Merseyside Criminal Justice Board sought a thorough review of how race hate crimes were dealt with in Merseyside by all aspects of the criminal justice system. A senior manager in the Merseyside Probation Service led the review, which came up with major recommendations covering the investigation, prosecution, sentencing and disposal of such cases. Merseyside Probation Area completely overhauled its racially motivated offender programme ('Against Human Dignity') as a result of the review, and the police created specialist hate crime investigation units in all its Basic Command Units. There is now a system in place that, it is hoped, will enable members of black and other racial minority communities to feel that the criminal justice system in Merseyside is taking their safety seriously.

Race and faith hate crime now, and their place in the criminal justice system are at the same stage that domestic violence was prior to the requirement issued to chief constables by the then Home Secretary, to introduce specialist domestic violence units to all their police forces. That was in the very early 1990s, and we know how much domestic violence has entered the mainstream of criminal justice processes.

George Santayana once wrote that those who cannot learn from history are doomed to repeat it. Regrettably, it is unlikely that racist murders will ever be eradicated. What we can do, however, is ensure that our responses to such crimes are swift, thorough and transparent and that perpetrators are brought to justice. We can also learn important lessons from domestic violence and apply them equally to the arena of race and faith hate crime. In that way, neither Emmett nor Stephen nor Anthony will have died completely in vain.

Harald Salomon – A Swedish Pioneer

Kerstin Svensson, Senior Lecturer, School of Social Work, Lund University, Sweden

Probation in Sweden has a history almost as long as the British. Philanthropic organisations were created throughout the country around 1850 on royal demand. In the late 19th-century, the public interest in organising help for offenders grew parallel to organisations for poverty, for children in need and other social issues. In 1906, the first legislation towards probation came in to operation when conditional sentences became possible. In this first law there was no supervision, no demand for any contact or supervision ('Social Work in the Criminal Justice System. An Ambiguous Exercise of Caring Power', Svensson (2003) in *Journal of Scandinavian Studies in Criminology and Crime Prevention*, 4:2). The offender had to manage by himself and prove that he could behave well.

The American criminologist Jonathan Simon argues that this early period in probation is characterised by 'surety of good behaviour'. He points at its connection to industrialisation and new forms of social control; probation grew as a way to control and correct, with the overall aim to shape useful workers. Many criminologists have pointed at the connection between social development and how the criminal justice system is formed. Nevertheless, in forming it, there are different ways it can be constructed. While the state may put the responsibility on the offender, civil servants who can see the difficulties in the situation for the offender can use their discretion creatively and that way influence history. Even if we in a long historical perspective see structural similarities and patterns, individuals' actions make differences through to the present day and thereby shape how we later will regard history.

That is what the Swedish judge, Harald Salomon, did. It is his story which shapes this 'Moment'.

Harald Salomon was a judge in a municipal town court in the early 20th-century. His father was a psychiatrist and had started philanthropic organisations in the mid and late 19th-century, which had influenced his son. Harald Salomon was also influenced by impressions from frequent travel. In his work as a judge these two aspects joined in a creative way (Salomon, 1916, 1917, 1937).

In 1906 he had visited the United States and heard about probation and supervision. When he came back home to Sweden, a new law with a conditional sentence was in operation. When he started to use the new law in sentencing, Salomon lacked something. He had learned about pre-sentence reports and supervision, but here he had neither of these tools available.

Salomon started to write pre-sentence reports on his own initiative. He contacted the offenders and asked them about their life and social situation, he transcribed what was said and handed his notes to the court. He was, though, unsuccessful. Pre-sentence reports were prepared but the court did not use them, since the court was not required to pay them any attention. In 1910 a philanthropic organisation, 'Skyddsvärnet', was established which Harald Salomon became a member of, as his ideas were in the same spirit as the organisations' aim. One of his colleagues in the organisation told him that since the police had to take every aspect that comes to their knowledge into the case, if a pre-sentence report was given to the police, it had to be acknowledged. So, Salomon started working in that way. He asked offenders if they would like their story to be heard in court; if so, he wrote the report and handed it to the police. As time went by, pre-sentence reports became something that were used more and more frequently in courts. Parallel to that, Salomon and this organisation also arranged supervision of offenders, also, after a time, acknowledged in court.

Harald Salomon often spoke about and acted for the need for help for offenders. When the first Swedish law on probation was enacted in 1917, it showed that his work and thoughts had had a great influence. This law was characterised by human belief that punishment could lead to improvement. Through help, education and work offenders were to be changed into law-obeying citizens and workers. His work contributed to this thinking.

References

Salomon, Harald (1916) Den villkorliga domen och dess socialpolitiska betydelse. *Social tidskrift*, häfte 9. [Conditional sentence and its socio-political value]

Salomon, Harald (1917) *Redogörelse för villkorligt dömda som varit föremål för behandling av föreningen Skyddsvärnets centralbyrå i Stockholm under tiden oktober 1910-1915.* bilaga till Betänkande med förslag till lag angående villkorlig straffdom m.m.. Stockholm: PA Norstedts & söner. [Report on persons with conditional sentence that were the object for treatment by Skyddsvärnet in Stockholm during the period 1910–1915]

Salomon, Harald (1937) *Människovård i stället för fångvård.* Stockholm: Norstedts. [Human care instead of prison care]

Finding Probation Useful ... Eventually

Mark Leech, Editor, Prisons Handbook

I am not sure that I can remember the first time that I was put 'on probation' nor, lamentably, do I even recall at this distance the reason why; but in one guise or another 'probation' pretty much supervised my entire life between the ages of 15 and 35, and it was an interesting relationship to say the least. Probation officers came across as such nice people, always there to confide in and willing to help, but having once told a prison probation officer I was going on the prison roof in protest – only to find myself half an hour later tossed unceremoniously in the back of a van whose next and only stop was Dartmoor Prison as a result – it was a mistake of confidence I never made a second time.

I was released from prison on parole twelve years ago, 28th March 1995, and spent 12 months on probation. It was at the time a largely tame experience of having to report weekly (weakly?) to a probation officer who had more cases than she could adequately deal with and it was usual for me to be in and out of her office within five minutes. "How are things? ... is work ok? ... any problems at home? ... ok, see you next week ..." Looking back there was no real engagement between us, boxes had to be ticked, my file picked up from a pile on one side of her desk, scribbled in and dropped onto the 'done' pile on the other side of her desk before I was ushered out of the door and next client took my place.

After visiting the probation officer weekly for a month, in which time we spent less than half an hour together, I was placed on monthly reporting and it was all pretty much downhill from then until, 11 months later, the order was discharged and I was on my own. Looking back there was never any real 'work' being done during the sessions I spent with the probation officer; while everyone looked busy, in reality, the Service as a whole was only just managing to tread professional water. The questions asked were not designed to seek out vulnerabilities, rather they were designed instead solely to enable the ticking of the right boxes, scribbling the right words and dropping the file on the right pile which saw the Key Performance Indictors hit so everyone could go home, happy, job done.

And there my probation experience should have ended; regrettably, it did not ...

A decade later, having been out on the town with friends I came out of a nightclub at 3am, it was raining, the taxi queue was long and foolishly I got into my car and drove off. Two hundred yards down the road the blue flashing lights in the rear-view mirror sobered me up quickly but the night spent in the police station seemed to last forever – that foolish decision cost me a 12-month driving ban, a £1,000 fine, a 12-month supervision order and a 16-week drink impaired drivers course: if I expected my earlier experience of probation to be repeated I was in for a huge shock – probation had come a long way in the decade I had been away from it.

For one thing the weekly visits to see the probation officer bore no resemblance to my earlier experience; each visit lasted at least half an hour and was much more searching in its scrutiny. My probation officer still suffered from an overload of cases but I came away from each session with a feeling that something real had been achieved. The sessions asked how had I got into this situation – clearly my reasoning and planning skills had hit an all-time low if I could get into a car when twice over-the-limit and the sessions were designed to ensure I became reacquainted with the fact that decisions I made had consequences, both to me and to others, and I would either reap the rewards of my foresight or pay the price for my foolishness depending on what decision I chose to make.

The drink impaired drivers course stretched me considerably, and this was no token exercise. Each week for 16 weeks I spent two and a half hours doing hard work and, four months after starting it, I came away with a much better and clearer picture in terms of planning ahead and 'generating alternatives' – strangely, however, the course failed to take it that further step by insisting that having generated an alternative you should then select one of them! My knowledge of alcohol, learning to think in terms of alcohol units rather than the number of drinks, the dangers of getting into 'rounds', the effects of alcohol on the body and learning to recognise emotional pressures have all been important lessons which I continue to put into action daily.

The Probation Service has come forward a huge distance in the last ten years, the fusion of the Carter 'silos' three years ago and the creation of NOMS that came about as a result marks out what I believe will be an even better future – and one I sincerely hope I can watch develop from the vantage point of an observer rather than being once more the client.

Statement of National Objectives and Priorities (1984): A 'Watershed' in Probation Service Accountability?

Lol Burke, Senior Lecturer in Criminal Justice,
Liverpool John Moores University, UK

Like any new entrant to an organisation, one is faced in the Probation Service with a dazzling array of new language and acronyms to comprehend. In contemporary practice there is OASys, C-NOMIS, NOMS, etc., and so it was in the mid-1980s when I joined the Service. The talk at the time in the probation office tearoom where I worked was of SNOP and SLOP: The first referred to the Statement of National Objectives and Priorities and the latter to the Statement of Local Objectives and Priorities. If the former sounded vaguely disconcerting then the latter sounded positively unpleasant. I had heard that 'slopping out' was something that prisoners did after mealtimes but the thought of having to do this in polite company frankly filled me with dread and would ensure that I stayed away from the probation staffroom for as long as possible!

As its title suggests, SNOP was perhaps the first attempt to produce a coherent framework of provision from what was essentially 54 locally organised probation areas. With hindsight, as Mair (1997) states, the document looks fairly innocuous but at the time it was a source of considerable apprehension within the Probation Service. My new colleagues talked about this as being the 'thin end of the wedge' and the end of probation as we knew it. In order to fully appreciate these reactions one has to appreciate the political context in which it was introduced. The Thatcher Government which had come to office in 1979 had signalled a tougher approach to crime and stressed the rule of law over welfare considerations. It marked the end of the post-war political consensus that had enabled rehabilitation through casework and by *de facto* the Probation Service to flourish. Like subsequent policy documents, SNOP emphasised the function of the Probation Service within the wider criminal justice system rather than the needs of individual offenders.

The document also has to be seen within the context of the Government's desire to import what it viewed as good practice in terms of accountability, effectiveness, and value for money from the private into the public sector. It placed a responsibility on chief probation officers to ensure that the services they provided were cost efficient. It outlined the main duties of the Probation Service as: the provision of advice to courts; the supervision of offenders in the community subject to probation, supervision and community service orders; the provision of welfare services to offenders in custody; and the after-care of offenders released from custody including the supervision of those on licence. In doing so, it set the parameters for the introduction of performance indicators so favoured by successive administrations since.

Raynor claims that possibly the most adventurous proposal was the suggestion that the Probation Service should become 'much more involved in the community and in promoting constructive community concern about crime' (1984: 44). Though SNOP appears somewhat vague in defining what forms this work would take, its intention reflects the crime reduction agenda which has dominated contemporary law and order discourses since. Yet perhaps an equally important driver for change was the fact that the use of imprisonment had continued to rise throughout the 1970s, placing a burden on public expenditure which coincided with a period of ongoing economic instability. As such, the underlying rationale of SNOP was diversionary through the provision of alternatives to custody. It de-prioritised after-care work with released prisoners except where such work was consistent with the main objective of implementing non-custodial measures for offenders who might otherwise receive custodial sentences. In the probation area where I worked, for example, we were told that officers could hold no more than 10% of after-care cases as part of their workload. Once this magical figure had been reached, help was to be refused regardless of need (although in practice many probation officers continued to oversee such cases on a 'voluntary' basis).

Today the language of SNOP seems somewhat tentative in that it 'hoped' Probation Committees (as was) and chief probation officers would take into account the objectives and priorities in developing local area plans and indeed a study by Lloyd (1986) found considerable diversity in the responses to SNOP amongst probation areas. My employing area at the time refused to prioritise its work on the grounds that it viewed all of its tasks as of equal importance! There is no doubt that SNOP was a radical document for the time and led to an era of increasing centralization, control and, ultimately, the politicalisation of the direction which the Probation Service would ultimately be required to take. It was to pave the way for a flood of legislation aimed at *'toughening up'* the image of the Probation Service as a deliverer of 'punishment in the community'. In this respect, it was merely the start rather than the culmination of a journey.

The Bill McWilliams Quartet

Dr Philip Whitehead, Senior Lecturer in Criminology, University of Teesside, UK

I cannot claim to have known Bill McWilliams or even to have met him. However our paths did cross when we had a telephone conversation in 1991/92. He had agreed to write the first chapter in a book on management issues in probation which, at the time, I was editing with Roger Statham. Of course, his chapter on the history of management thought was not the first or only contribution he made to probation theory and practice. On the contrary; he had been involved in researching and writing about probation matters for some time, he knew the Service well from the inside from his work as a probation officer. He was involved in researching the IMPACT experiment during the 1970s at a time when the rehabilitative ideal was under threat. By 1979, and against the background of the IMPACT findings, he contributed to a reworking of the rationale of probation with Tony Bottoms in the non-treatment paradigm.

Nevertheless, when I think about the work of Dr McWilliams I am drawn to his quartet of essays prepared for the Howard Journal published in 1983, 1985, 1986 and 1987. It is possible to approach probation from different historical perspectives; in fact, to do history in a variety of ways. The approach of Bill McWilliams was to explore the different ways in which the probation system had understood itself between 1876 and when he was undertaking this piece of work in the 1980s.

In the first paper of the quartet he explores the period 1876–1936, beginning with the missionary period and concluding with the third departmental committee report. According to this first paper the rationale of the police court missionaries was saving offenders' souls by divine grace. Consequently, the religious beginnings of the system are emphasised during a period when evangelical theology was a salient theme within Victorian Britain. However, by the 1930s, a theological understanding was slowly giving way to a more secular and scientific understanding; from religious amateurs to a greater emphasis on training and professionalism; from salvation via grace, through faith, to the modification of minds and behaviours through human intervention.

The 1930s–60s, the period covered by the second paper, brings into view a set of ideas associated with scientific endeavour, the medical model, and treatment. In fact, this was the period which saw the transition from understanding the offender within a framework of evangelical theology to offending behaviour as a manifestation of a psycho-social disease which was amenable to expert scientific assessment, diagnosis, intervention and cure, via what was referred to as a 'casework relationship'. By this time the initial missionary spirit was being attenuated, yet religion was to remain influential in the organisation for many decades to come.

The third paper looks in greater detail at the diagnostic ideal. He continues to analyse the shifts which were occurring in the Service and devotes much more space to explaining casework methodology, beginning with the Charity Organisation Society founded in 1869 as the forerunner of social work practice. In fact the acme of casework can be traced to the 1960s, which was endorsed by the fourth and last departmental committee of 1962.

The fourth and last paper in 1987 begins with a helpful summary of the first three. Moreover, he continues to analyse the transformations which were occurring in the organisation and argues that, by the 1980s, there were three main ideologies underpinning practice: personalism; a radical-Marxist approach; and rapidly emerging managerialism. McWilliams states that all three locate the offender within a framework of policy and that they were united in pursuing alternatives to custody (a politically supported goal which persisted until 1993).

For those interested in delving into and understanding the history of probation from the standpoint of underpinning and sustaining ideas, the McWilliams quartet is an invaluable resource. Since this body of work was completed in 1987, a period of profound and sustained disruption has enveloped probation work, particularly since 1997 in the name of modernisation. Where his 1987 tripartite typology is concerned it can be suggested that isolated pockets of personalism remain; radicalism has had its day; and the notion of managing the Service has given way to bureaucratic systems and processes.

Social Skills and Personal Problem Solving:
A Personal Review

Philip Priestley, Author of 'ONE-TO-ONE' Accredited Programme

I nearly never met James McGuire in 1974. His train to Glasgow was late and I was about to leave when he did arrive. I offered him a job on a project training prison officers to run Release Courses in Ranby and Ashwell prisons. Along with other project staff we developed packages that addressed pressing ex-prisoner needs like accommodation, employment, budgeting, and personal relations; a curriculum which at that time was coming to be called 'life skills'. (The materials were also used in the Sheffield Day Training Centre, but that is another story.)

We were greatly influenced in this work by a manual we came across written by Canadian psychologist Stuart Conger for use in the Saskatchewan New Start programme – targeting indigenous youth with educational and other disadvantages to help them into employment. He used self-auditing of 'saleable skills', problem-solving methods, and behavioural rehearsal.

'The Prison Project' – as we called it – was a most engaging experience, working with prison officers whose collective intelligence, integrity, and adaptability was a revelation to those of us with probation and psychology backgrounds. It demonstrated convincingly what existing prison staff could do when given the time, the training, and the materials for working creatively and constructively with prisoners.

In the end, despite impressive completion rates, and many reports of successful transitions to the community using the procedures learned in the Release Courses, the reconviction rates showed only slight improvements over those of men released from the same prisons at the same time without the benefit of the courses. The project came to an end, the programmes lingered on in prisons for a while, and then disappeared into history.

From our point of view, the project had two positive legacies. One was the insight that if you want to reduce offending behaviour maybe it is a good idea to address that topic directly, rather than only obliquely through all the other factors associated with re-offending. Furthermore, and more directly, we had approached the legendary Gill Davies, then publisher of the Tavistock list at Methuen, with a proposal for a book that would report the outcomes of the Prison Project. We enthused about the work of the prison officers and the methods they had used. That, she said, was the book she wanted – not the research, but a how-to-do-it guide to what the staff had actually done.

And that was the book we gave her – entitled *Social Skills and Personal Problem Solving* (Tavistock: 1978). It was a handbook of methods. It presented a problem-solving framework for addressing a wide range of problems in social work, education, mental health, and criminal justice; provided concrete examples of assessment methods, ways of setting goals, skills – including social skills – with which to achieve them, and evaluation, checking up on the results; all conceived as a cycle which fed back into its own earlier stages to maintain progress towards personal targets.

The book found favour with a wide readership; it was re-printed many times, and total sales reached around 30,000 units. James and I also spent many years training thousands of staff in many kinds of agencies in the use of the approach – including at least half of all probation officers in the 1970s and 1980s. With hindsight, we had written a cognitive-behavioural book before the words came into general use.

When authors revisit earlier work it is sometimes an occasion to reflect on the temporality of what they have written; many books end up as examples of preserved journalism, dealing with issues and ideas that are no longer with us. However, I believe that the principles of *Social Skills and Personal Problem Solving* have stood the test of time better than that. We would not write the same book now and lots of its detail would be different, but I still think that its rational structure and the spirit of respect, voluntarism, and empowerment it embodies remain relevant messages for the conduct of work with troubled people in the 21st-century.

Experiencing the DipPS

Jo Cox, Probation Officer/Deputy Manager, Town Moor Approved Premises, Doncaster (South Yorkshire Probation Area), UK

I had worked for the Probation Service since 1989 as an 'unqualified' probation service officer. When I made the decision to apply for the DipPs training in 2000, I thought that I had *done* and seen it all in terms of working with offenders. I was 'well-prepared' to make the progressive move onto professional training. I would sail through it – or so I thought! On reflection, nothing and no-one could have prepared me for the following two years of the intensive training programme that I was about to 'embrace'.

I have witnessed many changes during my time in Probation (South Yorkshire); some good, some not so good, but all that could be learned from. The Probation Service has come a long way from the 1984 Probation Rules and the duty of a probation officer to 'advise, assist and befriend' which existed when I first joined the Service. My experience, not only as a trainee probation officer but as a long standing employee of the Probation Service generally has taught me that change is essential within the 'survival process' (and tactics for survival are essential within the ever-changing processes). The term 'treading water' was how I might now describe how I felt at times as a trainee on the DipPS.

This article will focus on my experience as I commenced the DipPS, in particular, as a former PSO. I recall feeling confident, experienced and comfortable in my abilities as a PSO. My confidence took a battering when I learnt that for several months as a trainee I would become a mere 'observer' of practice. I really struggled with this and pleaded with my PDA for several months until she gave in and *allowed* me to become a 'practitioner' before I was really supposed to. Although, I can now reflect and recognise the need for me to take my practice back to the very basics, I felt, at the time, that this course of action did not necessarily help me as a former PSO. I missed that 'client' contact that I was used to and felt de-skilled and de-valued as a result. Once I began to engage in intervention it took some time for me to feel confident in my abilities, despite my extensive experience and transferable skills working with such a client group as a PSO.

Another blow to my confidence at the start of the course was the academic part. I was conscious of the fact that the majority of those starting the course from outside of the Probation Service had either come straight from university or already had attained a qualification at degree level. The handful of former employees of the Probation Service tended not to have the same academic experience and I was 'one of them'. There seemed, to me, to be so much emphasis placed by lecturers on previous degree attainment and a general assumption that we, the whole group, had experienced this route onto the DipPs training. I was in the minority group of those who had much relevant work experience but limited academic knowledge. I felt oppressed. It was a daunting experience for me to be faced by those whom I perceived were much more powerful than I through education alone. I have used this experience positively to frame my own practice in acknowledging and presenting an empathic approach to oppression and discrimination whilst intervening in the process of promoting positive change amongst offenders – good solid grounding for the Approved Premises (hostels) interventions that I am currently working in!

Over recent years there has been a vast growth in agency guidelines, procedures, practice instructions and policies. Although the organisation with its current 'business-like' approach places limits and constraints on the work of probation officers (perhaps now more than ever!), I remind myself that I *still* have a degree of autonomy in the interventions that I deliver. Handy (1999) writes 'supportive styles of leadership were found to be associated with higher-productive work groups'; I am extremely grateful to those managers whose leadership styles have reflected participative and democratic principles, particularly in my times as a trainee and subsequently as a newly-appointed PO. There is no doubt in my mind that the support that I received – in particular from the DipPS course leader and from my PDA – impacted positively on my learning experience. Their encouragement and support gave me the confidence to continue with the training at times when I felt like I was sinking fast. I have now been 'qualified' for six years and am Deputy Manager of a Probation Approved Premises. I am a bit of a 'rottweiler' at times when I feel the need to fight for my rights or those of others with whom I work – DipPS course leaders, tutors, PDAs and probation seniors – you did a good job!

Thank you.

Probation: A Personal Perspective

Peter Astle, ex-Offender

Most people take risks and make mistakes, but very few people end up on probation. In the late 90s I took a risk, committed a driving offence and was given an 18-month probation order by the courts. I was young, gung-ho and thought the sentence was probably appropriate to the crime but, at the same time, I thought it was a bit of a let-off.

The crime, by the way, was driving whilst disqualified. I had already lost my licence but chose to continue to drive. Following an accident, I was eventually placed in the dock.

The order given to me meant that I had to attend weekly meetings with an appointed probation officer and also attend group sessions in order to discuss offending behaviour with specific respect to driving offences.

Overall, it was not a fun experience; it was inconveniencing and sometimes highly condescending. I stood my corner in the debates and to some degree enjoyed the rhetoric of groupwork but, as the sessions stretched on, week by week, I did begin to see the value of their intention.

The punitive aspect to the probation order was made clear. Attendance was paramount. Unless we were present at the one-to-one meetings and groupwork sessions, we would be in breach of our probation order and potentially marched back to court.

Fortunately, I had an excellent officer. She was mature, astute and able to differentiate, taking into account my own personal background and experiences. She picked up nuances and recognised where I wanted to go rather than where I had come from. She did not judge me as an offender and did not harp on about my particular crime, but was refreshingly constructive and determined to move things forward. She spoke with me about my current situation, my aspirations to teach and gave sound advice as to how I might achieve my goals. We even had a laugh or two now and again.

On the downside, the sessions became a bind as the months continued because there was less and less to say. It became a signing-on session. There was very little advice left for her to give that had not already been given. Despite this, it was good to feel supported in the closing stages.

I thought that the groupwork sessions were somewhat patronising, but they did at least try to offer a supportive environment and provide a broad overview of the consequences of a variety of driving offences. They involved probation and police officers and offenders getting together to discuss the impact of driving offences and there was a lot of drinking tea from paper cups and sitting around in circles.

There was at times antipathy from some members of the group, including me – particularly when the traffic police showed their shock tactic blood and gore videos of roadcrash accidents and implied that all present were potentially killers – but, overall, the group-work sessions were sociable affairs and constructive in that there was an ostensible attempt to help us to learn from our mistakes.

We bonded with other risk-takers, criminals and mistake-makers and were given the opportunity to share our experiences in an open forum, which was sometimes cathartic and occasionally thought-provoking, despite the fact that we all came from different backgrounds. Most of us agreed that the decisions we had made, which led us to where we were, were bad ones.

At the same time, most of us in the group were fighting against the pious position of the probation officers who chaired the group. There was a sense that some of the probation officers and some of the police officers did have the tendency to treat the group, as a whole, like naughty children who needed to be taught a lesson, rather than as a group of rational adults. This seemingly endemic aspect to groupwork was difficult for me to accept at the time and I can only hope that practices have improved since then and that now group co-ordinators, or leaders, communicate more effectively and evenly with offenders in their working environment.

The groupwork sessions were viewed by most offenders as a necessary evil and a means to avoid a breach of the probation order. There was perhaps some positive value to them, but I felt that this value was lost to the majority in the same way that good lessons taught by the best teachers and the best lecturers throughout the country are lost on some students.

The weekly one-to-one sessions with my probation officer were, on the whole, useful in terms of motivation and reflection; my probation officer was supportive and was able to suggest ideas that would potentially enhance my future. These sessions were infinitely more valuable than groupwork because there was an opportunity for me to discuss things on a personal level and to take advice on appertaining issues.

I have come a long way from my time on probation and am now head of media in Further Education. I've never re-offended but still take risks and make mistakes of different kinds.

The NOMS Offender Management Model: A Radical Moment in Correctional Practice?

Susan Parkinson, Senior Lecturer,
Sheffield Hallam University, Sheffield, UK

In the late 1990s, the evidence-based practice agenda was introduced as a fairly credible initiative, which would effectively reduce offending. Based originally upon the three principles of 'risk, need and responsivity', this agenda seemed to make sense; the likelihood of a behaviour occurring together with the probable gravity of that behaviour, may be predicted, managed and reduced through assessment and intervention. This intervention, based upon offenders' criminogenic needs and their active participation in the change process, would lead to their eventual re-integration into the community.

With the development of risk technology and the introduction of its artefacts, such as the Offender Assessment System (OASys), this important assessment and intervention process appears to have been reduced to a fixation on formulating lists of offence-related factors and linking them, as far as possible, to group or individual cognitive behavioural programmes. The adoption of these 'technicist' working processes has seemed to limit the opportunity for probation staff to develop and use their expert knowledge around specific offence types and specific offenders, to formulate continuous assessments based upon the unique interplay of both static and dynamic risk factors and to deliver related interventions that genuinely engage the offender in becoming safe. Inspection and evaluation reports appear to bolster this supposition that probation staff are harnessed by managerialist interpretations of 'what works' to reduce offending.

In a thematic inspection of the Offender Assessment System (*Realising the Potential* (2005: HMIP)), staff highlighted that offenders rarely participated jointly in the production of sentence plans and that meaningful engagement with offenders was aggravated by the complex coding and user 'unfriendliness' of OASys, which reduced staff perceptions of the sentence planning process to a bureaucratic chore. One of the main overall findings of the inspection was that sentence plan formats were not relevant to the needs of offenders.

An Effective Supervision Inspection ('An Essential Element of Effective Practice' 2005. HMIP) found that more than half of the cases did not have an adequate assessment of accommodation issues and that insufficient time was allocated to senior managers to enable them to effectively engage with the Supporting People agenda (a government policy to address social inclusion, diversity and equality).

A recent evaluation of a Prolific and Priority Offenders Scheme (HCCJ, 2007) found that securing accommodation and accommodation advice were the most common problems reported by both offenders and their probation officers.

The revised version of the Offender Management Model, which began its roll-out in 2006, is said to be informed by 'new evidence and new learning' (Christine Knott, NOMS). As such, the NOMS Offender Management Model 2006 has, at its core, the ideas of an 'evidence-based, offender focused approach' and the development of 'personal relationships' with an offender. The 'new evidence' includes the recurring findings from the 'desistance' research which suggest that correctional practice must be tailored to each individual offender; that problem definition and supervision planning should be a participative endeavour; that assessment and intervention practices need to be reflexive and research-based and include 'pro-desistance factors' which focus on the identification and development of 'social' as well as 'individual' capital.

Critical accounts of the New Labour Third Way project, which illuminate how the discourse of social inclusion and exclusion acts as a subterfuge for the real experiences of social and economic power and inequality, throw into question the extent to which the development of offender social capital is achievable through the implementation of the National Offender Model. Dee Cook (2006) reminds us of the Social Exclusion Unit's strategy (2002) to reduce re-offending by ex-prisoners, through a programme aimed at developing their social capital, failed to be implemented. Bill Jordan (2006) presents the stark message from survey evidence that "Social Inclusion and empowerment have not been achieved by Third Way programmes". As such, attempts at offender-centred practices risk being foiled when implemented in an existing political and cultural context that seeks to manage – rather than eradicate – social exclusion.

A crucial moment in correctional practice will be when NOMS moves beyond the implementation of pragmatic responses to New Labour's policy claims and forges a political, as well as a professional, venture to challenge such rhetoric. An insistence upon a much more candid dialogue with the Government, which takes account of all aspects from the evidence base of effective practice with offenders (including that which acknowledges the entrenched social and economic disadvantage of the majority of offenders and the need for structural and ideological change), will mark the end of ineffective answers on how to deal with socially excluded 'problem' people. It will represent the beginning of a new principled and radical direction for working with those people who offend.

Probation in the 60s

Mike Worthington, Former Probation Officer

I trained as a probation officer between 1963 and 1966, first at Liverpool University and then the Home Office Training Course at Rainer House. The academic diet was Biesteck, Barbara Wootton, Florence Hollis, John Bowlby and, being at Liverpool, Penelope Hall and John Barron Mays. I started work in the Bolton County team, in the Lancashire South East Probation Area, on June 6th 1966 and for the next five years, my patch was the small, industrial, working class town of Farnworth – birthplace of Alan Ball and Frank Finlay. On my first day at work, I was handed a reduced caseload of 42 – 'difficult' cases and 'deadwood' having been weeded out. I eventually took responsibility for the adjacent small towns of Kearsley and Little Lever and, over the five years, my caseload averaged about 80 and I was reponsible for the preparation of over 100 social enquiry reports for the court each year. As an officer of the court, there were also a range of other statutory and non-statutory duties to perform – court duty, office duty, escort duties, serving the Domestic Court, etc.

A typical working week included two court duties – one in a Magistrates' court, one in a Juvenile court – two half-day office duties (daily office duty was 9.30–12.30, 2.00–5.00 and 5.30–7.30), two evening report centres, home visiting at least one afternoon and one evening, appointments at the office for social enquiry reports, approved school, detention centre, Borstal, remand centre and prison visits as necessary, plus supervision, meetings, records and administration. The week also included monthly court duty and office duty on a Saturday morning!

I was the sole probation officer in Farnworth (apart from my female colleague – who dealt with all females in the county area – male officers not being allowed to supervise female clients or prepare reports on female offenders) and, over five years, came to know my patch intimately. Without any 'partnership' planning, I developed strong links and good relationships with the local police station, social services office, schools, education welfare, youth clubs, employers, Labour Exchange, National Assistance Board, health visitors (always the best source of information!), voluntary, private and public sector accommodation providers, etc., etc.

I could also call on the skills and commitment provided by our Bolton volunteers, who could often 'reach the parts that professionals couldn't reach'.

As an officer of the court, central to my role were the relationships I established with the Magistrates and court staff. This was crucial in sustaining and developing both the credibility of the Service and my personal credibility, so that reports I prepared for court were received and read with confidence and recommendations I made were respected. I then had to report on my work at regular intervals to the Probation Case Committee, comprised of Magistrates acting on behalf of the Probation Committee, our employer.

Work undertaken with clients, as they were unquestioningly known, was centred on the duty, enshrined in the Probation Order, to 'advise, assist and befriend'. Qualifying training had taught me to 'start where the client is'. This involved gaining trust and attempting to understand the causes of an individual's offending behaviour and to do the best I could to address these causes. Often, there were a range of practical problems – accommodation, finance, employment, health, family relationships, leisure time activities – the list is familiar, I'm sure. A range of resources were developed through knowledge of the patch and consequently, many practical problems could be resolved quickly. More specialist help was available locally in the area, and sometimes nationally, to call on with more difficult and complex cases. I recognised that change for many of my clients was a slow and often painful process and through experience, I learnt to 'stay with' people. Breaching someone was a last resort – an action taken only when absolutely necessary.

I am not holding up probation in the 60s as the golden age. The climate in which we worked was different from today, more tolerant and understanding. The 'caseload', although high in numbers, did include many who could hardly be called heavy-end offenders – and many were juveniles. However, I do believe that the particular relationship we had with the courts, that knowledge and understanding we had of the communities in which our clients lived, that intimate knowledge of their homes and families, that natural recognition of the value of working with others and using the resources available to us, the value placed on the role volunteers can play, that person-centred approach to our work with clients – offenders – that willingness to go the extra mile, still represents the best of probation practice and made us the envy of the world.

The Good Society?

Bruce Hugman, PO and SPO, SYPACS during
1970s, currently Medical Communications Writer and
Consultant, based in Thailand

Two reports in my expatriate's *Guardian Weekly* have recently stunned me: first, that the UK is virtually at the bottom of the list of EU countries in terms of its children's quality of life in almost all respects; second, that 'slavery is widespread' in parts of the economy. While I am often incredulous at what I read about the state of the UK, these two damning accounts particularly impressed me.

It is often the case that a single piece of evidence will give you massive insight into larger matters (like the state of the toilets telling you almost all you need to know about an organisation or a hotel; the size of the prison population revealing a great deal about a country's vision of justice and social harmony). I wonder what we can learn from these two assessments of the neglect of our children and the enslavement of the vulnerable? And how do such facts relate to the state of criminal justice and society as a whole?

I see most of the problems arising from the lack of vision and the tyranny of short-termism in every aspect of government, welfare and commerce. Every problem requires an immediate macho response which satisfies the clamour of weak minds for instant solutions, without reference to any larger set of principles or long-term vision. It is exemplified in commerce: the increasing activities of private equity groups are driven by the urge for rapid, massive financial returns without regard to the history, integrity, purpose or future of the enterprises assimilated (listed companies have been no less greedy for high, short-term returns, but private equity is a new mechanism to accelerate the process). It is exemplified in public services: healthcare and public transport (two of the key elements in a free, open and just society) are reduced to commodities, subject to market forces as much as potatoes or steel, without regard to issues of access, equity or vision of their place in the good society.

So, inevitably with criminal justice: what is the radical, long-term vision behind the sweeping of increasing numbers of people into the dark cul-de-sac of prison? What is the radical, long-term vision behind increasing violation of privacy and the universal presence of CCTV cameras? Well, we know: there's no long-term vision – it is all to do with seeming active and macho to disguise utter emptiness in understanding of the vast and complex labyrinth of causes. It does not take much imagination to see that a country, whose children get such a raw deal, and whose citizens manage and tolerate slavery, is in a moral swamp beyond remedy with spoons and buckets. And, of course, it's not just a lack of understanding of causes, it's a complete lack of interest in even thinking about them.

I am now too far removed from the day-to-day life of criminal justice and probation in the UK to be clear what long-term vision – if any – might be lurking in the system or the Service, but I fear much of what happens is probably driven by political expediency and short-term political advantage, however passionate and visionary some (or many) of the individual participants may be.

A couple of years ago in Thailand, the pre-coup government trumpeted a crack-down on drug supply and use. Within a few weeks, more than two thousand citizens lay dead, mostly shot by zealous law enforcers following the enlightened leadership of the time. Of course, the massacre had next to no impact on drug supply and use, not least because we all know that drug supply is a many-headed Hydra which cannot simply be decapitated, and because large numbers of the victims had no proven association with drugs anyway.

Much social so-called policy round the world seems to be driven by a similar urge for extermination, or at least for impenetrable camouflage. It's very unlikely that the UK's children or its secret population of slaves will be well-served by such visionary strategy, or that the disturbing, multi-faceted phenomenon of crime will ever be understood or resolved by it.

Regional Staff Development (RSD)

Gordon Read, former RSDO Midland Region (1976–1981), CPO for Devon Probation (1981–1996) and Chair of ACOP (1990–1991)

In 1968 when May Irving was head of the training arm of the Probation Inspectorate (HMIP), the appointment of four Regional Training Officers (RTOs), initially for three years, formalised an inspired innovation in Probation, even though it took until September 1969 before all four were actually in post. Influenced by their different cultures and geography and the individuality of RTOs themselves (re-designated RSDOs in 1972), the four regions were located in the North (North East and North West England with North Wales); the Midlands; the South West (including Central and South Wales); and the South East (including Greater London). By 1995, only one – already re-designated as the Midlands Probation Training Consortium – remained. The reduction of the original proposal for eight such regions had resulted in entities too large and dispersed for effective management of the co-operation required. However, the germ of the idea survived in the nine post-1997 Regional Consortia for recruitment, selection and training along with a co-ordination mechanism RSD had lacked.

Arriving at the time of changes leading to the establishment of the Central Council for Education and Training in Social Work (CCETSW), RSD worked to enhance the training of probation officers with one year's training behind them. It may also have represented a muted flowering of an earlier aspiration for a probation college. At the three-year point, assistant RSDOs were appointed to help with increased numbers of staff and courses as well as the training responsibilities that CCETSW had requested RSDOs should undertake nationally for Direct Entrants (DEs), i.e. unqualified recruits. Various pressures, including RSDO concern that trainees would remain disadvantageously unqualified, led to the abandonment of DE appointments in 1974. By this time the RSDOs were beginning to apply their 'national' approach to the induction of the burgeoning numbers of senior probation officers. In this respect they were ideally placed because of their strong links with CCETSW, Higher and Further Education, NHS and Prison Service trainers, the National Marriage Guidance Council, management and group relations consultants and also inspired practitioners and managers from within probation areas.

Roy Taylor, a former Chief Inspector of Probation, suggests one of RSD's strengths was in working with the same sort of creative tension between conflicting interests as probation officers themselves. This would have been heightened by the fact that, in part, RSDOs operated in a competitive market place for staff development provision. That brought an additional pressure from what Malcolm Lacey, a former RSDO and Chief Probation Officer (CPO), describes as 'a tension between the requirements of policy driven skills and personal [professional] development'. Brought up to date that might be construed as a tension between developing a professional ethos (i.e. ethical or moral) and coping with an instrumental managerialism designed to constrain the discretion required when dealing with complex social and behavioural problems.

RSD also became a useful mechanism for co-ordinating and expanding approaches to new responsibilities like community service and day centres as well as hostel management, sexual offending and – in family court welfare – mediation and conciliation. Often this was undertaken on a workshop basis, or through regular monthly forums, allowing staff of all grades to develop a real authority when exchanging ideas and skills. In one region ventures were also made in international relations, an example being training exchanges with Poland. All this demonstrates that ,in spite of being difficult to manage, RSD was not only innovative but also eminently flexible and adaptable. It had a structure through which it could have been managed; however, CPOs and area committee representatives failed to capitalise on it. This was a missed opportunity. It could have provided the basis for a more formalised structure for the developing co-operation between area Probation Services already extending into research, measurement, the piloting of innovation and commissioning. The Probation Service, essentially community-based, might then have been less vulnerable to absorption within a heavily managerialised, centrally driven and unwieldy Corrections Service as well as subject to the potential chaos of contestability.

Expletive Almost Deleted:
A Moment About Bad Language

Mike Denton, National Probation Service
(HMYOI Thorn Cross), Cheshire Probation Area, UK

I was walking from the admin block to my office. Passing the entrance to the Health Care Centre, I heard a verbal altercation between a member of the HCC staff and a trainee of around 18 years of age:

"I've told you, you can't see the nurse just now."

"You're so f***ing unhelpful."

"Right! I'm putting you on report!"

"Do what you f***ing like."

This high-level exchange registered with me, as did another comment – made not quite at the same volume, and probably for my benefit – by the young man in question as he fell in behind me:

"F***ing slag!"

I stopped and gave him a look (the one that has been described as 'fierce'), and asked him:

"If the word f***ing didn't exist in the English language, do you think you would be able to hold a proper conversation?"

His reply was:

"Course I would!"

While I was at that moment almost prepared to believe him, he then spoiled it by adding:

"Don't you f***ing start!"

Well, that's one for the book of memories, which working in Probation has contributed to in no small measure. It made me think about how we use language, especially in the context of pro-social modelling.

Recently, I heard a prison officer talking to one of the trainees, who politely but jokingly had asked the officer for a cigarette. The officer responded in similar joking vein, but his reply to the request was littered with what we refer to as 'foul language'. Why? I know this man, and respect him for the way he carries out his job and I have not heard him swear in any of the conversations we have had, so the way he chose to speak to the young man surprised me.

Likewise, another member of staff, in dealing with an application for HDC, suddenly lost his usual articulateness and resorted to a string of expletives to reinforce the point he was making (which was actually about the importance of keeping probation appointments. Very laudable!). Again, why do people feel the need to resort to the use of expletives?

I do not know the answer to this, but could speculate that both people felt that that was the way to ensure they were understood. Maybe using language that young men in custody normally use is the key to communicating with them? I don't think so! Maybe the staff in question felt that this was the way to assert their authority? Possibly.

I have heard the equivalent of a verbal game of tennis on a few occasions. That's where two people seem to test the water in a conversation, starting it without a single swear word, but then subtly dropping one into the exchange. If the service is returned with a corresponding word, the game often descends into an attritional base-line rally, with the 'hits' becoming ever stronger. I don't know how this one is won or lost.

By now, I bet there are a few people thinking, 'So what? It's just words. They don't mean anything.'

Well, if it is 'just words', and the implication is that they do not signify anything much, then why use them? I also bet that most people neither resort to bad language in normal conversation, nor would want their children, partners, or families to hear them do so; furthermore, they would also really rather that young people didn't feel they had to use foul language either. So, what effect on young people does the use of foul language have, when used by those older and supposedly wiser than them? What does it tell them about us? Do we think its use is without consequence? Either we believe in pro-social modelling or we don't. I think I would quite enjoy listening to people trying to rationalise why using bad language is a better way of communicating.

Good grief! Did I really write that? Talk about f***ing over-intellectualising!

Key Influences: Hilary Walker and Bill Beaumont

Michael Teague, Senior Lecturer in Criminology,
University of Teesside, UK

When I made the choice to become a probation practitioner in the 1980s, I was not inspired by the thought of successfully achieving an endless list of key performance indicators. Nor did I passionately conclude that if only I was more outcome-focused, I might more effectively accomplish my targets. I was certainly not eagerly anticipating the privatisation of probation (or should I be using that more anodyne term *'contestability'*?) in order to achieve efficiency gains. With the absurd optimism of youth, what I was inspired by was the thought of helping people to change. I aimed to change not individual cognitions, nor particular behaviours, but to transform lives.

This (as it now seems) preposterously idealistic notion was heavily influenced by the work of Hillary Walker and Bill Beaumont. Their fluent and sustained socialist analysis of the Probation Service and its relationship to the wider social system explored how the Service (directly or indirectly) pressured clients to conform and acknowledge the legitimacy of authority.

I was not alone. Walker and Beaumont's seminal text *Probation Work: Critical Theory and Socialist Practice* (1981) exerted a substantial impact on many contemporary practitioners. Four years later, a companion volume edited by the same authors, *Working with Offenders*, shared the earlier book's theoretical standpoint but employed a sharper, empirical focus. All the contributors were experienced probation staff, able to integrate socialist theory with daily practice experience well. Quaint as it may sound today, the book was even published as part of the *Practical Social Work* series.

Walker and Beaumont rejected the individualisation of social problems. They were not convinced by explanations of offending which were rooted in the cognitions of individuals. As the introductory chapter declaimed, they did not accept:

> " ... the first assumption of the official account, a consensus view of society – we see society as riddled with inequality and injustice based on real, deep and enduring differences and conflicts of interests."

Rather than criminalising vulnerable individuals, thereby distracting attention from broader structural issues of poverty, economics, and discrimination, they emphasised the need to attend to those structural issues in work with clients. They acknowledged that the oppressive impact of social pressures might contribute towards propelling individuals towards offending.

Beaumont argued for a wide-ranging and unswerving commitment to social change by probation staff, while Walker's pioneering critique of probation practice from a feminist perspective anticipated current methods of anti-sexist practice. Paul Senior's account of groupwork intervention's potential for developing socialist probation practice was also ground-breaking. Other practitioners contributed radical analyses of court work, supervision, prison work and day centres.

Walker and Beaumont emphasised the unequal power imbalance which characterised the relationship between probation staff and their clients. They envisioned this power imbalance reflected in the dynamics of class, race and gender. While the theoretical context was central, what ultimately resonated with novice practitioners was their profound grasp of daily lived realities for clients. Their philosophical and ethical context for probation both demanded social justice and made sense for practitioners. Heretical as it may now seem in our target and compliance driven culture, attention was paid to exercising caution when considering breach; stressing the importance of welfare rights; and emphasising the value of community involvement and active campaigning.

Nowadays, the 'What Works' agenda defines the principles governing effective probation practice. A rigorous process of scrutiny led by the Correctional Services Accreditation Panel (whose members include a psychologist based in Sacramento and a professor of psychiatry from the University of Tennessee) ensures that we are swamped with evidence from meta-analytical studies to confirm which interventions might generate statistically significant reductions in re-offending. In the context of this brave new professionalism, radical socialist meditations on probation practice seem to possess the air of deeply outmoded and thoroughly unscientific ways of thought, not dissimilar to believing that the earth is flat.

Some twenty years after the publication of these seminal texts, I ran into one half of this dynamic duo of authors, Bill Beaumont. By then, I was no longer a novice probation worker and had deserted the coal face of front line practice, to seek refuge in the cosseted safety of academia. Old socialists with a probation background never die, it seems. They just go and work in a university. Bill was external examiner for the probation training course on which I was then lecturing. He teaches on a social work programme now.

References

Walker, H. and Beaumont, B. (1981). *Probation Work: Critical Theory and Socialist Practice*. Oxford, Blackwell.

Walker, H. and Beaumont, B. (ed.) (1985). *Working with Offenders*. London: BASW/Macmillan.

CSAP: *The Correctional Services Accreditation Panel Report 2005–2006*. (2006) London: NOMS.

My Moments from the 1970s

Andrew Bridges, HM Chief Inspector of Probation, UK

1972: It's my last year at university, and I'm thinking: "What about the Probation Service?" To enquire I visit the local Probation Office (York) and the bluff SPO there has two important pieces of advice: 1) "Wear a suit for the interview", and 2) "you get paid the same in Torquay as you do in Bradford". Perhaps because the Home Office is trying to encourage graduates into the Service I get in despite not wearing a suit …

1973: On the two-year Diploma in Social Work course at the University of Leicester, we are lectured by the already-venerable Mark Monger. He describes in graphic detail a horrendous crisis he had had to deal with on office duty years previously in his first ever week as a student, then looks up and tells us all that with all his subsequent study and experience he still doesn't know now what he should have done then.

1974: Lively debates, mostly ideological. Many argue that probation officers cannot do both care and control, and should not 'become screws on wheels'. Also it is the radical position to argue against the use of the term 'client' because it is inaccurate and patronising – years later, the radical position becomes to insist on retaining 'clients'.

1975: The work is varied. My last student placement task is a Divorce Court Welfare case where both parents have new partners, and both want custody of all four children, and the case eventually goes to a 3-day contested hearing. One of my first pieces of work is an Application for Consent to Marry. I inherit a probationer aged 17 who, at his first interview, looks at the Order and observes, "It says here that I have to come and see you any time you say, but there's nothing here about having to talk to you." This reinforces my view that with Probation, contact is compulsory but what you talk about is voluntary, an approach that becomes much harder to sustain 20 years later.

1976: We learn that the research results on intensive probation in London have been disappointing: intensive probation is no more beneficial than normal probation and, with first or second-time offenders, it can even be counter-productive. This is extremely disheartening (and it is probably fortunate that at the time I never hear about Martinson's 'Nothing Works').

1977: Our Chief Probation Officer is Lawrence Frayne, an utterly outstanding social work supervisor, and once every two years you spend a whole day with him discussing your work. A memorably uplifting learning experience for me, leaving me reflecting for a long time afterwards, "*How* did he do that?"

1978: A curiosity in the light of societal changes since then, but I swear this is true: Lawrence issues all POs in Wiltshire a statutory instruction that it is unacceptable to forbid a 'client' to smoke in your office during interview, essentially because we should show consideration to the 'client's' needs.

1979: Swindon is an expanding new town and the workload demands are great. I have 60+ cases, plus circa 130 social inquiry reports per year – but instead of National Standards each officer sets their own 'standards'. One of my probationers brings a friend in with her once and says, "What I want to know is: why do I have to come and see you every week, when my friend Angie here never has to see her probation officer at all?"

1980: In our team we radically organise ourselves into a report writer and court duty officer (me) and a group work and supervision group (my colleagues). Hence we get to entertain Home Secretary Willie Whitelaw in our tearoom when he visits Wiltshire Probation Service.

Other memories of main-grade work in Swindon – the sheer quantity of which I experience as an exhausting relentless treadmill of reports and cases for much of the time:

- A magistrates' court run with an iron fist by the Clerk, and a Crown Court with a singularly punitive judge sitting regularly. With no more than a handful of exceptions in six years, I start all non-custodial social inquiry reports with a home visit, usually in the evening, and a 'non-report' is virtually unheard of – I know that if the court thinks that a defendant is failing to co-operate with the Probation Service he or she will be remanded in custody for 3 weeks. Thus once I do a total of seven home visits to a delinquent young mother so that the court will get its report at the scheduled hearing.

- An outstandingly good Community Service scheme: brilliantly constructive, creative and entrepreneurial in its work placements, at the same time as successfully operating draconian enforcement – someone who fails to report for work at 9.00 am on a Saturday is prosecuted, sentenced and in Bristol Prison by the following Friday.

- A mother calling up the stairs after opening the door to me, "It's all right – it's only the probation officer …"

- Conducting interviews in living rooms, in my early days in competition with the TV, until I decide that drastic action is needed. I later learn that I have finally achieved something as a probation officer when a colleague reports back to me about a case where I had done a report – the mother told her, "Oh we remember Mr Bridges all right – he made us turn the telly off!"

Reflections on Probation's Lost Authority

Malcolm Lacey, former CPO, Dorset Probation (1982–1997), UK

There are 'moments' when things come together by chance and cause one to reflect. For me, this came from my reading of *The Guardian*.

On 30th May 2007, Eric Allison wrote an article about people on orders being recalled to prison for minor breaches. One was for missing an appointment, even though the man had phoned to apologise and re-arrange it. A friend has told me of a similar occurrence. Allison also reported another case of recall for swearing at a nurse in a unit specialising in brain injuries. Medical advice suggested this was behaviour consistent with the condition for which he had been admitted to the unit. These are three cases of the 9,000 recalled for breaches of their licence in 2005–6. This is the equivalent of nine large prisons.

Allison also wrote, 'a parolee can be recalled on the word of a single probation officer'. This led to a swift rebuttal from a probation officer, Ben Entwistle in HMP Risley (Letters to *The Guardian*, 1st June), pointing out that the probation officer's recommendation had to be endorsed all the way up the hierarchy and eventually ratified by the parole board.

A month later, on 4th July, the article series *'What else can I do?'* caught my eye. A 27-year old probation officer was looking to widen her experience. The details are insignificant but one of the suggestions was that she should consider moving to a voluntary drug intervention project *which would give her an insight into preventive work and take her away from focusing on enforcement.* (My italics.)

I find that very sad. If people are being driven to find other organisations where they can develop the knowledge and skills required for effective intervention, then it is difficult to understand how the continued use of the word 'probation' can be justified. It does, after all, mean the offender having the chance and the help to 'prove' that he or she can change, can, indeed, 'improve'.

I am not arguing that there is no need to enforce the order. What I am suggesting is that it is over-simple to suppose that the offender will immediately comply with the conditions. If he or she could, or would, obey, there would be no need for the order because the reason for the order is that they can't or won't. Their problem, and ours, is that they see no point in keeping to the rules. What an order does is to provide an arena where that failure can be addressed. Probation officers represent society and its rules and must never let go of that representation. They translate the need for rules from an abstract demand into a personal and human one. The person subject to the order can begin to experience the possibility of fulfilling his or her needs without transgressing the demands of civilised behaviour.

If the probation officer ignores the need to enforce the order, though not necessarily through breach action, then the offender may well experience this as neglect. Further misbehaviour is then likely, an adult form of childish attention seeking. In other words, the offender knows what the order is about even if he or she would find it hard to put into words. Too many authority figures – parents, teachers, supervisors – have already neglected them.

The current system weakens the probation officer's own authority because no scope is allowed for differential decision-making. If you cannot distinguish between the trivial and the serious, then you have no authority. You are powerless. The offender recognises this. The situation confirms their perception that there is little to be gained from keeping to the rules because the authority figure cannot see them as an individual or influence their situation. So, he or she may as well continue as they are, even if, deep down, they would like to 'improve'.

What can happen in a demanding and empathic interaction between probation officer and offender is that the offender begins to exercise authority over him or herself and begins to change into an 'ex-offender' and perhaps, in time, into a fully participating citizen. Yet what we have now is a bureaucracy which seems at every level incapable of exercising discretion. It wrings its hands at the increase in the prison population – even as crime levels fall – yet is powerless, again at every level, to modify its own behaviour.

There is an irony in this destruction of the probation officer's authority. In the beginning, a hundred years ago, the probation officer was appointed by – and was personally responsible to – the local bench. He or she was personally answerable for the differential decisions they had made. Without idealising the past, can we, hand on heart, say that probation officers now are more able to influence and reform those for whom they are responsible? Or, in a last quotation from *The Guardian*, is the Service now part "of a long-standing British tradition: let those who don't know manage those who know" (Professor Anthony Hopwood, University of Oxford)?

The Coming of Electronic Tagging

Mike Nellis, Professor of Criminal and Community Justice, Glasgow School of Social Work, UK

Tom Stacey (journalist, author, publisher and prison visitor) introduced the idea of electronic monitoring (EM) for offenders into British penal policy – and coined the word 'tagging' – in 1981, by writing a letter to *The Times* and founding the Offender's Tag Association. Despite being a true blue conservative he believed strongly in reducing the use of imprisonment in Britain but, more typically, he had limited faith in social work approaches to offender supervision. Given the then state of British prisons, he was nonetheless surprised that penal reform organisations and the Probation Service did not welcome tagging. However, even the Home Office initially rebuffed his efforts to interest them in the American EM schemes that had been running since 1982, changing tack only when they became apprehensive about the rising use and costs of imprisonment. In April 1987, after Lord Caithness had visited the US, the Home Affairs Select Committee recommended piloting its use.

To key spokespeople in the Probation Service, tagging seemed like an outrageous, self-evidently bad idea. NAPO's Criminal Justice Committee felt that even further research into it 'was an inappropriate use of internal time and resources'. They quickly recognised that the Home Office had become committed to it, and Harry Fletcher in particular became a significant opponent, arguing that it would be a discriminatory measure, used more on middle class offenders, who had the necessary landline telephone, than on poorer offenders, who would continue to receive custody. John Patten, the minister charged with introducing tagging, promoted it in the mainstream media throughout 1987, and intriguingly *The Guardian* broke with the prevailing liberal consensus and tentatively expressed support for it, on the grounds that prisoners themselves might well prefer it to incarceration. Specific proposals were announced in the Green Paper, *Punishment, Custody and the Community*, in July 1988. The Home Office was somewhat uncertain as to what was technologically feasible and suggested that EM might be used for 'tracking' as well as for confinement in one's own home (or a hostel). (Stacey's preferred approach was also to track movement rather than merely restrict an offender to one

place, but he had realised the limits of the then available technology.)
Either way, EM was envisaged as something obviously tougher – and
therefore better – than probation.

Three curfew-based pilot schemes were set up in Newcastle-upon-Tyne,
Tower Bridge (London) and Nottingham, aimed at using EM to reduce
the use of remands in custody. Marconi provided the technology for
two schemes, Racal Chubb for the third, with Securicor undertaking
installations. The schemes were a mixed success. They did target offenders
who would not otherwise have received bail, but take-up (50 cases) was
only one third of the level expected. Some offenders preferred remands in
custody because time spent on the tag was not discounted on subsequent
custodial sentences. 50% re-offended or breached, possibly because some
curfews were very long (20 hours per day in some instances). Re-offending
by Richard Hart, the first person in England to be tagged, received
particularly adverse publicity. The technology mostly worked well, but
not perfectly.

Fearing that the Home Office would expand EM regardless, the then
chairman of the Association of Chief Officers of Probation (ACOP),
Gordon Read, condemned EM because it 'brings carceral thinking into the
home of the offender: the place where he should be most human becomes
instead a prison'. He warned also that 'those who offend often treat other
people as objects of their own gratification. Electronic monitoring treats
them in turn as objects which may not be conducive to assisting them
to perceive their victims as people and take responsibility for the harm
done to them'. Sure enough, the Criminal Justice Act 1991 legislated
for curfew orders with EM as a sentence, but there was no immediate
implementation. NAPO wrongly took this to mean that Home Office
support had ebbed away and, in February 1993, prematurely announced
'tagging dumped – official'. By the end of the year, however, the new
Home Secretary Michael Howard was talking up new pilot schemes.
The Probation Service might once have been considered to run them (as
in Sweden) had it not been so hostile to EM and a decision was made
to tender for new private sector providers. In 1996 new pilots began in
Manchester, Norfolk and Reading and it was from these that the present
national schemes evolved under New Labour in 1999.

Hard Cases: A Probation TV Drama Series

Mike Nellis, Professor of Criminal and Community Justice, Glasgow School of Social Work, UK

Central Television's primetime drama, *Hard Cases*, set in a probation team somewhere in 'the Midlands' ran for two series in 1988/89, just as the 'punishment in the community' debate was beginning in England and Wales. It was devised by two friends, crime writer John Harvey and Graham Nicholls, then a probation officer in Nottinghamshire Probation Service, who also acted as its technical adviser. Nicholls, in particular – working as an information officer in the Service – wanted the series to be an authentic portrayal of probation practice, something to counter tabloid distortions of what supervision in the community entailed. Harvey, who was by then establishing himself as one of Britain's best and most realistic crime writers, wrote some of the early episodes. Central Television did indeed boldly claim that the series would 'look and sound right because the research that went into it would rival a Government enquiry'. (*TV Times* 16–22nd January 1988: p.18), but with its executive producer being Ted Childs, best known at that point for his action-oriented police series, *The Sweeney*, the prospect of *Hard Cases* being amped up was always high.

At the conclusion of *Hard Cases'* opening episode a senior probation officer has a nervous breakdown, and starts burning files. This precipitates a competition between two team members for his job – former lovers Martin (a rough-edged erstwhile radical) and Gill (an ambitious, feminist single mum). Jack, old school, ex-services, seemingly fonder of his dog than people (though he mellowed in the second series) becomes acting senior. The rest of the team comprised Ross, a young gay man; Leonie, young, very attractive, newly-qualified; Kevin, a student on placement, and a team secretary. (The actors playing the staff spent some time with real probation officers, and (allegedly) grew to respect them). In TV police dramas where probation officers occasionally appeared (there had not been many), the care/control, idealism/realism distinction was usually articulated as a clash between police and probation perspectives. In Hard Cases the clash was articulated within the probation office itself, each wing of the argument represented by a different generation of probation officer, without recourse to a significant police counterfoil. Elements of traditional police-probation tension remained, however; Gill has her naïveté about a black teenager's behaviour shattered by a policewoman, while Ross is saved from a shotgun blast by an Asian police officer.

The characters and attitudes of the various probation team members, and the internal team politics, were mostly convincing. The programme did genuinely capture something of the ethos of probation as it was then, but to make it dramatic and exciting an excess of implausible action was introduced in many episodes, and there were some rather too outlandish villains under supervision. That said, there were some convincing clients too – the emotionally deprived rich kid, the burnt-out ageing armed robber – and some pertinent, compassionate comments on sex offenders and on the value of family therapy. Opinion in the Service nonetheless varied as to the series' accuracy and value. Geoffrey Parkinson, a shrewd observer of probation affairs, considered it 'not bad' and particularly liked the way it had 'been decided by the writers that the staff will have their feet on the ground and their hearts in the sky'. Some thought it accurate enough in parts to be used in training videos, but complaints of inaccuracy and poor characterisation were far more common. Some thought it the first time probation had been dramatised on TV but, in fact, there had been an equally short-lived series, set in London, running in 1959/60.

Neither the TV series, nor the novelisation of *Hard Cases* by John Harvey, captured the public imagination, despite borrowing the then rather original idea of multiple lead characters and multiple, entwined stories (rather than single plots per episode) from Casualty and Hill Street Blues. Ultimately, there is no certain way of knowing what messages 'lay' audiences got, but a TV series does not have to be a massive popular success to do some good, and while it would have been helpful to the Service if Martin or Gill had become as iconic in the mind of the public as say, Rumpole or Inspector Morse, it was arguably sufficient that they did come over, convincingly, not only as people of skill, compassion and integrity but also all too human. The series should not be judged as a documentary and any occupation-based-but-fictional television series, whether about police, lawyers, doctors, nurses, firefighters, teachers or probation officers will inevitably skew the realities on which it draws for dramatic effect. Graham Nicholls (now chief officer of Lincoln Probation Area) received considerable flack for his involvement in the series, but Hard Cases was a perfectly honourable piece of work which did the Service reasonably proud, and I know of at least two probation trainees whose inclination to join the Service had either been triggered or cemented by watching it.

A Defining Moment

Mike Worthington, former Chief Probation Officer

1st April 2001 was probably the most important date in the history of the Probation Service since the Probation of Offenders Act was implemented in 1907. So fundamental were the changes which came onstream on that date that some have said that it marked the end of the Probation Service which had developed, incrementally, over almost a century.

Why were the changes so far-reaching? Well, many words have been written on this subject over the past six years, some with passion, some with clarity, some with both. For me, there are four underlying reasons for the fundamental nature of the change and, in a series of articles marking the centenary of the Probation Service, the story would not be complete without spelling them out.

Firstly, the core of the Probation Service, set out in the 1907 Act, was the Probation Order. It encapsulated the concept of a second chance for the offender. It articulated the role of the probation officer as to 'advise, assist and befriend' the offender under his or her supervision. It became the cornerstone of the values which underpinned the practice of probation officers throughout the 20th-century. How much more fundamental a change can you imagine than the removal of the Probation Order from the statute book, to be replaced by strictly enforced 'community punishment'?

The Probation Order also enshrined the principle of the probation officer's professional authority. The Order stipulated supervision by a named officer. Now that individual professional authority has been removed and replaced by an authority given to a remote and faceless national body. The probation officer is merely an agent of that national body. And the consequence? A contribution to a prison population which stands at an all-time high.

Secondly, the 1907 Act identified the Probation Service as a court-based service. In its developing, confident, post-war era, probation officers were the social workers of the courts – preparing Social Enquiry and Family Court Welfare reports, supervising offenders and others on Court Orders (both criminal and civil), being on duty daily throughout criminal court sittings – at juvenile, magistrates' and Crown courts. The service provided to the court was statutory and visible. Post 2001, the probation officer is accountable, through a maze of ever-changing and ever-increasing management, through bureaucracy at local, regional and national levels, to a National Director, who is directly accountable to the Minister.

This leads on to my third fundamental change. From 1907 until 1948, probation officers were appointed directly by courts, to serve in a particular Petty Sessional Division. In 1948, with the growth in the Service and with a belief in its future growth, PSDs were combined and probation officers were appointed by and accountable to local Probation Committees, initially made up of magistrates. The history of Probation Committees is a fascinating story in itself but through various changes, the concept of local accountability was sustained – through a committee membership comprising local magistrates, a Judge, local authority and community representatives – with a budget made up of 80% central and 20% local funding. All this created a strong sense of a local Service, with local pride and accountability to local courts, councils and communities. The ethos of the Service recognised the essential need to work with others in the community – other agencies, statutory, voluntary and private – if offenders were to be successfully rehabilitated. From 1966, when the after-care of prisoners became a statutory responsibility, local volunteers were recruited to befriend prisoners on release, particularly those not subject to statutory supervision.

Finally, 2001 politicised the Probation Service. By removing professional judgement and replacing it with meeting central government targets, by replacing local leadership with national direction, by substituting the provision of a service with the overriding need to operate within budget, by reacting to the worst excesses of the tabloid media and the 'tough on crime' lobby with increasingly frequent, often ill-thought through and punitive legislation, a Probation Service which was once proudly proclaimed as 'the world leader' was reduced to "chaos" by 2004, according to a feature article in *The Guardian*. And who am I to disagree? From 1907 until 1994, Home Secretaries had valued the unique role of the Service as the 'welfare' arm of the criminal justice system. As crime became more politicised and Home Secretaries more punitive, the Service not only ceased to be valued but became a political football by its translation into an agency of punishment, not rehabilitation. And throughout this period, the level of recorded crime has been decreasing!

How does one summarise the impact of these fundamental changes, which in my view – and the view of many others – have destroyed a once professional, creative, caring and proud Service? For me, it was summed up in an e-mail, sent to me by one of my former officers, on his retirement last year. He wrote:

> "I left the Service feeling very low and undervalued by NOMS, the Home Office and certain people at Head Office. The comments in your card reassure me that I did make a difference in my 31 years in Probation – 29 of which I enjoyed going to work. I think the rot started to set in when what's-her-name became Head Honcho in London and released a statement on 1st April 2001 saying some drivel about forgetting the past, probation starts here. It still makes me angry. Ever since then, we've been told that we're useless and can't be trusted to work with offenders without ticky box guidelines, assessment tools and other such b*****ks, which only serve to take time away from face-to-face work with offenders. You can go into any probation office in my area – or the bleedin' country for that matter, and you'll see highly skilled workers sitting tappy-lappying on friggin' computers, instead of doing the job they were trained to do."

Sadly, this retired officer died recently but his words are a fitting epitaph.

NAPO fought hard to retain the name 'Probation Service' in the led up to the 2001 changes. Its victory, however laudable, was a hollow one though. The organisation we have today bears little relation to the Probation Service of 1907–2001 and the concept of 'Probation – the Second Chance' has all but disappeared from statutory criminal justice in England and Wales ... at least until wiser and more tolerant counsel prevails.

Glancing Back and Looking Forward: A Final Moment of Reflection

Paul Senior, probation officer, probation trainer, probation consultant, probation researcher and professor of probation studies

My defining moment during the year of the Century of Probation came on the 17th March 2007 when, in my hotel room in Hong Kong at midnight (still working!), I waited for my colleague, Ian, to tell me that another Moment had arrived. 72 Moments had arrived thus far, filling each and every day of 2007. I had cajoled, bullied, pleaded, persuaded, bribed, enticed and begged busy people to contribute. Ian, the Portal Manager, had harried them for photos and we had succeeded in achieving my impossible target (we all have targets now!) of one a day throughout the year. Alas, the continuity was broken that night. The collective voice of the Probation Service – past and present – was fast ebbing away. But I have great pride in what we achieved in those first three months and the number of Moments continued to rise throughout the year (see the dates of the Moments), swelling to 99 for the year of 2007.

It is fitting that a book which celebrates a century of probation that this, the final Moment, should be the hundredth. For those of you who are cricket lovers as I am, that last single to take the total to a well-deserved century is most satisfying. A simple but heartfelt thank you to all who participated.

These Moments are rich vignettes from individuals capturing the essence of and experience in and with probation which typifies what probation means to them and to us all. In these pages we have highlighted events, legislation, policy changes, different innovations to practice, differential interpretations of the same event and collectively a memory of a range of moments documenting the history of probation. These are, in brief, some of the oral histories of 75 practitioners, commentators, critical friends and academics concerned with probation. They express collectively the continuities and changes which is, paradoxically maybe, a constant and ever-changing feature of probation practice. They breathe life into the term 'getting probation'.

The collection makes no pretensions about comprehensiveness or representativeness. The process of invite was inclusive and a number of the contributions were simply sent in by interested observers. We printed all those which were sent thus rejecting no perspective. In that sense, the contributions stand on their own as unique insights into probation across the century. We were promised many more but, sadly, the exigencies of time and other commitments meant some never got to the cutting table but maybe, encouraged by the appearance of this volume, might engender a second series in the future. (You can stop ignoring my e-mails now I have given up chasing you for the Moment!) We were grateful for some international contributors and would have welcomed more. Capturing the essence of a complex organisation like probation is never easy and we have to leave it to you to decide if we achieved it. In the modernised Probation Service or 'trust' we have standardised, over-managed and uniform responses to questions of policy and practice. The changing role of probation demands changing practices and we must continue to be influenced by research insights provided they genuinely capture what is best in current approaches.

There is a real risk that we might lose some of the essence we have captured here, some of the principles and values which remain pertinent whatever the particular configuration or organisational structure. The centrality of relationships is crucial. Probation has always been a people-centred service relating to vulnerable individuals and as such Barton [Jan 10], Wells [15 Jan], Watson [Feb 5], Ögren [Feb 12], Hugman [Feb 15] and Watt [Mar 9] are particularly redolent of that central concern. The need to innovate around our core work to improve our responses is many and varied as exemplified by Harding [Jan 11], Feasey [Feb 6], Knott [Feb 16], Cosgrove [Mar 3], Buchanan [Apr 18] and Priestley [July 5], amongst others. The need to listen to the voices of others such as our former clients epitomized by Leech [Jul 2] and Astle [Jul 10]. The need to look outward at our European and global partners and learn from such as Nilsson [Jan 28], Walters [Jan 22] and Lindholm [Feb 1]. The need to ensure training and staff development is maintained to ensure we can reflect on and thus improve our practice reflected on by Worthington [Feb 7 and Feb 8] and Boswell [Mar 12], just to name a few. All the Moments have their points to make, their impact to create and I commend them all to you.

I was walking down the street of the village I now live in, just a few months ago, when a figure came up to me. I recognised him as a probation client circa 1979. He had been put on probation for using recreational drugs at all-night parties and this proved a real shock to him and to his 'respectable' family. I was not going to acknowledge our prior relationship. It was a long time on and he may not want to be reminded of it. But he stopped, linked me with his past and talked freely of the way in which probation had helped him take stock of how his life was drifting and how he had been able to move on into his now successful life. I don't really know how much part I played in that and he would now be described, in modern case management parlance, as a low-risk case and probably only demand routine surveillance as a result. However, I was pleased he had remembered me and that he wanted, in some way, to acknowledge that time. In these pages many colleagues have written of the uncertainty of what they were doing and whether it had impact. And sometimes good research and evaluation is absent from our work even today. Yet so many people cannot simply be wrong. They did the best they could, buttressed by values which stemmed from roots as far apart as former Franciscan monks and (former?) Marxist anarchists but sharing a belief that probation occupied a necessary middle ground in what is often a bleak and for many punitive criminal justice system.

I cannot list all 99 Moments in this brief piece but all of them have reminded me and stimulated me to reflect on the past. There is a tendency in Government today to adopt something of an historical amnesia to the achievements of the past. Ideas are re-shaped and re-badged as if they represent completely original approaches to practice and policy. I do not doubt that circumstances do change and the difficulties that probation officers and other staff face today are qualitatively different from previous eras. Nevertheless, the human condition is such that responses fashioned in other eras still have a resonance and applicability in today's dilemmas and social battles. Capturing good practice as we are doing in this series is also about not losing the many good practices and the keen engagement shown by lots of dedicated people in making the best of the job they loved and saw as their vocation. Celebrating this is not just nostalgic but gives us clues about how we can understand today's dilemmas and fashion solutions which draw on the best from the past.

A Final Challenge

If you have enjoyed this volume and regret your tentative refusal to do a Moment or simply you did not realise you could or, with pen in hand, you want to write yours now, it is never too late. Send me your Moments and we will publish them on the Community Justice Portal and when we reach our second hundred, we will persuade the publishers to produce a second volume. Prove me wrong, I am not sure we can find another hundred!

End Note

E-mails should be sent to p.g.senior@shu.ac.uk